Plastic Tagore

Plastic Tagore

Thinking After Yesterday

RANJAN GHOSH

OXFORD
UNIVERSITY PRESS

OXFORD
UNIVERSITY PRESS

Great Clarendon Street, Oxford, OX2 6DP,
United Kingdom

Oxford University Press is a department of the University of Oxford.
It furthers the University's objective of excellence in research, scholarship,
and education by publishing worldwide. Oxford is a registered trade mark of
Oxford University Press in the UK and in certain other countries

Published in the United States of America by Oxford University Press
198 Madison Avenue, New York, NY 10016, United States of America

British Library Cataloguing in Publication Data

Data available

Library of Congress Control Number is on file at the Library of Congress

ISBN 9780198922964

DOI: 10.1093/9780198922995.001.0001

Printed and bound in India by
Replika Press Pvt. Ltd.

Contents

1

A Plastic Kavi?

If 'ineffable' was one of Rabindranath Tagore's favourite words, says Robert Frost, 'lost' was another. He has a 'beyondness', Frost notes, 'something that you just come up to the edge of'.[1] He is more contemplative than meditative—' "meditation" is meditating something to do; and "contemplation" is something to be lost in; to lose yourself in, so as to find yourself';[2] he, Frost mentions, is always playing with 'paradoxes'.[3] Did the kavi, like Frost's old farmer, believe that 'there is always something more to everything'? The kavi exists in dynamical plasticity caught within the reign of the ineffable, beyonding, a state of being lost, the 'something beyond, beyond, beyond—beyond the rational'.[4] Did Frost miss saying that Tagore was plastic?

We are born incomplete; we evolve incomplete; we die incomplete. This makes our being a point of expectation, formation, and possibility all the time. Is plasticity a form of incompletion, and a plastic kavi an event in failing? If art and living are expression, they bring out two forms of plasticity—one that 'passively receives form already present in the world of ideas' and the other where new forms are created emphasizing the creativeness, the urge, and possibility of the surplus.[5] Guido Cusinato explains that first 'by plasticity as change' we mean the 'capacity to acquire a new shape due to an external pressure or in order to adapt to the external environment. It may be the plasticity of a malleable piece of clay,

---

[1] Robert Frost, 'Remarks on the Occasion of the Tagore Centenary', *Poetry*, 99, no. 2 (November 1961): 107.

[2] Ibid., 109.

[3] Ibid., 111.

[4] Ibid., 119.

[5] In the second volume of his *Schriften zur Morphologie* (1824), Goethe explains that the nature of an organism is not confined to an essence or an immutable shape (*Bild*, *Gestalt*), but is characterized by a dynamic process of formation (*Bildung*). Johann Wolfgang von Goethe, *Schriften zur Morphologie* (CreateSpace Independent Publishing Platform, 2014).

Plastic Tagore. Ranjan Ghosh, Oxford University Press. © Ranjan Ghosh 2024.
DOI: 10.1093/9780198922995.003.0001

the plasticity of an elastic material that recovers its initial shape when the external pressures have ceased, the mimetic plasticity of a chameleon or of an individual opportunistically adapting to a specific environment.' By 'plasticity as transformation', Cusinato means 'the capacity of an organic, social or personal system to increase in its complexity in a specific way: in this case, the change in the equilibrium of one's own system or the distancing from oneself gives way to the birth of a new shape, that is to say, a new process of formation in the sense of a development, growth or blossom'. [6] It is plasticity as transformation that brings us before an incompletion which is mostly about 'forming', as Catherine Malabou argues; plasticity is about giving, receiving, and destroying form.[7] Malabou, working against a reified understanding of Hegel where Spirit is seen as subsuming everything into a systematic whole, identifies a 'future of Hegel' through plasticity as possibility. Hegel, she observes through her interpretative elan, can be read more expansively and accommodatively through flashpoints of possibility challenging the confinement of spirit—Hegel, she notes, 'rips [plasticity] away from' the traditional 'strict aesthetic ties (or sculptural ties, to be precise), definitively conferring the metaphysical dignity of an essential characteristic of subjectivity upon it'.[8] Plasticity is the performance of moulding, forming, sculpting, and an articulation on the refashioning of habit. Plasticity, as the substantive and accident, is inherent in all desires and projections of critical understanding; it 'wounds' our ways of thinking, helping a subject-project to have a future. This future is not simply about a temporal trajectory traced from a past. The event of future is the sign, the possibility, the enactment that stands before us in acts of recuperation, reintervention, and reacknowledgement. The future is about stealing a narrative from the monotone of the present, about an epigenetic life in the making which is what we can interpret as the recuperative moments of the present. The recuperative potencies of the future in the present make for plastic habit.

[6] G. Cusinato, 'Hunger for Being Born Completely: Plasticity and Desire', *Philarchive.org*, (2017), https://philarchive.org/archive/CUSHFB.

[7] Catherine Malabou, *Plasticity at the Dusk of Writing: Dialectic, Destruction, Deconstruction* (New York: Columbia University Press, 2010).

[8] Ibid., 13; quoted in Thomas Wormald, 'On Plasticity's Own Conceptual Epigenesis: Malabou on the Origin and History of Plasticity', *Cosmos and History: The Journal of Natural and Social Philosophy* 16, no. 1 (2020): 105.

Within such a repremising of the 'future', the Hegel for the hypothetical student in Malabou's 'Who Is Afraid of Hegelian Wolves?' initiates 'regulated explosion of an energy free of all fixity, an economy of fluidity of the real and of thinking; that she is particularly interested in Hegel's preoccupation with "fluidifying solidified thinking", with dispossessing consciousness of its mastery'.[9] There is the explosion, the subject of plastic explosive, the unpacking of flashpoints. Gregor Moder, working through Malabou's understanding of plastic as explosion— 'the annihilation of all form'[10]—explains:

> In the French expression 'plastic' which denotes plastic explosive and 'plasticage' which denotes an explosion of the plastic explosive, the difference between an explosive and something plastic is obscured. One should note, however, that both of these terms originate from the English expression 'plastic explosive'. And surely, what is plastic about plastic explosive is some plastic material that can be molded, just like Plasticine or dough. This substance is added to the explosive precisely because of its plasticity. To make it quite clear: plastic explosive is a mixture of two substances, the explosive and the plasticizer. But even if we consider plastic explosive as one substance, we should still distinguish its characteristic of being plastic from its characteristic of being explosive. Not everything that is plastic explodes, just as not everything that is explosive is plastic (moldable, fluid).[11]

Plastic understanding, by this logic, is not merely an understanding in explosive patterns of interpretation and revelations. It forms, experiences the forming, and experiences annihilation. A plastic kavi exists in the singularities of plastic moments where the flashpoints in thinking and formation are explosions that construct forms, develop their points of ignition from forms that are difficult to destroy, and initiate differentiations in critical thinking and aesthetic-ethical experiences. They help produce

---

[9] Catherine Malabou, 'Who Is Afraid of Hegelian Wolves?', in *Deleuze: A Critical Reader*, ed. Paul Patton (London: Wiley-Blackwell, 1997), 114–38; quoted in Gregor Moder, 'Catherine Malabou's Hegel: One or Several Plasticities?', *Filozofija I Drustvo* 4 (2015): 814.

[10] Catherine Malabou, *The Future of Hegel: Plasticity, Temporality and Dialectic*, trans. Lisabeth During (New York: Routledge, 2005), 12.

[11] Moder, 'Catherine Malabou's Hegel', 813.

and evolve a desiring being: a creative genius whose desires for the form and the formless are often 'plastic explosives' on the limits of finitude. Desire speaks of desiring alterity, constellating thoughts and ideas beyond oneself, making one's subjectivity manifest in a splatter. The Latin verb *desiderare* (to desire), as Cusinato shows us, 'is composed of the particle "de"—denoting a lack, or a destructive action—and the term *sidus*, *sideris* (pl. *sidera*), meaning "star". Thus, desire could correspond to the feeling one has when sensing a "lack of the stars"—that is not the lack of one star, but rather, of a cluster of stars. Now, it is widely acknowledged that, since antiquity, stars were assembled in constellations in order to decipher the starry sky.'[12] A plastic kavi as a desiring being is plastic Tagore, the desiring Tagore, who in his detachment, restlessness, and loneliness, senses the lack of stars—the constellation, orientation, and its annihilation. Also, 'desire expresses two different meanings according to how the particle "de" is interpreted: 1) as the feeling of a "lack of constellations", that is to say, of orientation parameters—accepting this, desire would denote a nostalgia for points of reference that are missing; 2) the attempt to destroy ("de-") the constellation of stars ("sidera") that limit my existence, determining my destiny'.[13] The missing, mysterious, hidden, and elusive build the desire for 'stars' unseen, unrecorded, and overlooked. A desiring Tagore is deeply incomplete, dissatisfied, and often disoriented in a positive way to plasticize a move away from the 'blocked' to the realms of new constellation. He does not live by years (specifically and incidentally not the eighty years that Tagore lived) but manifests through a profoundly plastic process of availability, accommodation, alteration, and formation. This is an affective space with its cross-cutting and tangential drives as plastic Tagore reshapes and accommodates to produce further levels of meaning and revelation. This book taps into the possibilities of Tagore to be other than what he is considered to be and what he thought he possibly could be. Plastic Tagore is the love for a Tagore who has always been restive, tensional, withdrawn, and recluse—a creative surplus that meant more but communicated less, achieved less in meaning but produced possibilities of agonistic life worlds.

---

[12] Cusinato, 'Hunger for Being Born Completely'.
[13] Ibid.

Plastic Tagore is a fresh involvement in 'thought', increasing the capacity to think, and is drawn towards what *withdraws* in Rabindranath Tagore, leaving us exposed to the being considered a 'sign'; often being considered as signs, plastic Tagore projects and points to multiple directions, for instance, his understanding of world literature corresponds with the contemporary discourses on the notion of the world and the rationale of the comparative or his thoughts on education connect deeply with transcultural educational plasticity or his historical consciousness hinges on the principles of transhistoricality. Plastic Tagore is the sign(s) that we did not read and missed reading in the Rabindranath Tagore we have come to know and acknowledge. As a Deleuzian 'outside', he is the power of the 'unthought', rather, the provocation to think the unthought. In fact, the discordance and rapprochement ringing out of these engagements with the unthought is what determines the plastic explosives. Deleuze writes in *Proust and Signs* that 'we are not physicists or metaphysicians; we must be Egyptologists. For there are no mechanical laws between things or voluntary communications between minds. Everything is implicated, everything is complicated, everything is sign, meaning, essence. Everything exists in those obscure zones that we penetrate as into crypts, in order to decipher hieroglyphs and secret languages. The Egyptologist, in all things, is the man who undergoes an initiation—the apprentice.'[14] Deleuze observes that 'what is essential is outside of thought, in what forces us to think'[15] and thinking for him is involuntary and always-already involves extraneous elements.[16] Plastic Tagore addresses his 'desert in thought'; he is an event in the incalculable and the construction of him is also an event of 'unconcealing'. If such a reading emerges out of the 'unthought', it is also an act in stupidity (*connerie*). He is stupid and, hence, he is the poesis of the possible: 'the possible or I shall suffocate', as Deleuze says.[17] Possibilities make the plastic Tagore.

[14] Gilles Deleuze, *Proust and Signs*, trans. R. Howard (Minneapolis: University of Minnesota Press, 2000), 92.

[15] Ibid., 95.

[16] Gilles Deleuze, *Difference and Repetition*, trans. P. Patton (New York: Columbia University Press, 1994), 147. B. Dillet, 'What Is Called Thinking?: When Deleuze Walks along Heideggerian Paths', *Deleuze Studies* 7, no. 2 (2013): 250–74.

[17] Gilles Deleuze, *Negotiations: 1972–1990*, trans. M. Joughin (New York: Columbia University Press, 1995), 177.

The 'possibles'—the stars awaiting constellation, the flashpoints of unthought—are Tagore's stupidity which, in fact, is a way of thinking, of finding plasticities of representation, narration, and truth. Deleuze sees philosophical thinking as harming stupidity, making it embarrassing and inspirational for a transcendence of state.[18] Not as opposition to thinking, but a form of thinking that has its baseness and shame but not without the seeds of transcendence and the countercurrents to inspire forms of exposure. Plastic Tagore is about revitalizing and repoliticizing thinking, of making understanding not a handmaiden of a violent institution whether that be a nation state or an ashram school or custom or an ideology. The stupidity of Tagore is about getting expelled from the baseness of thought, the confirmed and inert conditions of thinking and existence; this is not a journey to wisdom but a condition that energizes him to 'move beyond'. Understanding with stupidity cannot come on the sole condition of a truce with the Kantian pure will which does not encourage any restlessness but demands objectivity and lesser intensity of interrogation. Stupidity is the sedate acceptance of limits; it is also the reflexive desire to deconstruct the existent. Stupidity as creation comes with restlessness and surplus.

The surplus in Tagore is the individuation that interrogates Tagore incessantly about what he writes and what he means and tries to mean. The Tagore that he is, the 'be', is tensional by this surplus, resulting in a formative being whose desire 'to be' calls on various levels of plasticity. It is the 'tomorrow'—not as a linear temporal extension of the yesterday—in which we discover Tagore; this is a state of 'to-come', a state of future-present. Valeria Maggiore writes that 'the Greek term for accident (συμβεβηχός) derives from the verb συμβαίνω which has a lot of meanings like to agree with, to correspond, but also to happen and to occur. If the two first meanings are connected to the Goethean principle of a permanent bond between Nature and its observer, the two other lead us back to an expression that Catherine Malabou defines in her works as synonymous of plasticity: *voir venir*.'[19] Plastic Tagore is an event in the 'coming', of something coming to us. Maggiore explains further that 'the

---

[18] See Gilles Deleuze, *Nietzsche and Philosophy*, trans. H. Tomlinson (London: Continuum, 2002).

[19] Valeria Maggiore, 'Is Aesthetic Mind a Plastic Mind? Reflections on Goethe and Catherine Malabou', *Aisthesis: Pratiche, linguaggi e saperi dell'estetico* 12, no. 1 (2019): 55–60.

voir venir indicates the act of vision which sees what is coming, namely what we can anticipate or what we guess on the basis of what we see (for example our capacity to depict future evolutionary changes of species), but it also indicates the capacity of seeing what is unexpected and unpredictable. *Voir venir* is therefore the ability to account for plastic novelties and indicates a mental vision that opens to the contingent and the unthinkable.'[20] Being in the present is being actively anticipative; *voir venir* encourages the plastic kavi to *exist* in the 'coming', where waiting is not hanging around but a faith in the indeterminacy of the future in the acts of the present. This future leaps out of the unreckoning, the unbidden, and builds its own surplus before a plastic kavi.

In a state that is present and 'yet to come', plastic Tagore stays alive as frustrated, dynamic, inquisitive, and insightful, largely distanced from what Rabindranath Tagore is paradigmatically thought of and institutionally interpreted as; he is self-reflexive, committed to the possible and not unwelcoming of the impossible, but not uncannily decontextualized. Cusinato explains that 'Kant pictures the human as "crooked timber" that the pure will tries to straighten out according to what it ought to be, but never succeeds completely. What he proposes is an "orthopedic" scheme. Human beings are faulty and lacking and for this reason they try to conform to an ideal, unattainable and utterly transcendent "ought-to-be".'[21] The imperfection of Tagore, the crooked timberhood as it were, inspires the plastic Tagore. The orthopaedic desire to straighten the imperfection, to reach the 'ought to be', falters to become the 'yet to be'. Plastic Tagore is the manifestation of the 'lack' in Tagore. Is desire only about achieving something new, like a school, a university, visiting foreign lands, composing music and songs? Can desire also mean rethinking the contemporary at the cross-points of where one has been and what one might end up doing? Is desire again the plasticity that makes one relive a fresh birthing? It is from this relentless effort to straighten the orthopaedic crookedness of thinking and desire, the lack as the seedbed of promise, and the failing in 'yet to come' that the plastic Tagore is born.

Rabindranath Tagore detests theory and systematic philosophizing and believes in the text and the performance of expression. Plastic Tagore

[20] Ibid., 59.
[21] Cusinato, 'Hunger for Being Born Completely'.

sees no distinction between the two: text is as much theory as theory is text. Is *Sadhana* a theoretical text? How deeply theoretical is Tagore's poem 'Ami'? How is a supposedly theoretical text, 'What Is Art?', poetical and metaphorical in its constitutive complexities? Tagore may have antagonized theory but his writings in their metaphorical, abstractive, analogical, and figurative ways produce a plasticity, an anarchism, that is at once alluring and meaningful. He tries hard to theorize methodologically; fortunately, he fails and this failing renders an incompletion to his aesthetic, unschooling him in the process. Kenneth Stunkel notes approvingly that

> theoreticians who are not poets fear inconsistency and probably endure sleepless nights trying to detect it in themselves. For artists, the messiness of life affords little protection from it (for Michel de Montaigne, in his *Essais*, inconsistency and human nature are one). Better to face the rugged tumultuousness of existence than to impose a clean logical order on it. . . . It is likely that Tagore's own indisputable theorizing in books and essays is half-hearted because genuine rigor for him would have been like pinning butterflies to the wall or damming up the flow of experience. Rarely was he inclined to build and extend arguments to make a palpable case for ideas. In his prose, the appeal is usually imaginative, emotive, and suggestive.[22]

Inconsistent, wavering, conceptually undulating, Tagore is a plastic theorist; the rhythm he seeks to realize and believes he knows and often does not know, is less a *hodos* (method) and more in the nature of a *poros* (porosity) that makes theory gain its sustaining charm and revisionary ambit. Although it is accepted that Tagore did not believe in frameworking a strict method for the construction of a poem or a novel—something that one can argue as a *hodos* required to substantiate a particular genre or style of writing and composition—the lingering and persuasive question remains as to why we should consider theory in such a narrow sense. Tagore is deeply theoretical; he struggles to make the distinctions between a critic (theorist) and a creative artist (simplistically seen as

---

[22] Kenneth R. Stunkel, 'Rabindranath Tagore and the Aesthetics of Postmodernism', *International Journal of Politics, Culture and Society* 17, no. 2 (Winter 2003): 248.

non-theorist) and keeps investing in an enfolding phenomenon where the whole idea of theory comes to acquire a different valence and experience. All kinds of creative acts *are* theoretical. The plasticities in creation contribute to the plasticity of the critical discourses, and theory survives and thrives on such inherent and manifest plasticities. Tagore has for me changed the ambience and resonance of plastic arts.

Is a plastic kavi analytical without being systematic, digressive and yet fluent, critical and yet not pedantically rigorous? Is he often positional without being assertive and impositional, abstract and intriguing and yet insistent on not being explanatory, conceptually rich but refusing to call this theory when theory is about perception, the power and uniqueness of *seeing*? Does he have an apparent lucidity without a deeply complicated sensibility that appreciates life on terms unique to the poet and somewhat obscure to the common mind? *Seeing* is not staying fixed; *seeing* builds a view and asks for questioning the habits of seeing; *seeing* makes an event or an experience a passage that takes one to the other side without pitching the understanding in permanent props of settlement. Goethe considers 'seeing' as active and considers his perception itself as thinking and thinking as perception.[23] Like Goethe for whom thinking is deeply founded in varieties of seeing (*Vorstellungsarten*), Tagore puts his faith in the event of emergence, borrowings, and dynamic conceiving of things. Theory is living with an idea that changes us. The changes in seeing become the acts of heightening (*Steigerung*) and perception. If theory does not metamorphose the seeing person, it is never theoretical in a good and gestaltic way. The *Steigerung* implicates enhancement and ascension which clearly indicates theory's inherent abilities to plasticize. In a plastic kavi there is always a seeing of thought coming, as Malabou has argued. It is about being in a thought when it is a plan and a promise and yet more.[24] This act of seeing or perceiving is about trying to claim what escapes us, attempts to help resurface what keeps on escaping us all the time—a struggle in thinking by committing to the very nature of thought. Goethe sees this as trans-formation where attaining form and being in a form is seeing a metamorphosis coming; this is the plasticity that he finds in the

---

[23] Johann Wolfgang von Goethe, *Goethe Edition*, vol. 12, *Scientific Studies*, ed. D. Miller (New York: Suhrkamp, 1988), 39.
[24] See Catherine Malabou, 'An Eye at the Edge of Discourse', *Communication Theory* 17, no.1 (2007): 16–25.

workings of nature. Plasticity is 'the thought of a sculpture of the self with that of transdifferentiation.'[25] An idea then is like a sculptor's clay which shapes with the will of the agency and leaves out a remainder to produce something. The clay is a promise of metamorphosis and escaping where what exists is never outside the chance of being formed differently. The transformation escapes the existing to introduce new modes of emergence and manifestation only to know that escaping from the earlier form is no guarantee of its stability. A plastic kavi is a sculpture in process, a formation in transdifferentiation. Tagore as a plastic kavi is the theorist we have always missed, for theory, as conventionally and conservatively understood, has often failed to understand its own inherent pleasures of plasticity. Tagore is theoretical because he is plastic.

Being Plastic

Tagore is romantic in that, like romanticism which does not have a precise premise to enunciate, he 'left no system nor is there potential in his work to systematize his thought.'[26] There is a *prantik*[27] (marginal, on the fence) self to his aesthetic, intellectual, and psychological being; and a restlessness too: 'I sometimes feel within myself the conflict of two opposite forces, the one of which beckons me always to cessation and fulfilment, while the other would not simply let me rest. The dynamism of Europe has ever been impinging on the quietism of my Indian nature— hence anguish on the one hand and resignation on the other; poetry here, philosophy there; . . . on the one side, the pull of action, on the other, the magnetism of thought.'[28] V. S. Naravane sees an underlying 'aesthetic humanism' to Tagore's metaphysical, philosophical, and religious

[25] Catherine Malabou, *What Should We Do with Our Brain?*, trans. S. Rand (New York: Fordham University Press, 2008), 79.

[26] Ellen Goldberg, 'The Romanticism of Rabindranath Tagore: Poetry as Sadhana', *Indian Literature* 45, no. 4 (July–August 2001): 196.

[27] *Prantik* is a collection of eighteen poems that address the theme of the borderland. As Ghose observes, this work is marked by 'spots of illumination set against a background of gloom'. Sisir Kumar Ghose, 'Rabindranath and Modernism', *Indian Literature* 11, no. 3 (July– September 1968): 81. The poems reveal a psychological journey as if he is living on the borderland or margins.

[28] Tagore in his letter to Pramatha Chaudhuri, 29 January 1898. See Prabhakar Machwe, 'Tagore: The Oriental and Modern', *Indian Literature* 19, no. 5 (SeptemberOctober 1976): 80.

ideas, arguing that the kavi projects a very personal understanding of the problem of elusiveness, appearance and reality, pluralism, God and man as artists ('the world as an art-work'[29]), maya ('The world as an art is "Maya". It "is" and "is not". Its sole explanation is that it seems to be what it is. The ingredients are elusive. Call them maya, disbelieve them as you will, the Great Artist, the *Mayavin*, is not hurt'[30]), the profound relationship between humanity and divinity, and the infinite. The failure to appreciate an aesthetic foundation to his conceptual and ethical expositions creates a deeply divided school of reading the poet:

> The result is that Tagore's philosophy is mechanically categorised into 'sections' or 'stages', and this in its turn leads to all kinds of dichotomies—Upanishadic versus Vaishnava, rational versus intuitional, theistic versus pantheistic, and so on. Clearly, this procedure can only culminate in two alternatives: either we attribute to Tagore a particular theory or set of theories with the help of forced and farfetched interpretations, or we belittle his philosophical achievement in one way or another.[31]

However, the aesthetic and its inherent and manifest plasticities make for a different experience of Tagore, outside any strict categorization of him being a Hegelian, adaitavadist, romantic, Vedantic, and any other school-sponsored projections. It is a poet's religion which is never dogmatic but, as he explains, 'fluid, like the atmosphere round the earth where lights and shadows play hide-and-seek, and the wind like a shepherd boy plays upon its reeds among flocks of clouds. It never undertakes to lead anybody to a solid conclusion; yet it reveals endless spheres of light, because it has no walls round itself.'[32] This religion exists to be projected, revised, formed, and transformed; it is, undeniably, deeply plastic. Such a plastic philosophy with its failings will always fall short of a heuristic and hermeneutic finality for the plastic kavi knows that such a religion is 'too

---

[29] Tagore, 'The Religion of an Artist', in *On Art and Aesthetics: A Selection of Lectures, Essays and Letters* (Kolkata: Orient Longmans, 1961), 48.

[30] Ibid., 48–49.

[31] V. S. Naravane, 'The Place of Aesthetics in Tagore's Thought', *Indian Literature* 4, no. 1/2 (October 1960–September 1961): 147.

[32] Ibid., 153.

elastic and indefinite'—'no doubt it is so, but only because its ambition is not to shackle the Infinite . . . but rather to help our consciousness emancipate itself. It is as indefinite as the morning, and yet as luminous; it calls our thoughts, feelings and actions into freedom, and feeds them with light.'[33] The plastic aesthetic believes in form and forming, context and transcontextualization, the dialectic of definiteness and suggestiveness, and restraint and freedom in a constructive disharmony.

Sisir Kumar Ghose writes that Tagore's last years were 'riven with cosmic queries and agonies, a psychic upheaval. Questions trooped in and, with the passion of purgation, tore and trained him to a greater intensity and austerity than any he had known so far. There is enough evidence left through the chinks and crevices of the poetic consciousness and through new turns of interest and emphasis, as, for instance, in the frequent use of the simple word "Keno".[34] It is the relevance and interpretative heft of *keno* (why) that helps us to make a case for the plastic kavi in his negotiation with modernism. Modern mind, Tagore contends, is often a 'hasty tourist' in that it succumbs to flamboyance and meretricious experimentation. He complains about the dulling of 'natural sensibility for simple aspects of existence' by 'constant preoccupation that diverts it'.[35] With a strong dislike for 'fashions in literature' that tire very easily as they don't emerge from the 'depth', Tagore for me misses a distinct rhythm of literature. All experiments are not boisterousness where, as he argues, the strain of maintaining the outwardness 'exhausts' the 'inner development'. And the plastic rhythm espouses and exposes an aesthetic of surplus achieved through modernist experiments in the form of surprises and paradoxes. Modernism with its vagaries and variations is not without wisdom; however, it is the cleverness that annoys the kavi for he feels that the serenity of wisdom is missed and a relentless drive to hold the attention of the crowd impairs the depth and delicacy of a rhythm that genuine plasticity is expected to introduce and sustain.

It is this attitude to art that makes the understanding of plasticity restrictive. What does he mean by the expression of feelings 'that are usual in a form that is unique and yet not abnormal'?[36] How can an evening

[33] Ibid., 154.
[34] Ghose, 'Rabindranath and Modernism', 18.
[35] Tagore, 'The Religion of an Artist', in *On Art and Aesthetics*, 51.
[36] Ibid., 52.

be only an expression of beauty within a poetics of experience that normal minds can connect with? What jars Tagore's sensibilities is a modernist description, for example, where the 'coming out of the stars in the evening is described as the sudden eruption of disease in the bloated body of darkness'.[37] He explains that 'the writer seems afraid to own the feeling of a cool purity in the star-sprinkled night which is *usual*, lest he should be found out as commonplace'.[38] The very act of italicizing 'usual' is part of Tagore's somewhat inconsistent philosophy of life and art. How usual, I am tempted to ask back, is it to look out over a barren, near inhospitable, tract of land and think of building a school and then an international university? How usual it is to begin doodling and painting in an obsessive submission to lines and images at the wrong side of one's sixties without a formal training in art? How usual it is to get aggressively grounded in Vedantic philosophy and judge and critique life and art almost monocularly? Is equilibrium as against surplus to be considered usual? The individual politics and critical position in Tagore's adjectival apathetic outbursts—'jerky shriek', 'desperate dexterity', 'glare of sensation', 'spurious novelty', 'palsied taste', 'pungency of indecency', 'tingling touch of intemperance', 'tyranny of fashion'—commentate, to an extent, on modernist experiments and innovations but cannot qualify as a comprehensive and incisive critique of the temper. This failing in his aesthetical understanding of art declares a lack (when deficit is a kind of surplus) that contributes to the formation of a plastic kavi. More than being restrictive in their claims on art, these concerns exude anxieties over the plastic rhythm that sits at the heart of all writing and creation. What he misses under the spell of a certain conservative understanding is the nature of plasticization of art made possible through, say, T. S. Eliot's 'The Waste Land' or James Joyce's *Ulysses*. They are not instances of 'fanaticism of virility' and 'brawny athleticism'.[39] All art minted and produced through shocks, risk, and unbounded energy in the modernist era is not meant for 'circus': these texts are not reactions against a particular mannerism; they are not building a 'militant fashion' but have repremised the rhythm in art formation through an engagement with the unaccustomed

---

[37] Ibid.
[38] Ibid.
[39] Ibid., 53.

emotion and a shock and tremble in understanding. Tagore's explanation of proportion in art makes all art formation that is outside his own dominant tenor of understanding become a 'trick'. Eliot's expression of the evening as a patient etherized on a table does not make any 'false claim to reality'.[40] Shock as surplus comes in a variety of ways, be it the transfiguration of the obvious, the epiphanous moments of revelation, alethic manifestation, or experiments without lurid restlessness. Aren't Tagore's paintings anything less than a shock, an experiment with (dis)proportion? Trick or tyranny of fashion cannot be art; but shock does not necessarily come from tricks alone. A genuine and perceptive intervention on the proportion that art has with its environment can also build its shock moments, generating plasticity of an unaccustomed kind.

Tagore's failings strike hard in his misunderstanding and underdeveloped appreciation of the unconscious in art. How does one interpret this series of events without the power and presence of the unconscious— a deeply engraved loneliness and solitude in writing, the barriers of the windows separating the child Rabindranath from the wondrous external world as it made imaginative and playful inroads into his growing mind, the deprivation of the intimacy with the outer world, the deficit of attention and affection in the family, the servocracy of supervision as he grew up in disciplinary modes of restraint, the detachment and solitariness ingrained in the making of a personality ('somewhere deep in me I am impersonal—aloof. If it had not been so, if I had allowed myself to become enmeshed, then I should have been ruined [. . .]. In my mind, I am for ever alone, detached—from boyhood, and even from childhood, I was like that'[41]), the coming of a poem not wholly obligated to the mind and subjectivity of the poet, the image coming out of lines often carelessly drawn, the mask of faces in self-portraits concealing more than we expect them to reveal, an unaware drive and Eros that made a mind think that seven acres of barren land could ever turn into an international university? Unlike science, which he thinks we dominantly understand through intellect, art is realized through personality. This attaches 'mystery' to

---

[40] Ibid., 54.

[41] Maitraye Devi, *Tagore by Fireside* (Kolkata: Rupa, 2002), 154–55; originally published in Bengali as *Mungpute Rabindranath* (Kolkata: Prajna Prakashani, 1943).

art—an endless mystery that we cannot 'analyse' or 'measure'.[42] Tagore puts it interestingly—'Here you are'.[43]

The plasticity of Tagore builds again on the contradiction around his repudiation of psychoanalysis as a source of literature and the unknowingness of art's emergence: the mystery. Amit Chaudhuri sees 'accident and chance' in Tagore's system of expression and understanding that ensure 'unpredictable and life-transforming' outcomes: 'his embrace of life, of chance, of play, makes Tagore stand out in the intellectual and moral ethos of late romanticism and modernism— an ethos with which Tagore shares several obsessions (time, memory, the moment, the nature of reality, poetic form), but whose metaphysics he constantly refutes'.[44] The contradictions introduce the play; the chance and the element of the unknown make his understanding grow into ever-altering unities and wholes. Art, Tagore notes, 'has grown by its own impulse, and man has taken his pleasure in it without definitely knowing what it is. And we could safely leave it there, in the *subsoil of consciousness*, where things that are of life are nourished in the dark.'[45] There is an acknowledgement of the 'unconscious process' of living that contributes to a plasticity of art life outside the glare of the 'scrutiny of our knowledge'.[46] He disapproves of the 'zeal for definition' and metaphorizes art as a 'wheel in motion'[47] where the importance is in 'the velocity of motion' and not on the spokes waiting to be counted. The kavi's insistence on analogizing art as the 'imperfect definition of the wheel' fits into two realms of its emergence—the conscious reasons of its existence and, also, what seeps deep, invisibly, into the recesses of its formation. It is the processes and emergence of the unconscious that produce a kind of fractality that Tagore never realized—rather, does not bother to realize. Here again the inconsistency in Tagore's thought-system arises as to whether art is outside judgement of productions and parameters of contextual and historical understanding or simply a matter of emergence, coming into bloom outside any verdict of evaluation, in a making purely of its own. These inconsistencies settle

---

[42] Tagore, 'What is Art?', in *On Art and Aesthetics*, 12.
[43] Ibid.
[44] Amit Chaudhuri, 'Foreword: Poetry as Polemic', in *The Essential Tagore*, ed. Fakrul Alam (Cambridge, MA: Harvard University Press, 2014), xxv.
[45] Tagore, 'What is Art?', in *On Art and Aesthetics*, 12; my italics.
[46] Ibid., 23.
[47] Ibid.

him into a plastic consciousness that fails to decide the definition of art and leaves the question about the status of art as transversal. More ambivalences mark his plasticity. Tagore who glories in the productive power of imagination speaks about the coming of a poem through utter detachment as it transcends the material and emotional mood of the author. He writes that the 'poem gains its freedom from any biographical bondage by taking a rhythmic perfection which is precious to its own exclusive merit.'[48] Tagore is contradictory in his exposition when he envisages the fashioning of the poem as freedom from its genesis and then proposes, in the same breath, to minimize its history to emphasize its independence. The blur remains over simultaneous claims of liberty from all biographical freedom, and again the efforts to minimalize historical contextualization and the formation of an image through the unity of the emotions and the objects of engagement. Was he claiming in some form the separation of the mind that creates from the mind that suffers? A proposition as deeply metaphoric and theoretical as this—'a dewdrop is a perfect integrity that has no filial memory of its parentage'[49]—raises several contradictions. Tagore writes that 'when I use the word creation, I mean that through it some imponderable abstractions have assumed a concrete unity in its relation to us. Its substance can be analyzed but not its *unity* which is in its self-introduction. Literature as an art offers us mystery which is in its unity.'[50] By bringing unity and mystery in the same stretch of thought, Tagore implicates the expression of unity as a baffling concept to pin down. He notes that 'in the creation of art, therefore, the energy of an emotional ideal is necessary; as its unity is not like that of a crystal, passive and inert, but actively expressive.'[51] The unity is a rhythm which Tagore argues is not a 'measured blending of words' but a 'significant adjustment of ideas, in a music of thought produced by a subtle principle of distribution which is not primarily logical but evidential.'[52] The 'distribution' leads to a combination that might not make for a decent balanced representation; it still can claim a 'dynamic vigour

[48] Tagore, 'The Religion of an Artist', in *On Art and Aesthetics*, 54.

[49] Ibid., 55.

[50] Ibid.; my italics.

[51] Tagore, 'The Creative Ideal', in *The Complete Works of Rabindranath Tagore* (New Delhi: New Delhi General Press, 2017), not available in this edition.

[52] Tagore, 'The Religion of an Artist', in *On Art and Aesthetics*, 56.

in its totality which claims recognition, often against our wishes for the assent of our reason.'[53] When Tagore argues that an 'avalanche has more mystery to it and much more possibilities than a huge mound of snow', he means a poem has a 'massive movement', profound possibilities that are not always within the domain of reason and logicality. A poem is like a dewdrop, a mystery, and does not encourage any investigation in parts for in trying to 'torture out a confession' the poem 'departs like the gentle wind, silently, inevitably. No one knows how it exceeds all its parts, transcends all its laws, and communicates with the person. The significance which is in unity is an eternal wonder.'[54] To lose all filial memory of its parentage, leaves the poem in a difficult and contradictory relationship with what Tagore means by 'rhythm of relation'. Isn't the coming into being of a poem both preindividuation and individuation? Tagore clearly cannot see the emergence of literature as severance from the past and sees its substantiation through borrowings and networks of cultural and epistemic correspondences. It is a growth not to be seen in aggregation but in plasticities, not enlargement which is 'merely adding to the dimensions of incompleteness'; it is, as Tagore argues, 'the movement of a whole towards a yet fuller wholeness', a process in synthesis and not additions.[55]

He is romantic with a transfigural and associative imagination that initiates a unity among disparate elements; he comes close to being New Critical through the refutation of biography, modernist in his faith in relationality and intertextuality, and anti-modern in being antagonistic towards all forms of shock and innovative understanding of life and art; he is evocritical in seeing the importance of past and the productive potencies of tradition and post-romantic in considering art as mystery; he is anti-New Critical in resisting all efforts to opening up a poem into parts within a confinement of interpretative density and, then, again, deconstructive in seeing frames of understanding outside the lines of perceptible creation. Amiya Kumar Bagchi nails the contradiction further when he observes that 'it is only when we grasp Rabindranath Tagore's ceaseless quest for connectivity and creativity that we can understand, however imperfectly, how he could be at one and the same time intensely

---

[53] Ibid.
[54] Ibid., 55.
[55] Tagore, 'The Creative Ideal', n.p.

secular and profoundly religious, punctilious in his public performance, yet able to portray the nonconformist in so many ways, traditional in the bedrock of his knowledge and some of his philosophical perspectives and yet more modernist than most Indian litterateurs and artists of his century and ours.[56] The expression of the unity of his personality and the aesthetic workshop of this antinomial and anarchic mind unhinges on *keno*. As Frost's swinger of birches, moving from one end to the other, staying in motion to stay alive in separate positions, the stabs of *keno* have prevented him from being reductive and doxic; ironically, his inconsistencies and prejudices have become fragile targets for further interrogations. Is this a plastic unity that dithers on the revisionary aesthetics of experiencing life, philosophy, and art? What kind of a plastic art are we faced with?

Becoming Plastic

Abstraction and, in a certain sense, abstruseness confront Tagore's exposition on art. For him the ultimate truth of art is the expression of universal man (*manava prakash*) where intelligence and feelings, cravings and experiences melt into a harmonic composite of personality.[57] For him, when art focuses on nature, it is a humanized nature in relationship with man touched by human emotions that forms its content. Never did art go beyond man. Yet the non-private self, the surplus in man—Schiller's *aesthetische Zugabe* (the aesthetic supplement)—was the source of creation. The deepening of world-consciousness is coterminous with self-consciousness—art owes its origin and texturing to a 'connect' between the artist's self and the Greater Being or the Great Further—a process more invested in 'becoming' (a sense of the 'not-yet') than 'knowing'. Tagore saw poetry as more real than fact; poetic reality embodied a vision that encompassed matter and spirit, being and non-being. This vision was due to a 'superabundance' which was free from Platonic doubt, free

---

[56] Amiya Kumar Bagchi, 'Rabindranath Tagore and the Human Condition', *Economic and Political Weekly* 49, no. 12 (2014): 39.

[57] Ranjan Ghosh, 'Introducing a Surplus', *South Asia: Journal of South Asian Studies* 35, no. 1 (2012): 7–12.

to 'perform' beyond 'the claims of necessity, the thrift of usefulness'[58] For Tagore, utility was just a state of dark heat. The excess of 'pure utility' was like white heat, which is expressive. The excess ensured access to creativity and the surplus was instrumental to aesthetic un-concealment, the disclosive power of art. Leading to the formation of plastic art, this *excédentaire* (excess) translates into *ananda*, 'the power of feeling delight'[59] in the doing of art and what art itself alethically exudes (*ananda* is not to be considered as having an antonymic presence against unhappiness; *ananda* is in happiness as much as in emancipative suffering). So *ananda* is not in withholding, but in submitting to an infinite, thus revealing that 'aspect of our personality which overflows in excess of all our creaturely needs and [is] exhausted by all pressures of practical living. It is this excess in which man is most truly revealed'.[60] This excess inspires the plasticity of forms and the lines of creation; it is manifested through a tryst with the 'infinite'. Even though Tagore sees the Supreme Person present in man's creation, this manifestation is always incomplete. Its lack of completion generates new premises where although the reality of life does not change much, the reality of poetic truth and truth in art keeps changing form and expression. Tagore's 'infinite' is redolent of deconstructive presences. The surplus keeps deconstructing the poet in man and gives art a plastic power. Thus, creativity is a continual deconstruction of the artist's personality—the 'encroachment of man's personality has no limit'[61]—manifested by renouncing oneself to align instead with the Everlasting: the finding of the 'personal me' as it dissolves to evolve ceaselessly in the course of art's disclosures. The contestation and conflation with the Infinite result in the 'giving', as Tagore notes, which is a process that 'can be classified and generalized by science' but was itself 'not the gift'.[62] Beyond reason in logic, and generated through reason in surplus, the personality encounters the pressure of 'emotional surplus'. The point remains that the poet strives to remove the 'stranger-tag' from his being, and yet the 'play' of the Master, the Infinite, makes him ever so

[58] Tagore, 'What Is Art?', in *Personality* (London: Macmillan & Co., 1945), 17.
[59] Ibid., 8.
[60] Tagore, 'Universal Literature', in *Angel of Surplus*, ed. Sisirkumar Ghose (Kolkata: Visva Bharati, 1978), 101.
[61] Tagore, 'What Is Art?', 29.
[62] Tagore, 'The World of Personality', in *Personality*, 69.

strange to the manifestations of art and his understanding of the world. This is a deep realization of being a plastic kavi who attends to this continual strangeness about him, subjected as he is to the pleasures and play of forms and formations, and relishes the subjection to states of certain incomprehensibility and unknowing. The Master, as the muse of excess, as a plastic force, keeps playing a variety of tunes and rhythms through the poet, and art is manifested through this surplus in mystery, incomprehension, and confused throbs of *ananda*.

Although Tagore finds that 'in music man is revealed, and not in noise',[63] the reality of trying to find harmony in music reveals the inherent reality of disharmony which inspired man's repeated visits in order to discover greater avenues of music. Man scores music; the Master plays it. Man enacts the Drama, the Master dreams the Drama. The finite inherited the music, the Infinite revealed the music. Creativity is, thus, man's 'cooperation' with the Infinite. The struggle to connect with the Infinite is endowed with the surplus of imagination which is love, a love that is transformative and enabling. The plasticities involved in the love of the Infinite—not to forget its emergence from the desire of the finite—are both exhausting and fulfilling. In such antinomy there is an extinction and an exfoliation, a loss 'which leads to greater gain'. This love for the Infinite 'turns the emptiness of renunciation into fulfillment by his own fullness'.[64] It is the procreative separation that art uses for its emergence and survival— the complexities invested in 'what is in us and what is beyond us; between what is in the moment and what is ever to come'.[65] The creative unity seeking harmonization of the divergent elements of the cosmos fails to resolve the contradiction arising between the 'present' in us and the 'presencing' (the Logos of the moment and the *avenir*, yet to come). The plasticity in surplus is true because it is where the Infinite resides. Loving as joy is the means of loving more, of finding 'abounding joy' and ways of enhancing love. This love has a 'rhythm' which, for instance, does not encourage knowledge of a rose through merely learning about the pulp of its petals, but plasticizes the experience and sensing of

---

[63] See Tagore, 'The Music Maker', in *The Religion of Man* (London: George Allen & Unwin Limited, 1958), 127–28.

[64] Tagore, 'The Religion of an Artist', in *A Tagore Reader*, ed. Amiya Chakravarty (New York: Macmillan, 1961), 234.

[65] Tagore, 'The Second Birth', in *Personality*, 83–84.

the rose as maya, an image whose 'finality has the touch of the infinite' in it.[66] And the plastic rhythm for Tagore, the quality of finding proportion in apparent irrelevancies, is the 'presence' where art, deeply inscribed in 'surplus', is like the 'stars which in their seeming stillness are never still, like a motionless flame that is nothing but movement'.[67] The plastic principle in Tagore's idea of art makes a case for 'lack' which is not the exhaustion of meaning but the 'surplus'; art survives by expressing itself and by continually 'guarding' itself too. This 'guarding' attests to a continuity that plastic art survives on, but about which man is never quite sure. Plastic art for Tagore is the expression of freedom, of freeing man from his finitude, but such un-barring, such efforts at un-bounding oneself, are embedded in an anxiety begotten through the enchainment that art produces in its limitation. The striving for freedom is an unconscious exposure to a chamber with whose walls man could never be content.

This leaves us with a plastic kavi who ensures that a discontinuity is inscribed at the point of art's manifestation, preventing a wholesome unconcealment; instead, the sundering, the shock, generated at the point of man's creative manifestation prevent the 'paradox of the infinite' from assuming finitude. The Infinite that is ontologically plastic transcribes the 'everyday', while the 'plus' in 'sur-plus' is the Deleuzian 'and',[68] where the repetition of a sight (say, watching the sun rise and set every day) and the differences in experience and manifestation cohabit with infinite possibilities. The problem with Tagore was his somewhat restrictive understanding of art in terms of the Upanishadic tradition; his eternal, the Brahma, the Supreme Personality, the Infinite, are clearly alienable categories, deeply abstractive in one's understanding of the production of art. This alienation, however, eases the complicated emergence of a plastic kavi. Although the kavi states that forms must always move and change, that 'they must necessarily die to reveal the deathless',[69] the point remains that such a 'deathless' category is beyond human comprehension. And this incomprehensibility and the incommensurability generated

---

[66] Tagore, 'The Religion of an Artist', 234.

[67] Ibid., 234–35.

[68] Gilles Deleuze uses the topology of 'And' to bring about the dialectic of 'difference' and 'repetition' related to the ever-mounting hermeneutic possibilities. The politics and aesthetics of 'plus' are intriguingly pertinent here.

[69] Tagore, 'The World of Personality', 60.

through man's engagement with the Infinite is what produces art. In a strange paradox, this 'nebulousness' (to quote Tagore) is what inspired the living in the 'delight' and the possible ways of fusion—finitization of the Infinite—which, again, is clearly the doings of a profusion.

Such plastic figurations vindicate what Tagore has called the 'freedom of the outcast'[70]—an invitation and compulsion to build one's own world with one's 'own thoughts and energy of mind'. His sense of plastic figurality is deep: 'no poet should borrow his medium ready-made from some shop of orthodox respectability. He should not only have his own seeds but *prepare* his own soil' and 'when forms become fixed, the spirit either weakly accepts its imprisonment within them or rebels'.[71] There is a power within us, argues Tagore, which refuses domination, challenges all forms of oppression to express itself—an innate transformative figural and transcendental power. This conative plasticity makes forms fluid, inspires form-making, and makes form-ation possible. What makes a plastic kavi is a belief in the untapped, the conviction in the excess of energy within that is 'vastly in excess of his need',[72] the 'ananda in productions that are unnecessary to him and therefore representing his extravagance'. Art, hence, is seen as a product of abundance that 'seeks its freedom in forms of perfection'.[73] Plasticity lies in the 'self-revealing'[74]—the 'immediate consciousness of reality in its purest form, unobscured by the shadow of self-interest, irrespective of moral or utilitarian recommendation, gives us joy'.[75] The joy is the product of the excess in the kavi; this joy builds the love that plasticizes all experiences into forms of harmony that are intriguingly impermanent and yet real in their worth and making. There are worlds that exist outside us, argues the kavi; he is like a passenger in a railway compartment who knows that the world outside exists but the railway carriage is more important to him in that moment. He also knows a world that exists outside the carriage is dimly visible through the window of the illuminated compartment.

Bird and Eckersley see speculation as the 'artist's capital'. This is 'art's capacity to bring about new frames of reference—new kinds of questions,

---

[70] Tagore, 'The Religion of an Artist', in *On Art and Aesthetics*, 36.
[71] Ibid., 37.
[72] Ibid., 45.
[73] Ibid., 45.
[74] Ibid., 46.
[75] Ibid.

experiences, events or encounters—to leverage difference in order to open onto an indeterminate future'.[76] Outside the relentless accumulation and delivery of capitalist surplus, this speculation is rooted in the affective and the material dimensions of emergence and manifestation— a 'processual surplus-value as an affective excess that differs in kind from the surpluses of capital accumulation'.[77] This surplus comes from a speculative value in zones of indeterminacy, an artistic will and aimlessness. Often the conditioned emergence of a thought and an actualization of circumstances cannot come with surplus which is mostly about exceeding the 'empirical conditions'. Plastic Tagore is always caught in a *process* whether as a poet-educator or radical painter or unsystematic philosopher. Brian Massumi observes that 'process is the immanent outside of the in-between of systems. Since it is unbounded by any given system or set of systems, that immanent outside overspills systematicity as such. Considered in itself, this in-between is a wide-open. It is the expanded field of where systems' becoming may go, beyond where and what they are now. It is the fielding of potential. Process is by nature in excess over system'.[78] A plastic kavi is invested in the surplus-value—as with art so with literature, as with politics so with religion. And this is indeterminate and immeasurable. It can be called the plastic-value which is in its indeterminate totality turns over on itself: 'rhythmically overspilling its own systematicity to dip into the processual outside in order to avail itself of the self-constituting potential to be found there'.[79] This brings us before the ever-alive potencies of a plastic kavi and the 'moreness' of affective-value in creative-critical thinking. Massumi mentions 'mutant flows' that do not go 'from known to known' but from 'metamorphosis to metamorphosis'. A plastic kavi lives the mutant flows intensely and, in the words of Massumi, this is not free from 'systemic/processual, systolic/ diastolic asymmetry'.[80]

---

[76] A. Eckersley and T. Bird, 'Speculation as Surplus-Value', *MaHKUscript: Journal of Fine Art Research* 3, no. 1 (2019): 6.

[77] Ibid., 1.

[78] Brian Massumi, *99 Theses on the Revaluation of Value: A Post-Capitalist Manifesto* (Minneapolis: University of Minnesota Press, 2019); Brian Massumi, 'Virtual Ecology and Questions of Value', in *General Ecology: The New Ecological Paradigm*, ed. Erich Hörl with James Burton (London: Bloomsbury, 2017), 345–73.

[79] Massumi, *99 Theses on the Revaluation of Value*, 15.

[80] Ibid., 16.

Tagore writes that 'when a reader feels particularly interested in some passage of a book, he underlines it. Although the words are not his own, he feels a kind of proprietary right to them by the intensity of his realization of their meaning. And he wishes to mark them out for all times. That kind of underlining or marking out may be called Art.'[81] This right to possess what is essentially not one's own speaks of a surplus: an intensity of possession where the original thought and ownership are disrupted into new spaces and affordances. Such 'underlining' marks all artistic realization where a deep plastic consciousness turns what is apparently external to oneself into an experience which the kavi can call his very own. This owning and the worlding of the existent produce the art: the surplus inspires new lines from what is underlined. This is what makes Art say: 'I perceive.'[82] A separate vein of 'perceiving' makes the artist-plastic kavi relish the continuity of such perceiving as flights of lines make for separate frames of the canvas. The poet recounts an incident: 'When in China I had a Chinese poet for my friend and companion. He would nudge at me excitedly as we journeyed in a car and shout: "Look there goes a donkey".'[83] The inanity and prosaicness of the donkey translate into an impactful experience in the poet's mind that cultivates an 'excited awareness' to 'bear upon his picture of the donkey.'[84] The plasticity of artistic consciousness connects with the ordinary sight of the donkey in inexplicable ways, generating an awareness that transforms the donkey from what it is meant to be and thought as into a separate aesthetic life world. This is another instance of 'underlining'—a plastic becoming—as the donkey is repossessed into the artistic consciousness in terms that are singularly subjective and deeply perceptive. The donkey requires 'perceiving' to be possessed as art, art-experience and art-emotion. Anne Sauvagnargues argues that

> the relation to territory is always a provisional balancing act, a rhythmic formation of a milieu, so it must not be considered a place but an expressive habitation. This involves describing balancing movements that are formed from the outside (deterritorialization), in an exploration

---

[81]   Tagore, 'A Random Discourse', in *On Art and Aesthetics*, 65.
[82]   Ibid., 69.
[83]   Ibid.
[84]   Ibid., 70.

toward (territorialization), or in a return to (reterritorialization); we would also be mistaken if we assumed that a territory is given. It is rhythmically constructed by movements that territorialize, deterritorialize, or reterritorialize—movements or vectors that either tend to stratify beings and things and contain their becomings by binding them in stratified organizations, or in movements that tend to undo them by placing value on their intensive axis.[85]

For the kavi it is the intensity and affectivity that set the rhythm where both the art and the artist, the rose and the poet-who-names-the-rose are caught in a play of territories. Watching the donkey in the act of perceiving is the 'capture' (in the words of Deleuze) that abducts a moment of delight and exclusivity that is not assimilative with the milieu. The rhythm of perceiving and aesthetic awareness is constructive and provisional, expressive habitation and exposed to reframing—in short, plastic.

Tagore writes that 'Art is the response of man's creative soul to the call of the real'.[86] What is the 'real'? For this real to be realized there cannot be a confinement to a tradition, a thought, and a state of reality. This disrupts the rhythm of the real; it is not about meeting the incompletion or being nudged by 'the warning elbow of classifiers in their choice of inspiration'.[87] The real finds the rhythm in the 'intermingling' of traditions and thought—the 'borrowings' and territorializations that generate the creative surplus. These borrowings have their plastic rhythm for they are both conscious appropriations and events without the definitive knowing of the artist. Such intertextual plasticities make for the real and the freedom in borrowing signals a 'debt', a gift, a *sambandha*. The reality of national inheritance and its outside are forms of expression that make for 'comprehensive sensiteveness'.[88] The real is in the surplus where acknowledging the 'freedom of entry' leaves art as 'alive and awake'. Sāhitya cannot exist without such *sambandha*—a profound plasticity in changing understanding of one's borders of thinking and expression in correspondences with the possibilities and allowances of others. The plastic

[85] Anne Sauvagnargues, *Deleuze and Art*, trans. Samantha Bankston (London: Bloomsbury, 2005), 119.
[86] Tagore, 'Art and Tradition', in *On Art and Aesthetics*, 58.
[87] Ibid., 59.
[88] Ibid., 70.

kavi proposes 'daring experiments'[89] and encourages venturing 'out into the open road in the face of all risks'. He advises defying 'unholy prohibitions preached by prudent little critics'[90] and relishes the experience of not behaving like 'good children' who never cross the 'threshold of their school-room'. It is this threshold defiance, the experimentative energy, the unconventional rhythm in acts and modes, and school-breaking urge that make room for a plastic kavi to breathe. The plastic kavi sees individuality and solitude in art-emotion and art formation assimilating 'various experiences, unclassifiable and uncatalogued, continually'.[91] The plasticity of habit dilates the radius of receptivity as art can have its Indianness as an 'inner quality' and not as an 'artificially fostered formalism'.[92] Transplasticity of artistic habit makes the kavi create forms that have surprises and 'unknown shrines of reality'.[93] As a plastic kavi he refuses to hold on to habits that discourage 'allurements of all adventure'[94] and settlements into repetitive and ungenerative modes of functioning (cultivating 'a monotonously easy success by means of some hoarded patrimony of tradition'[95]).

Tagore notes:

> When something in art, which is too peculiar in its presentment, shows an incorrigible tendency to repeat itself we may be sure that it is a sign of the waning life. If it is a fact that some standard of invariable formalism has for ages been following the course of arts in India, making it possible for them to be classified as specially Indian, then it must be confessed that the creative mind which inevitably breaks out in individual *variations* has lain dead or dormant for those torpid centuries. All traditional structures of art must have sufficient degree of *elasticity* to allow it to respond to varied impulse of life, delicate or virile; to *grow* with its growth, to *dance* with its rhythm.[96]

---

[89] Ibid.
[90] Ibid., 60.
[91] Ibid., 61.
[92] Ibid.
[93] Ibid., 62.
[94] Ibid.
[95] Ibid., 63.
[96] Ibid., 63; my italics.

Tradition serves the frontiers of difference with its inherent elasticity: in fact, for our conceptual precision, this elasticity is not what distends and on being extended has the promise to return to its shape; not having resilience always, this elasticity is opposed to itself in that it both unforms and annihilates the forming. It becomes the plasticity that is 'diametrically opposed to form' where, paradoxically, it creates and is the force of destruction and 'very annihilation of all forms.'[97] On such a plastic principle, whether with Marx or Freud or Max Weber, tradition is considered as a dead lump that needs to be transcended; this demands plasticization of an 'unreflective habit' that impedes progression by shouting out from the dead. The ghost of the past cannot be blind, says the plastic kavi. Amit Chaudhuri is right to note that 'for Tagore, tradition is at once contemporary and immediate, and inaccessible and disjunctive.'[98] Habits, Tagore argues, may not have the sole effect of deadening our mind: 'the bee's life in its channel of habit has no opening; it revolves within a narrow circle of perfection. Man's life has time-honoured institutions which are its organized habits. When these act as enclosures, then the result may be perfect, like a bee-hive of wonderful precision of form, but unsuitable for the mind which has unlimited possibilities of progress.'[99] His understanding of tradition is clearly about trans-plastic-habit. N. Eisenstadt sees tradition and innovation in an interesting relationship: for him, tradition is creativity—'the most enduring element in the collective social and cultural construction of reality.'[100] Tradition and modernity—what we know as 'co-existence' theory[101]—work into and against each other. Most often they transform each other. Edward Shils dwells on this conceptual and performative tension. For Shils, experienced sentiment, 'state of sensation at a given moment', rational judgement, an action, visual perception, a prayer, a scientific proposition, a process of industrial production, and an act of exercise of authority are not 'tradition'. He argues, none of these ideas is a tradition. None of them in itself is a tradition. But all of them can in various ways be transmitted as traditions; they can become traditions.

---

[97] Tyler Williams, 'Plasticity, In Retrospect: Changing the Future of The Humanities', *Diacritics* 41, no. 1 (2013): 6–25.
[98] Chaudhuri, 'Foreword', in *The Essential Tagore*, xxiii.
[99] Tagore, 'Art and Tradition', in *On Art and Aesthetics*, 64.
[100] Quoted in Ranjan Ghosh, *Trans(in)fusion: Reflections for Critical Thinking* (New York: Routledge, 2020), 8.
[101] Ibid., 9.

They nearly always occur in forms affected or determined in varying degrees by tradition. They recur because they are carried as traditions which are 'You Cannot Value Him Alone' re-enacted. The re-enactment is not the tradition—the tradition is the pattern which guides the re-enactment.[102] Tradition comes both with adaptation and re-enactment. The plasticity of tradition is a flow and in a flow; an act of performance of transmission where re-enactment, assimilation, encoding, normativeness, and imagination are put together in a complicated process of 'handing down'. For a plastic kavi, tradition is thinking; it is mostly about attachment that is both reasonable and intangible—a direct association and the understanding of the past as it unfolds and comes as inherited. It is an 'associative past' which speaks more about 'pastness' and spots of time than anything else. Transmission is past and pastness; it is the tangibility of following one's predecessors and their thinking—the filiative. It is also what 'retires' into or 'goes away' into the stream of existence and thought—the affiliative, the amateurism. Shils interprets it well:

> The interpretation of the text does not remain the same equally among all the recipients at a given time or among the recipients who succeed each other in time A rule of conduct, explicitly articulated or implied in a pattern of conduct, or a belief about the soul, or a philosophical idea about the common good does not remain identical through its career of transmissions over generations. An artistic style does not remain the same over its transmissions even though each of the particular paintings or statues in which it has been embodied does remain the same. Constellations of symbols, clusters of images, are received and modified. They change in the process of transmission as interpretations.[103]

Tradition constellates. It challenges the 'present': it patternizes the accepted and reified, provokes thinking imaginatively through the 'received'. It is in the transplasticity of habit—whether through the ashram education and its experimentations or understanding of transhistoricality or worldings of sāhitya—that the rhythm in the surplus comes into being; this is a disruptive rhythm that challenges reified habits of performance

---

[102] Quoted ibid., 10.
[103] Quoted ibid., 114.

and infuses an excess that dismantles conceptual equilibrium and institutional statis.

Tagore writes that the 'personality in me is a self-conscious principle of
a living unity; it at once comprehends and yet transcends all the details of
facts that are individually mine'.[104] Deeply Vedantic, and yet deconstruc-
tionist, this living principle is the plastic principle that clearly assists in co-
hering knowledge, feeling, wish and will, memory, hope, love, activities and
all other 'belongings', and again transcending them. Understanding finitude
and failing to understand the unlimiting potencies of finitude make rhythm
problematic. There is the unpredictability and lack in all forms of expression as Tagore argues that we 'can never be sure that we have come to know
the final character of anything that there is'.[105] Plastic figurality rests on finitude where crossing the finitude is realization of art. Is finitude the limit that
Tagore chooses to theorize? Can such crossings be read close to what Jean-
Luc Nancy points out about literature or art? In such crossings one pushes
the limits of artistic finality, creating forms that are invested in 'joy'—a joy
that is somewhat definable and again that defies definition. Reaching a form
is crossing limits, a passing, a kinesis, where the plastic principle of expression makes us aware of a living unity but never the finality of understanding.
Nancy writes:

Let us forget 'philosophy, literature, myth, wisdom', let us forget knowledge and belief. There is only one expectation: I want to pass. I do not
want to be or know, I want to pass and feel myself passing. Or you—it
amounts to the same thing. To pass—the limit, of course. To pass the limit
of the interrupted and the uninterrupted. Neither completion nor incompletion. Neither conclusion nor suspension. But the passage we expect.
Perhaps the expectation must be divided before it can be heard: from philosophy to literature and from literature to philosophy.[106]

Tagore is deeply invested in crossing when he claims that 'limitation of
the unlimited is personality'.[107] Accepting the limits, understanding the

---

[104] Tagore, 'The Religion of an Artist', in *On Art and Aesthetics*, 47.
[105] Ibid., 48.
[106] Jean-Luc Nancy, *Expectations*, trans. Jean Michel Rabate (New York: Fordham University Press, 2017), 23.
[107] Tagore, 'The Religion of an Artist', in *On Art and Aesthetics*, 48.

limits through recognition, is the inspiration to 'crossing' as the law of limits undoes its premises to become the field of play. The plastic kavi claims a world for art and allows art to claim a world for us within a play where image-making is a deeply complicated process. One *passes* into the other. If art is maya, as Tagore argues, it is never an experience in completion or incompletion, conclusion or suspension. In a commitment to plastic becoming, it is the surplus that declares the 'passing' and as maya it 'mocks even its own definition and plays the game of hide-and-seek through its constant flight in changes'.[108]

Plastic Figurality

The transition in art, the 'constant flight' as art's religion, and finitude as provocation bring the painter and the doodle artist in Tagore to our zone of argument. Aida Wong explains that in

> Tagore's rendition of the human face, one can trace an interest in the uncanny that does not shy away from the grotesque and forms that are not conventionally beautiful. In the portraits that arose in the 1930s, the human face closely resembles a mask that could have been inspired from his predilection for theatre, masked dances within performances and rituals. These faces appear frequently whether as paintings or illustrations to his text and seem to inhabit the shadowy world between reality and dreams. The face forms a visage that often smiles, or quietly contemplates the viewer.[109]

The ontogenesis of his art forms is deeply founded in silence, in expressions that do not need explanations—I call them 'talking plastic images'. What makes masks develop into a leitmotif of Tagore's pictures, grow as a canvas which screams back a challenge at our understanding, and become an inscrutability that is less a babble and more an emergence from the doodle? In one of the plates from *Rabindra Chitravali* (Self-Portraits),

---

[108] Ibid., 49.
[109] Aida Yuen Wong, 'Rabindranath Tagore's Mysterious Faces and India's Encounter with Modernism', in *Behind the Masks of Modernism: Global and Transnational Perspectives*, ed. Andrew Reynolds and Bonnie Roos (Gainesville, FL: University Press of Florida, 2016), 14.

'he has transformed his bearded face into that of a kind of monster; in another, into a woman. No one can look at this series and not comprehend something of Tagore's mercurial complexity, his "myriad-mindedness". Caught in plastic figurality that is less about Said and more about Saying, the self-portraits exist in plastic images that are greatly removed 'from the saintly, tedious image of him';[110] the self-portraits leave us with 'a man who recognises the savage in himself and is grappling with it'.[111] Being left in the Saying, Tagore's self-portraits emerge as entangled politics of surface, depths, visuality, and inner truth. Interested in essentiality in art and its multiple representations, self-portraits, in a meaningful way, can only emerge as less or more than the original. It is the unselfing of the self through an extension and breakdown of the frames that determines what the artist looks through his art.

Paul Klee's first pedagogical notebook *The Thinking Eye* has an observation that contributes to my arguments on plasticity:

There are some who will not be able to acknowledge the truth of my mirror. They should bear in mind that I am not here to reflect the surface (a photographic plate can do that) but must look within. I reflect the innermost heart. I write the words on the forehead and around the corners of the mouth. My human faces are truer than real ones. If I were to paint a really truthful self-portrait, you would see an odd shell. Inside it as everyone should be made to understand, would be myself, like the kernel in a nut. Such a work might also be called an allegory of crust formation.[112]

Self-perception, self-deception, self-distortion, and self-reflexivity mark the plastic rhythm here. This is the beyonding in self-representation. Plasticity is not in mirroring and self-portraiture; Klee notes and Tagore implies that self-portrait does not have 'mirror function', building a sense of inadequacy and wandering. Galen Johnson shows us how

---

[110] Andrew Robinson, *The Art of Rabindranath Tagore*, vols. 1–4, foreword by Satyajit Ray (London: Andre Deutsch, 1989), 195.

[111] R. Siva Kumar, *Rabindra Chitravali: Paintings of Rabindranath Tagore*, vols. 1–4 (Kolkata: Pratikshan, in association with Visva Bharati (Santiniketan) and Ministry of Culture, Government of India, New Delhi, 2011), 383, 389, 395.

[112] Paul Klee, *Notebooks*, vol. 1, *The Thinking Eye*, ed. Jurg Spiller, trans. Ralph Manheim (London: Lund Humphries, 1961), 20.

Merleau-Ponty's philosophy of art acknowledges this displacement and aesthetic slippage. In 'Indirect Language and the Voices of Silence', Merleau-Ponty writes that the modern painters 'want nothing to do with a truth defined as the resemblance of painting and the world. They would accept the idea of a truth defined as a painting's cohesion with itself, the presence of a unique principle in it which affects each means of expression with a certain contextual value. [W]hat replaces the object is not the subject—it is the allusive logic of the perceived world'.[113] The plastic kavi believes in the allusive, yes-ing the 'not' before the obvious and literal world, and committing to an innermost image that is elusive, epochal, detached, transitive, and—hence—deeply plastic. It is here that painting loses its borders with poem. As Klee, in a flash of realization, notes: 'The recognition that at bottom I am a poet, after all, should be no hindrance in the plastic arts!'[114] The plastic kavi has always been a painter ever since he began to ink his first lines of poetry. This painter-poet ensemble has its own plastic poesis; it is as true with Klee as with Tagore. Michel Foucault asserts that Klee annuls 'one of the two defining principles of Western painting since the Renaissance—the separation between "plastic representation" and "linguistic reference"—by showing the juxtaposition of shapes and the syntax of lines in an uncertain reversible, floating space (simultaneously page and canvas, plane and volume, map and chronicle)'.[115] In Klee's work, writes Foucault, we see 'the intersection, within the same medium, of representation by resemblance and of representation by signs. Which presupposes that they meet in quite another space than that of painting.'[116] Such plasticities—the contradiction and oppositional rhythm between 'poetic' painting and what Klee calls the 'pure plastic art'—make allowance for the post-literary. The inherent and restless poetic in the overlapping of the two dispositions builds the surplus (crossings) that keeps art in a state of *passing*.

Caught in an appropriative and disjunctive tradition (never in line with the Bengal School of Painting) and existing as an outsider to all forms of

---

[113] Quoted in Galen A. Johnson, 'On the Origin(s) of Truth in Art: Merleau-Ponty, Klee, and Cézanne', *Research in Phenomenology* 43, no. 3 (2013): 475–515.

[114] K. Porter Aichele, *Paul Klee, Poet/Painter* (Rochester, NY: Camden House, 2006).

[115] Cited in Annie Bourneuf, *Paul Klee: The Visible and the Legible* (Chicago: University of Chicago Press, 2015), 4.

[116] Cited ibid., 5.

legacy, these images figuralize plasticity of an enthralling order; this perhaps inspires the artist Nandalal Bose to speak about a re-education 'into
the fundamental values of art' and also makes him declare that 'none can
do it better than he who is creating before our very eyes forms whose
vigour baffles our classification and whose vigour compels the admiration of the artist'.[117] In an implicit acknowledgement of dynamic plasticity, he observes that 'if Rabindranath seems rough and destructive, it
is because he is breaking the ground anew for us that our future flowers
may be more surely assured of their sap'.[118] The Chitrakar's anguish leads
him to ignore all interpretation from others and express a kind of disin-
terest to see meaning in his paintings.[119] This makes for a separate logic
of sense. Destructive and deconstructive, Tagore, as Wong notes, 'wel-
comed any comparison with Western masters but remarked how some of
their works seemed either too doctrinaire or too deliberate in imparting
a primitive quality that was not inherently their own. He was generally
skeptical of Western uses of its cultural Other, even though he was aware
of his own complicity in this project.'[120] Wong writes that

Tagore's encounter with modernism as a received tradition afforded
him the opportunity for a double masquerade. To the world, he could
be seen as hiding behind his non-Western 'otherness', contesting, as did
the European avant-gardes, old concepts of representation. His enigmatic mask belonged to an 'Oriental' who understood the quandaries
of positivism and rationalism. The rhetoric of the Orient, despite its
Eurocentric connotations, empowered Tagore to affirm repeatedly,
after having won the Nobel Prize, the intellectual, artistic, and spiritual
worth of his people. At the same time, as part of a strategy to subvert a
nationalism that was predicated upon a hermetic selfhood, which he
compared to 'masks with exaggerated grimaces that fail to respond to

---

[117] Nandalal Bose, in E. Gladstone Solomon, 'Indian Art in London', *The Times of India* (4
January 1939): 18.
[118] Nandalal Bose, in W. G. Archer, 'The Paintings of Tagore', *East and West* 12, no. 2/3 (June–
September 1961): 151.
[119] In a letter to Suniti Kumar Chatterji dated 20 December 1929, Tagore expressed reservations about subjecting his art to local evaluation. See *Selected Letters of Rabindranath Tagore*, ed.
Krishna Dutta and Andrew Robinson (Cambridge: Cambridge University Press, 1997), 367.
[120] Wong, 'Rabindranath Tagore's Mysterious Faces and India's Encounter with
Modernism', 24.

the ever-changing play of life,' Tagore therefore did not paint Indian history and legends. Tying these two potentially contradictory positions together is the strength of his ambiguity.[121]

This plasticity in art space—ambiguity, shadowiness, masking, radical vigour, irreverence—complicates the identity of Tagore; and the elusiveness, non-authoritative canvas-identity, personality-confrontationist narratives, and the diffusion of art-life emotions, reclaim more grounds for the genesis of a plastic kavi.

Plastic figuralizations allows the kavi-Chitrakar to 'occupy'. It is a very special way of occupation which is not a mere response to something or some force and, also, not a simple act of adding thoughts or experiences to the existent. This is about a declaration of excess that new affective affordances bring, claiming a territory of fresh desire and figures of form and ecology. To occupy is an act that is deeply creative, materializing subjectivities and singularities. The plastic kavi's indulgence in lines and the enigmatic radicalism of self-portraits are about 'occupation'. Rick Dolphijn argues that 'it is art that occupies, that releases the suppressed and that takes over and thus has the power to stage another world. Art realizes occupation as it thinks through involvement like any other "persona" by involving the flows of matter (from paint to the hand of the painter) and the network of ideas linked to it (from fear to jealousy, from subjectivity to objectivity).'[122] When art is more than its presence, it exceeds the artist in a new kind of rhythm of the unsayable and the unperceived. This makes the declaration of Tagore—'I see'—come through with different resonances and tonality.

Gladstone Solomon, writing on Tagore's paintings for *The Times of India*, points out that 'some call them "apotheosis of the doodle" and newspaper mentions it as "aboriginal hauntings" . . . they have been termed as "metamorphosis of the blot" . . . it is all very elusive and very remote. Somewhere in the heart of this medley of the grave and the fantastic, the sinister and the bizarre, one feels that beauty is enshrined'.[123] Such hauntings and metamorphosis make for the plasticization of figures

[121] Ibid.
[122] Rosi Braidotti and Rick Dolphijn, eds., *This Deleuzian Century: Art, Activism, Life* (Leiden: Brill, 2015), 192.
[123] Gladstone Solomon, 'Indian Art in London', 18.

and invite certain irresistible convergences between Paul Klee and plastic Tagore. Klee's observations here are somewhat of an echo of Tagore's concerns: 'At first I was not capable of producing very much, because the discrepancy between initial inspiration and final expression was too great for me to overcome. I had to keep on waiting... I preferred to do nothing until I was sure of the pure form and until the work forced itself upon me ...'[124] This waiting—the pause and the caesura between the dots and the lining of the dots—is crucial to developing the plastic forms that overflow his canvas and pages later. The waiting and its emergence from a long and deep gestation come to life through lines, the rhythm of lines that scarcely bind a plastic kavi to rigid structures and conventions of expression; the plastic rhythm infects his consciousness with a flush and flow that, most often, fail to trace its precise origins. The unfolding and folding-in bring over an experience whose freshness is recurrent. Tagore thought he had 'it' in him ever since he got drawn to the wonders of the surroundings, making him grow in an 'eye hunger'. Paritosh Sen is right to see the correspondence between Klee's observation—'I place myself at a remote starting point of creation whence I state a priori formulae for men, beasts, plants, stones and the elements and for all the whirling forces. In my work, I do not belong to the species, but am a cosmic point of reference'—and Tagore's understanding of art-rhythm. 'Both artists', Sen notes, 'treated the picture surface as two-dimensional, and used line as an important element to delineate forms. An undercurrent of lyricism pervades their expression.'[125] For plastic Tagore, however, there is more fun, and surely less professionalism as he writes: 'I have great fun with my pictures. As you can see, I do not lay on colour all at once. First, I do a light-and-shade sketch, rubbing the pencil, soft or hard. Thereafter, when colour is laid on, it becomes accentuated to a degree.'[126] This fun brings anxiety importing discontent which, invariably, leverages a fresh flush of creativity. The plastic urge to reform, re-present, gets him to dismiss his own art, making him believe in deconstructing himself aesthetically— 'When I do a beautiful picture, that is, when other people call it (nice),

---

[124] Quoted in Paritosh Sen, 'Pandora's Box: The Original Art of Rabindranath Tagore', *India International Centre Quarterly* 17, no. 3/4 (Winter 1990–91): 274.

[125] Klee, *The Diaries of Paul Klee 1898–1918*, ed. Ralph Klee (Berkeley and Los Angeles: University of California Press, 1964), no. 1008, pp. 343–44.

[126] Tagore, quoted in Sen, 'Pandora's Box', 275–76.

I forthwith manage to spoil it. I spill some ink on it or scratch haphazard lines across. Then after it is thoroughly spoilt, I start salvaging it until it assumes some other form.'[127] Salvaging the intentionally and dispiritedly 'spoilt' forms plasticizes other formations, territorializing fresh levels of occupancy.

What Klee looks to find in 'transcendent visible', the plastic kavi sees in the surplus of the Infinite. There is a process and a kinesis to *make* 'visible' possible, an intransitivity that Jean-Luc Nancy has called the 'taking place'. Art like religion is mostly devoted to the unknown, the coming into being of what we never thought was possible or considered as invisible. Alfred Whitehead points out that 'art is a message from the Unseen. It unlooses depths of feeling from behind the frontier where precision of consciousness fails'.[128] Art aims at a reality beside itself— 'something which is real, and yet waiting *to be* realized; something which is a remote possibility, and yet the greatest of present facts; something that gives meaning to all that *passes*, and yet eludes apprehension; something whose possession is the final good, and yet is beyond all reach; something which is the ultimate ideal, and . . . quest'.[129] This is less about making something visible and more about coming into the experience and frames of the visible. The experience is not about what plastic arts make possible or visible; it is the plasticity of art formation, the poetic, that makes itself visible. It announces an experience outside the literary. Plasticity processualizes without making anything rushed—the processual flow has its rhythm. There is a growth, some calibrated, and some unmeasured and unmeasurable. The unity of creation for Klee and plastic Tagore is formed by a sheer depth of feeling and a vision that sees the whole as slightly in excess of the aggregating parts. This excess is the non-guaranteed quotient of a transcendent realization of creativity—as Whitehead notes, the 'habit of art is the habit of enjoying vivid values'.[130] It, again, is not an invitation to disequilibrium; rather, Tagore sees a rhythm in disparity, in contrast and the forces of opposition. Klee, Whitehead, and Tagore submit to a

---

[127] Tagore, quoted ibid., 275.

[128] Alfred North Whitehead, *Adventures of Ideas* (New York: Macmillan, 1961), 349.

[129] Alfred North Whitehead, *Science and the Modern World* (New York: Macmillan, 1954), 275; my italics.

[130] Ibid., 287; Angelo Caranfa, 'Into the Unseen, the Unsaying, the Unknowing: Whitehead's Mystical Aesthetics in Paul Klee', *American Journal of Theology & Philosophy* 39, no. 3 (September 2018): 5–28.

creative event that harmonizes without being a statis; a rhythm whose grounding condition is in plasticizing apparent incongruence and incoherence through the transformative agency of the artist and the mystery of great art that knows its way of balance, assimilation, and interconnection. To an extent, all plastic arts are maya.

A plastic art for Tagore grows in lines, play, fun, a distinct spirit in doing and becoming with unmistakable self-denial and self-interrogation: 'I am no artist, don't you know? My mind has no part in my painting. To paint or seek to do some painting deliberately and give it definite form are just beyond me. Most often it is my doodles which assume some form. Would you call such a one an artist?'[131] Indeed, we can; a plastic artist. The kavi doodles; the doodling kavi is intensely plastic. His one-time secretary Leonard K. Elmhirst sent him a pen from England to encourage his doodling to which Tagore responded: 'You have expressed your hope that this pen of yours will help me in the flowering season of my *eccentricity* which comes from an *excess* of dream energy [. . .]. Of late I have occasionally been compelled to write prose compositions with tracks across them of scratches—the hasty burial places of errors—but they remain there undisturbed like a maze of deserted trenches in a shell-ravaged battlefield.'[132] The handwritten texts of collections of poems like *Purobi* and *Kheya* and the play *Rakta Karabi* are prominent territories for these eccentricities and excess. They 'take the shape of unfurled ribbons, or free hand symbolism, arabesques and ornamental patterns. Of particular interest are the scribbles that took on a zoomorphic resemblance. However, the animals are not bound by rules of naturalism, but rather are creatures plucked from the poet's imagination. Similar to the doodles, his paintings of beasts and birds seem primitive, like primeval, fabled animals of nature.'[133] Forms fascinated Tagore as he spent a lifetime in creating and appreciating forms. The acts of doodling—arguably unintentionally—threw open an 'art-nouveau-like arabesque' which Victoria Ocampo considered as a play with erasures, as a kind of movement from verse to

---

[131] Tagore, quoted in Sen, 'Pandora's Box', 280.

[132] Tagore to Elmhirst, 4 October 1925; cited in *Selected Letters of Rabindranath Tagore*, 323–24; my italics.

[133] Chandrika Acharya, 'Rabindranath Tagore's Sky of Colours' *Artery India*, 8 May 2021. https://arteryindia.com/blog/post/sky-of-colours-rabindranath-tagore?artist=rabindranath-tagore.

verse with his pen 'making lines that suddenly jumped into life out of this play: prehistoric monsters, birds, faces appeared.'[134] The lines form and transform; this 'play of forms' and the acts of 'assembling different forms together'[135] evoke the plastic forms which are realized in figures assuming 'the temperate exaggeration of a probable animal that had unaccountably missed its chance of existence, some a bird that only can soar in our dreams and find its nest in some hospitable lines that we may offer it in our canvas.'[136] The conceptual cluster formed around words— exaggeration, probable, missed, chance, soar, hospitable—does not miss speaking about the flight of lines. Sibyl Moholy-Nagy explains that the first part of Paul Klee's *Pedagogical Sketchbook* (Sections 1.1–1.13) 'introduces the transformation of the static dot into linear dynamics. The line, being successive dot progression, walks, circumscribes, creates passive-blank and active-filled planes.'[137] Adventures and eccentricities in doodles as plastic art are non-presuppositive, unpremeditated acts, which build their own realities; these manifestations are accidental and unexpected emergences where Tagore sees a representation—the continent of the probable and a sudden engagement with the unknown. The doodles discover a plastic kavi as much as they represent the plastic Tagore. The doodled emergences—calligraphic erasures—speak of an imaginary of plastic forms whose enchantment lies in staying invoked with mystery and sublimity.

Although the etymological parentage of the English word 'doodling' would insist on classification that it has against 'scribble', the French *gribouiller*, the Polish *gryzmoli*, and the German *kritzeln* translate into 'scribble' rather than 'dawdle' or 'simpleton'.[138] In Tagore's vernacular it is হিজিবিজি কাটা (aimless lines and scratches). But, Matthew Battles argues,

scribbling is not doodling, because scribbles are marks made in haste or by an uncertain hand. Doodling, by contrast, is beyond craft and

---

[134] Victoria Ocampo, cited in https://sujnaturelover.wordpress.com/2013/07/17/the-last-harvest/ Also see the exhibition in New York, 'Rabindranath Tagore: The Last Harvest', Asia Society, n.d. https://asiasociety.org/new-york/rabindranath-tagore-last-harvest.

[135] Tagore, 'Letter', in *On Art and Aesthetics*, 91.

[136] Tagore, 'My Pictures' (II), in *On Art and Aesthetics*, 101.

[137] Paul Klee, *Pedagogical Sketchbook*, ed. and trans. Sibyl Moholy-Nagy (New York: Frederick A. Praeger, 1960).

[138] Leo Rockas, 'The Rhetoric of Doodle', *College English* 40, no. 2 (October 1978): 139–44.

criticism; it belongs to us all; it's impossible to do it badly—or well. It springs from that flourishing thicket, common to everyone, where mind shoots forth its florid branches from the rootstock of the animal brain. Its intent, if it has one, differs from the pre-liminary brainstorming of sketching and the territorial mark-making of graffiti: it is the graphic expression of ennui, an existential criticism of the world-as-such.'[139]

Even if doodling casts self-doubt in Tagore about his artistic skills and status as an artist, doodles for him don't exist in silence. Resonating with what Erasmus says—'For just as nothing is more trivial than to treat trivial matters in a serious way, so too nothing is more delightful than to treat trifles in such a way that you do not seem to be trifling at all'[140]— Tagore's seeming trifles plasticize a world of thought, are profoundly interpretative, and caught in a deep simplicity. On a comparative note, Oscar Wilde 'was an incorrigible doodler'. Thomas Wright points out that 'he covered his writing papers and notebooks in a deluge of arabesque decorative patterns, desultory drawings, geometric and architectural designs. He often poured out these images in prodigal profusion, at a rate of one, two, three, four, five, even six doodles a page' (p. 80). Wilde's 'Poems Notebook' (tentatively dated 1874–81) is 'a cornucopia of drawings and decorations. On one page you'll see, in the margin of some verse, pictures of jewels, clothes, pianos. On another you'll find, between Wilde's lines, intricate patterns or sketches of rivers, boats, butterflies.'[141] Competence and adroitness are not the key items here; but a kind of active indulgence, artistic lethargy, an inertia of absentmindedness crept into these doodles.[142] Doodles speak of figural plasticity as we know how 'Leonardo Da Vinci scribbled sketches and calligraphic designs all over his notebooks in the belief that doodling would liberate his imagination, encouraging a free flow of images, words, and ideas', how Flaubert loved 'to sketch boxes in his mss and then shade them in with parallel lines; Keats drew flowers in his student notes; Dostoyevsky covered his papers

---

[139] Matthew Battles, 'In Praise of Doodling', *The American Scholar* 73, no. 4 (Autumn 2004): 105–8.

[140] Quoted in Jessica Stevenson Stewart, 'Toward a Hermeneutics of Doodling in The Era of Folly', *Word & Image* 29, no. 4 (2013): 409–27.

[141] Thomas Wright, 'Wilde the Doodle Dandy: A Scholarly Doodle', *The Wildean: Journal of the Oscar Wilde Society* 47 (July 2015): 65–89.

[142] Ibid.

with architectural designs, while Lewis Carroll enjoyed sketching human figures and profiles'.[143] For the plastic kavi হিজিবিজি কাটা is not mere indulgent random; here reflection leads to a release. I disagree with Wright that these are merely 'decorative and illustrative art in their own right', and not to be placed 'within conventional artistic traditions—alongside, say, illuminated medieval manuscripts or the illustrated poetry mss of William Blake'.[144] Even if they don't have a very high literary value, the lines and images are too subtle and provocative to remain as mere embellishments and prettifying. There is no escaping from the lines, admits Tagore: 'Every day they are revealing themselves anew in ever new shapes and attitudes. There is no end to this mystery'.[145] Through 'irrelevant caprice of forms',[146] indulgence and truancy, the plastic kavi has no settlement in those plastic lines since some show 'anger, some placid benevolence' and some 'essential laughter' as forms and formations can often be accidents. Abstract passion and subtle suggestions make for the plasticity of the mind that joins the lines and creates images of 'non-deliberate origin'. It is here that conspicuous subjectivity responsible for the growth in the canvas meets with a challenge as Tagore experiences his art without words and finds music without words too. There is a release from the chains of discursivity, a linguistic schema, as indefiniteness becomes the motif of representation. Plasticity emerges out of such independence, a space that forgets its subservience to justification, validity, and sensible meaning-making. Plastic lines conceal stories—unconscious, psychoanalytical, recessive, articulation in alternative forms of expressions—well beyond the ambit of the pages that hold them in fascinatingly unfamiliar shapes and appearances. Such involvement and investment in lines and dots, in images and intentions, in appearance and surprises, make for trans-plastic habits in aesthetic failings and affective affordances. Words can often prove incomplete and images and illustrations fill out a deficit; this is not about compensating for the verbal lack and choke and may be completely disconnected from the text whose territory it physically occupies. This disconnection may speak about another version of plastic behaviour.

---

[143] Ibid., 80.
[144] Ibid., 83.
[145] Tagore, 'Letter', in *On Art and Aesthetics*, 91.
[146] Tagore, 'My Mistress of the Line', in *On Art and Aesthetics*, 87.

Tagore admits his training in rhythm—the rhythm in thought, the rhythm in sound. It is rhythm that determines the surplus, the expression and occupation; it gives any desultoriness a reality, redeems irrelevance. A plastic kavi knows that all scribbles, daubs, and tinkering have their rhythm—a rescue that only rhythm can pull off. The poetics of figural plasticity is an understanding in rhythm. It is in the declaration of the untrained hand, the unconscious self, the wanton movements and the wander; the danger of not being visually meaningful underlines a rhythm: the plastic rhythm. This rhythm was Tagore's only training since those days when words and ideas started to pursue and settle in him. He knew that 'rhythm gives reality to that which is desultory, which is insignificant to itself'.[147] Although Tagore is annoyed by what the 'scattered scratches' in his manuscripts do—'they represent regrettable mischance, like a gapingly foolish crowd stuck in a wrong place, undecided as to how or where to move on'—the plastic kavi knows how the apparent unrelatedness, random, and erraticism speak of a rhythm that builds sense quite removed from how we understand it as the mere antonym of nonsense. Williams and Taylor point out that

the brief mental vacation afforded by drawing may have allowed the writer's conscious mind to rest while the subconscious surmounted the difficulty; and examination may in fact reveal some connection between the text and the doodle, although not necessarily a linear or logical one. Although both creative activities, writing is linear, logical, and left-brain, whereas doodling is intuitive, spontaneous, and right-brain. Because the doodler is somewhat absent-minded, the writing implement is moved more or less autonomously, and the resulting drawings may reveal more, perhaps, than more consciously crafted artistic creations.[148]

The rhythm inscribed in such lines of seeming moreness, drift, and frivolity—existing as mute eloquence—produces a disinterested pleasure; in works of such reclamation and rescue, the revenge of aesthetics is born.

---

[147] Ibid., 97.
[148] Dave Williams and Chris Taylor, 'Peripheral Expressions: Samuel Beckett's Marginal Drawings in Endgame', *Journal of Beckett Studies* 19, no. 1 (April 2010): 29–55.

The plastic rhythm prepares the 'salvation' for the apparent irrelevance and sporadic scratches in his manuscript—a kind of rescue performed through a 'finality of rhythm'.

In a quaint way, the woman writer in Tamura Toshiko's short story 'A Woman Writer' ('Onna sakusha', 1913), never writes but doodles—not words but lines and curves as the only metaphoric or symptomatic performatives:

> This woman writer's head was filled with residues, the very last remnants of her squeezed brain, and no matter how much she compressed positions her head-bag, neither a word with flesh nor a fragment with the smell of blood would come out. She had been tossing around her idea for a commission by a publisher since the very end of last year. Every day she sat behind her desk and did nothing but doodle flax leaves and vertical lines in the grids of the ruled paper.[149]

There is a plasticity in staging and play that exceeds a mere act in lines; it has a motivation, somewhat indistinct, a sense of production with the lingering shadows of waste, and a triviality with a touch of seriousness. Interestingly, for a plastic kavi words are struck through into lines—an unveiling that words under erasure could make possible. A certain careless liberty of the imagination and a submission to the vagaries of emotion construct a series of plastic moments for Tagore—moments that aspire to a 'fitness of cadence' and figure a poetics of relationality. The surplus through plastic rhythm engenders 'forms' that baffle; and such bafflement is perpetuated through heterogenous strokes of emotional and ideational intervention and the struggle to fit into the 'interrelated balance of fulfilment'. Creation breathes the best in crisis. It is never the best when 'interpretation of an idea or representation of a fact'[150] govern its emergence and status. Within such plasticities of experience and emergences, meaning ceases and often eases into 'sense'—the presence of meaning. Within a plastic poesis, the burden of meaning or unmeaningness (which again analytically leads to meaning) does not exist. These

---

[149] Shu Kuge, 'Politics of Doodling: Tamura Toshiko's "A Woman Writer"', *positions: east asia cultures critique* 15, no. 3 (Winter 2007): 487–509.

[150] Tagore, 'Pictures (I)', in *On Art and Aesthetics*, 98.

plastic lines are not symbolic or signifying and yet not reckless, signifying nothing. The plasticity here is deeply complex in that the lines have their initiation and the kinesis that helps a drawing to come through but not without a semi-randomness; it aligns with a 'continuity, and without succumbing to disorder at the same time'. When asked about the meaning of his pictures, Tagore maintains that they are silent as he is; 'it is for them to express and not to explain'.[151] In positive plasticity (the giving, in Malabou's words) it is a passion for the 'irrelevance' and speaks about the 'unconscious courage of the unsophisticated'; revelling in individuation, in negative plasticity (in receiving, in annihilation), they are lines that 'perpetually disturb peace'.[152]

Tim Ingold writes that 'people inhabit a world that consists, in the first place, not of things but of lines. After all, what is a thing, or indeed a person, if not a tying together of the lines—the paths of growth and movement—of all the many constituents gathered there? Originally, "thing" meant a gathering of people, and a place where they would meet to resolve their affairs. As the derivation of the word suggests, everything is a parliament of lines'.[153] It is not just everything being a parliament of lines but it is about imagining the universe as 'a universe of lines which in their movements and combinations pass on their signals of existence along the interminable *chain of moments*. The rocks and clouds, the trees, the waterfalls, the dance of the fiery orbs, the endless procession of life send up across silent eternity and limitless space a symphony of gestures with which mingles the dumb wail of lines that are widowed gypsies roaming about for a *chance* union of fulfilment'.[154] Do those lines, coursing and collapsing into each other, create forms of anti-art? The factoring of chance and the rhythm of lack in the expression 'widowed gypsies' make for a kind of plasticity responsible for the possible fulfilment of art and creativity. It is the lack in art, the insufficiency of meaning, the sense of being bereft, and a feeling of being deficient that form the passage between an idea and creation. The plastic kavi's 'manuscript of creation' has 'erring lines and erasures, solitary incongruities'[155]

---

[151] Tagore, 'My Pictures (III)', in *On Art and Aesthetics*, 104.
[152] Tagore, 'My Pictures (II)', in *On Art and Aesthetics*, 100.
[153] Tim Ingold, *Lines: A Brief History* (Abingdon: Routledge, 2007), 5.
[154] Tagore, 'My Pictures (II)', in *On Art and Aesthetics*, 100; emphasis mine.
[155] Ibid.

against the 'principle of beauty and balance'; and, instead of what Tagore thinks as 'condemnation', they bear out rhythm of indiscipline, indiscrimination, vagrancy, and flight. The 'casualties'[156] of his manuscript, the certain abstractness of expressions, the flights of his metaphors and words, the deep imagination, aberrative curiosities come together to put a productive plasticity in force, projecting a plastic kavi in expressive and interpretative frames. The challenging religio-aesthetic dimension of this line-art-space comes from the poet's faith in the Infinite as artist: the inexhaustible plastic reality of the Infinite delighting in 'drawing lines upon lines to set a limit to himself'.[157] The intriguing paradox in the coming together of inexhaustibility and limits is not without forming and a sense of proportion. This proportion builds around a 'joy' as lines flow, overflow, and yet are not reckless and indiscriminate beyond restraint. Plastic lines have a reason for their outflow and measure of their seeming measurelessness. Art has its surplus in reason; plasticity in artistic consciousness comes with an inherent sense of proportion.

The plasticity of Tagore's artistic effusions and, often, his writings, hinge on causality and structuration. They are neither about an enchainment to a certain tradition of structural growth nor an inflexible allegiance to a system of thinking. Tagore's near submersion into Vedantic thinking does not make him philosophically monistic; a transversality and relationality inform his philosophy of art and life. There is a certain 'metastable field individuation'[158] that informs sāhitya and notions of art in their becoming. A plastic kavi cannot afford to reduce all aesthetic experiences to interpretation, to a systematization of norms and principles of expression. This is why I prefer to see him working from the margins, creating a 'minor' effect on opening up different forms of expression and truth-experiences. His plasticity is not in interpretation as explanation and decoding; it is in transversality, the ante-border mode of disciplinary experiences and conceptual overlappings. Tagore is never so intense and committed to transversality as Deleuze and Guattari are but, with him as with them, experimentation replaces interpretation to a large extent.

---

[156] Ibid., 101.

[157] Tagore, 'Letter', in *On Art and Aesthetics*, 91.

[158] Anne Sauvagnargues, *Deleuze and Art*, trans. Samantha Bankston (London: Bloomsbury, 2005), 74.

In doodles and paintings, in music and philosophy of sāhitya, it is an inherent transversality that prioritizes relations over rigid structures. There is, in his plastic arts, a sense of incompletion that is not without proportion, a restlessness that is never without order. This is what I see as an extra-corporeality in art and thinking—it is 'alloplastic'. The transversality in thinking through life and art through *sadhana*, understanding sāhitya and image-making through *tapasya*, blocks certain accepted interpretative truths of understanding. Tagore as a plastic kavi has built its own entry and take-off points.

The refusal to see meaning and being pinned with a meaning leads to a swarm of senses, a sensing beyond meaning. Finding sense through the infinite, love and surplus is not about finding meaning through the formal premises of understanding, lexically, taxonomically, and paradigmatically. The meaning is experienced through a 'mobility of sense'.[159] Sense is not always in making the sensible; sense is circulation. 'We know that this great world-verse, that runs from sky to sky,' writes Tagore, 'is not made for the mere enumeration of facts—it is not "Thirty days hath September"—it has its direct revelation in our delight. That delight gives us the key to the truth of existence; it is personality acting upon personalities through incessant manifestations'.[160] The delight through sense inhabits the liminality between a generation of meaning world that is not readily accessible to common understanding and an understanding that believes in the surfeit, the excess of being, and the 'what is' which is difficult to negotiate. The productive plasticity of letting the world be known through sense—both the sense of the world and world of sense—and not always in certitude and 'regime of signification' contributes to Tagore's tireless agenda of 'I see'. 'Relation' (seeing 'I see' as sense making and sense generation) is the conceptual platform that connects Nancy with Tagore; not that, necessarily and expectedly, the connections and enunciation are similar but it constructs a 'sensization' of the world that breaks the interior with the exterior, bringing both into a hand-shaking distance. It is the 'to' that for both is a strong prepositional mobility—not the 'to' that becomes the 'signifying relay or directional sending', the index of a finality of perception and understanding. The plasticity here

---

[159] Verena Andermatt Conley, 'Nancy's Worlds', *Diacritics* 42, no. 2 (2014): 84–98.
[160] Tagore, 'The Creative Ideal', n.p.

connects with the 'signifying hinge of the preposition "to" (à)' that 'acti-
vates the empowering indeterminacy of "coming into being" (passage à
l'acte)'.[161] Nancy and Tagore think deeply around 'to' where sense exceeds
signification as all things cannot be mechanically calculated to aggre-
gate into a meaning and reduced to a form of explanatory analysis (Latin
explano, in the sense of flattening or spread out). A plastic kavi believes
in the openness to others, being exposed to other forms of manifestation,
to time, language, and affect. This is the centrality of 'relation' that for
both maintains 'to' and 'an infinite toward'.[162] As in art, so in doodles
and sāhitya, it is about discovering 'how we can desire something else,
or desire differently'.[163] The desire working on an 'element of unpredictability'[164] helps plastic art to build on a 'hint of a line' and then keep the
desire alive to see the lime becoming a form—'As I watch the trees, I seem
to see so much of them'.[165] Since Tagore's lines are wanderings, plastic
arts in the form of his projects, social and educational, are events in wandering too. Nancy notes that 'wandering and method, method of wandering, methodical wandering, way that is not traced but is itself the trace
of an advancing step, a step about to pass by, about to awaken for itself the
possibility of a direction, a destination, a desire. Just making known its
desire, which invents itself with every step, although being merely the desire of the step itself—which is, all in all, only the essence of desiring. Just
desire'.[166] Desire inheres deep in plastic arts and the desiring kavi could
never leave his wanderings. All forms of plastic art are founded in aesthetic genesis which is ontogenetic and has its own epigenetic nature. In
such relationality lies the plastic rhythm, leaving us exposed to encounters whose resonance, connection, and network leave behind forms that
Nancy sees as presence, access to excess, and Tagore as surplus.

World, for Nancy, argues Verena Conley, 'bears the attributes of
"being-to" or "being forward" as rapport, relation, address, sending, donation, presentation in a relation where entities and existents relate to

[161] Timothy Murray, 'Prepositional Oscillations: Politics, Ontology, Poetics', *Diacritics* 43,
no. 4 (2015): 3.
[162] Philip Armstrong, Jason Smith, and Jean-Luc Nancy, 'Politics and Beyond: An Interview
with Jean-Luc Nancy', *Diacritics* 43, no. 4 (2015): 96.
[163] Ibid., 95.
[164] Tagore, 'Letter', in *On Art and Aesthetics*, 89.
[165] Ibid., 91.
[166] Nancy, *Expectations*, 34.

each other'.[167] A plastic kavi, much like Nancy's philosopher, believes in how the 'relational virtue of sense is one where transformation is possible'. The worldization of sense and sens-ing is in *anandadhara bohiche bhuvaneh*, in *lila*, in doodles, that flow out as flights of determination and the unconscious and create images that are never what we would accept as true representation: so, extension, excess, and exceeding inform such image making and understanding. The world is 'coextensive with taking-place of all existing, of existing in its singularity' and 'coextensive', Conley explains, 'in the double sense of co-extended (co-spaced, co-opened) and co-tendered, co-arriving, co-expressing. The world is always a plurality of *worlds*'.[168] For plastic Tagore the world is profoundly *worlds* where worlding is presence and presencing, indexing meaning and making sense, being part of sense and allowing a sense-ability that creates truths of understanding. Nancy writes that 'as soon as a world appears to me as a world, I already share something of it: I share a part of its inner resonances . . . A world is space in which a certain tonality resonates'.[169] Sharing for both Nancy and plastic Tagore is about presencing and relationality and the world is in inhabiting it and not mere simple dwelling (*séjour*). Conley explains further that '"to inhabit" recalls the ghost of the philologist whispering in his ear. The infinitive is close to habitus and ethos, that is, a manner of being-in-the-world. *Habitare* and habitus come from habere, to hold and to keep oneself. To occupy a place is to have a way of relating to it and to have a value of being'.[170] Transplastic (in)habitation is about making and generating sense and a plastic kavi never exists outside such generation. Where the poet is the *mayavin*, and the world and reality have their own *lila*, and *ananda* flows and folds into every atom of our being and being with the world, there is an immanence, collapsing homes that separate and encompassing homes that connect.

Paul Klee writes that

we have worked hard: but genius is not hard work, despite the proverb. Genius is not even partly hard work, as might be claimed on the ground

---

[167] Conley, 'Nancy's Worlds', 89.
[168] Ibid.
[169] Jean-Luc Nancy, *The Creation of the World or Globalization*, trans. François Raffoul and David Petigrew (Albany, NY: State University of New York, 2007), 42.
[170] Conley, 'Nancy's Worlds', 92.

that geniuses have worked hard, in spite of their genius. Genius is genius. Grace; *it is without beginning and end.* It is creation. Genius cannot be taught, because it is not a norm but an exception. It is hard to reckon with the *unexpected.* And yet as leader it is always far ahead. It bursts ahead in the same direction or in another direction. This very day, perhaps, it is already in a place we seldom think of. For from the standpoint of dogma, genius is often a *heretic.* It has no law other than itself. The school had best keep quiet about genius; it had best keep a respectful distance.[171]

In being a heretic, exceptional and irreverent, the genius is plastic. This claims sufficient grounds for what I argue as Tagore's 'plastic art' as it unfolds and exhibits the range of its understanding through a distinct understanding of sāhitya, the building of the ashram school and later the university (Visva Bharati), his historical and political consciousness, and the unique engagements with nature, the Infinite, and love. In conceiving, narrating, and executing his plastic art, Tagore fails to write and think in a way that fits him into a discursive pattern to be able to get categorized—mostly outside the DNA of understanding. His plastic art holds a sheer amount of 'belonging', and the challenge to negotiate his arguments outside certain well-entrenched principles of ideation and execution accumulates a power and pervasiveness—a deep invitation into a narrative of thought and action that any stodgy and staid understanding of world and art would never have been able to manage. Plastic art leaves all experience on the edge, a little short of a pointed and deeply categorized understanding: it fails the readers and leaves open a criticism that inspires thinking beyond thought. The plastic Tagore is processed out of such a thinking. Within such a premise of plastic art, Tagore is deeply theoretical with a difference. Plastic Tagore, as this book commits to reveal, is part of a movement of thinking.

---

[171] Paul Klee, *Paul Klee* (New York: Parkstone International, 2013), 159; my italics.

2

Plastic Pedagogy

When can critical understanding reach a 'flashpoint'? Can interpretation be explosive? If in chemistry a flashpoint refers to the temperature at which a particular organic compound ignites, how do
we configure the flashpoints in the performance and articulation of
philosophical-literary-cultural-pedagogical thinking? Critical thinking
is conflictual and combustible; it is inherently hostile, changing its temperature and transition points for possible 'flare-ups'. It is the volatility
and conflagratory properties—the bursting into something from something else—that make a critical understanding plastic. What I call plastic
pedagogy is innately combustible and inflammatory. Like the chemical
compound that needs the temperature (fire point) and the exposure to air
to ignite, plastic pedagogy throws up several units of thinking and intervention in the form of a concept having a breaking point, thoughts in
crisis and volatility, the 'peaking' of critical understanding, emergence
of critical moments, turning points and tension, and critical discourse
suffering its own vicissitudes and threshold threats. It jeopardizes conventional habitations, builds critical thought-precarity, generates in-
spirations to venture, constructs exposure, and cultivates vulnerability.
In fact, habits make us vulnerable; and plastic pedagogy owes to trans-
plastic habituality.

Catherine Malabou in her reading of habit through Hegel finds
genuine plasticity in a restive transaction between essence and form,
contingency and accident, necessity and the possible. In *The Future of
Hegel*, she writes that 'in the etymology of the word "habit" we discover
the Latin word *habere*: "habit" is a way of "having", and in this sense, a
kind of possession, a property'.[1] Malabou argues that

---

[1] Catherine Malabou, *The Future of Hegel: Plasticity, Temporality and Dialectic*, trans.
Lisabeth During (New York: Routledge, 2005), 37.

Plastic Tagore. Ranjan Ghosh, Oxford University Press. © Ranjan Ghosh 2024.
DOI: 10.1093/9780198922995.003.0002

Hegel brings out here the sense of a 'having' derived from a 'mechanism'. Habit is in truth 'mechanism of self-feeling' (*Mechanismus des Selbstgefühls*).

It is habit which gives the soul the possibility of escaping from the two kinds of mania previously described: idiocy—the self over-concentrated on itself—and alienation—where a particular part of the self is clung to. Habit emerges as a liberating process, saving the soul from the two forms of dissolution—either lost in the emptiness of ideality or absorbed in a determinate part isolated from the whole.[2]

However, this 'having' is exposed to sculpting which is about not allowing the marble to stay at rest. The marble is itself an invitation, a culture, to habits of change and recontouring and, as Malabou argues, 'plastic individuality makes it possible to imagine the "conformity" of singularity with the universal by means of a perspective totally different from that of pure and simple subordination'.[3] Singularities of the self learn to overcome the substance-fixity of the soul-corporeal unity; this learning creates the possibilities for the self. Through a *Bildung*, it horizonizes the possibilities differently. The subject is liberated to 'see' what is there and what is coming and starts to live in the 'to come'.

Habit has the nature of seamlessly becoming the self through a process that Malabou describes as 'disappearing subject' or a 'self-absenting'. Habit makes the subject lose its own history into a self-feeling that makes it become the identity, as something that has always been there. This is the 'having': 'Habit murders man. And it does so as surely as it makes man live.'[4] But habit is inherently plastic for it took a habit to grow and make a leap from the contingent to the essential; but then the essential can be challenged again, revised and readdressed, to make it affirmative in a different way. Once a property, habit can also be lost and repossessed differently, taking forms, reclaimed as a property again, that can surprise its status of the essential. Plastic Tagore finds his home by being not-at-home in the world. His thinkings on education and educational projects are all habitations in 'thoughts to come'—a future lived in the present and the

[2] Ibid.
[3] Ibid., 26.
[4] Ibid., 76.

living in futurity through the present. Reformulative pedagogy is about unmaking habits where making home for oneself is plasticizing a home with others: a world under trans-plastic habits is a state of forming. The alienation of the plastic kavi comes from accidentalities and contingencies which stem from the disappearance of an educator into the 'coming' of a poet-educator. This comes close to Nietzsche's spirit of revenge. Malabou explains that for Nietzsche 'revenge is essentially another name for repetition. Revenge, taking revenge, wreaking, meaning to push, drive, herd, pursue, persecute . . . The human is the only being that seeks revenge after an offense. This should not be confused with, for example, divine punishment, for gods can punish men, but they don't seek revenge proper. It has nothing to do with struggle or conflict either: animals can fight and kill each other, but it does not occur out of vengeful instinct. Revenge is human, all too human.'[5] However, this revenge as repetition is not rigidification, not iteratively mechanical. It is not always a submission to finitude although waiting to die is repeating oneself to avenge the suffering of living. It is a spirit of revenge against Law, against transiency and the relentless passing of time: 'We are humans, seeking revenge for being human.' But Nietzsche's Overman is the plastic man; 'instead of thinking of repetition as the return of the same—that "most abysmal thought"—he learns to recognize that the space for difference it opens. That is, he learns to affirm what is repeated, thus transforming repetition itself. Instead of passively bearing what happens, one can desire it, plastically.'[6] Plastic Tagore sees the differentialities in the revenge of living where the repetitive educator self-explodes (destructive plasticity) into a return of being whose relationship with time, values, and law is fresh and radical. There is a joy in the revenge, implying an 'openness to what makes the routine of time explode, that is, the event'. The plastic explosion in the routine of time produces contraction of habits as the 'being-at-home' state of habit-performance is exposed to a refashioning or resculpting into other forms of habitation and homecoming.

Malabou points out that 'thought's very life depends on its power to awaken that vital energy which tends to "mortify" itself, to become

---

[5] Catherine Malabou, 'Superhumanity', e-flux, February 2018, https://www.e-flux.com/archi tecture/superhumanity/179166/repetition-revenge-plasticity/.

[6] Ibid.

sedimented into fixed and rigid positions. The outcome that will follow depends on this awakening: thought has nothing to do but wait for the habitués to look at their habits.[7] Is plastic Tagore here the non-habitués? His politics of counter leave him as 'not-at-home, the improper, propertyless, nonaccommodated, the refused, the foreclosed'. He is 'the excluded, the expropriated: if habit is the "sculptor" of plasticity, then the nonhabitués are those who have had their ontological right to shaping a world in which they can be at home with, which is the "proper," stolen, re-fused; their instruments blunted, chances taken, and possibilities muted. And it is this very expropriation, this impossibility, which acts as the ongoing possibility of the habitués' world. The nonhabitués thus force a critical reappraisal of habit and plasticity.[8] Plastic pedagogy, by this logic, is not merely an understanding in explosive patterns of pedagogical understanding. It forms, experiences the forming, and experiences anni-hilation. Flashpoints in thinking and formation are explosions that con-struct forms, develop their points of ignition from forms that are difficult to destroy, and initiate differentiations in critical thinking and aesthetic-ethical experiences.

This chapter identifies two forms of plastic habits as pedagogical per-formatives: one in Rabindranath Tagore's delicately dynamic under-standing of eco-corporeal pedagogy and the second in his ideas of counter-institutionality as revealed through the establishment of an international university called Visva Bharati. It would be almost a 'cate-gory mistake' if we were to read Rabindranath Tagore as merely an Indian subcontinental thinker. His wide interdisciplinary interests, extensive travels in Asia, Europe, and America, and his extraordinary range of in-tellectual sympathy enabled him to absorb all that he found was essen-tial and significant in Western and Eastern thought. It is on this note of transversality that Tagore's thoughts on education, in this chapter, come to get interpreted through flashpoint moments as revealed through a fresh understanding of body pedagogy and institution-formation. His plasticity of understanding and approach to education emerged from a space of a poet-educator as the 'unbounded cosmopolitanism' in him

---

[7] Malabou, *The Future of Hegel*, 190.
[8] Thomas Wormald, 'Habitués', in *Thinking Catherine Malabou: Passionate Detachments*, ed. Thomas Wormald and Isabell Dahms (New York: Rowman and Littlefield, 2018), 123–38.

combined with an 'existential engagement with one's tradition and the constellations of traditions that constitute the world'.[9] Saranindranath Tagore rightly observes that the 'Tagorean conception of rationality does not merely yield postmodern toleration of alterity, but aspires to dissolve instances of otherness altogether by enriching one's own tradition through hermeneutic absorption and assimilation'.[10] Tagore's understanding of reason encouraged talks across cultures and put the local in communication with the global, the home and world coming together into a cross-traffic of enabling discourses of knowledge and ideas. His ethics and aesthetics of educational thinking and philosophy demand that he be read in the cross-traffic of traditions, plasticities of knowledge systems, and flashpoints of epistemic understanding. He has left behind a legacy of cross-traditional thinking and remarkable congeries of ideas that have percolated beyond his immediate context and culture of understanding. Reading Tagore now is more about reading Tagore 'with'—in a productive hyphen. The 'with' inspires the pedagogical flashpoints. We are *with* plastic Tagore. He addresses the figures of non-homogeneity whether in the concept of his ashram or the construction of the university through a fluidification that keeps challenging the unitary wholeness of colonial educational system, the set ideologies of instructive teaching, the teacher–student dialogism and materialist-instrumentalist purchase from a uni-centric pedagogy. Plastic Tagore cannot afford to see his projects as models of preformationism—objects and realities waiting to be discovered and amassed. Malabou's Hegel is plastic Tagore's school with no guarantee of concepts in advance to pursue and realize—the unpacking of wolves of ideas and structures. The chest was scarcely there to be excavated and possessed. Education can never be poetry without speculative trial, accident, gradual differentiation, and the secret index of the future.

As an artist-intellectual Tagore had always argued for cultural refinement, an emancipatory ferment and a dynamic consciousness that connected the home and the world—the public and the private—and eclectically problematized the relation between tradition and modernity.

---

[9] Saranindranath Tagore, 'Tagore's Conception of Cosmopolitanism: A Reconstruction', *University of Toronto Quarterly* 77, no. 4 (2008): 1081.

[10] Ibid., 1078.

He works from within a Vedantic and Hindu tradition which is richly diverse, and yet is not unmindful of the ways in which other traditions in their heterogeneity impinge on his own. Tradition have always appeared to Tagore as creative: his appropriations have been aesthetic, dynamic, non-adversarial, and dialogic.[11] He chooses to settle on a busy confluence—flashpoints of vibrant possibilities—to realize the universal nature of the artist in him, excavating in the process the transnational intellectual which he quintessentially is. Bundles of habits crack and crackle when the dream, the spirit of projection, has a sublime power and the inspiration to swim through currents and not resist them. His work is meaningfully opposed to hegemonic universalism and deeply oppositional to the imposition of one local set of beliefs and customs on everyone else. Instead, he has an unwavering support for empathic universalism—a universalism that does not impose dogma but fosters a sense of common humanity across the many particularisms that define our daily lives. As an artist of creative humanism, Tagore believes that the final nature of the world does not depend upon the comprehension of an individual person; rather, comprehension is associated with the universal human mind which has the power to plasticize the limits of knowledge, power, love, and enjoyment, allowing Tagore to remain on course to approach the universal.[12] The spirit of the artist is not an abstraction from the world; it draws upon the worldliness. It feeds on a dynamic aesthetic of wholeness, working out a vision which refutes 'absolute divisions between body and mind, matter and life, individual and

---

[11] Tagore writes, 'The tradition which is helpful is like a channel that helps the current to flow. It is open where the water runs onward, guarding it only where there is danger in deviation. The bee's life in its channel of habit has no opening: it revolves within a narrow circle of perfection. Man's life has time-honoured institutions which are its organised habits. When these act as enclosures, then the result may be perfect, like a bee-hive of wonderful precision of form but unsuitable for the mind which has unlimited possibilities of progress.' See Rabindranath Tagore, 'Art and Tradition', in *Angel of Surplus*, ed. Sisirkumar Ghose (Kolkata: Visva Bharati, 1978), 50–51.

[12] Tagore's understanding of the 'universal' is not precise, a concept and experience that can be formulated with determinate grounds of understanding. Universal is Tagore's infinite, a totality, an Eternity, that awaits being realized and approached. This is inexhaustible and recurrent—not homogenous and totalitarian but generative, surplusive, and a unique manifestation of expression.

society, community and nation, and empire and the world'.[13] This is the artistic aspiration for the universal, the continual intellectual striving to partner the local with the global, and also the reasoned articulation emerging from a profound understanding of Indian culture which he always wanted to see as removed from self-containment and insularity.

The two sections in this chapter—one on body-eco-pedagogy and the other on the making of an unconventional university—speak of a plastic pedagogical philosophy that claims that schooling can often begin when the school is under suspension. Jan Masschelein observes that 'it is formative and transformative: a world takes place, "things" appear, but in their appearing also the individual is transformed and co-appears and an interest in the sense of inter-esse can develop'. This leads us to the vexed issue of caring for the self 'as being a care for what inter-ests'. For plastic Tagore, within the metaphysics of *scholé*, knowing the world was as important as what the world tells me or us—a conjugality in 'being exposed together'.[14] The interventions in trying to see the trans-praxiality of body, nature, and pedagogy and the deeply oppositional forces in the coming into being of a university or a school construct their own flashpoints; this announces a plastic pedagogy that thrives and performs in the 'leading out': not always the outside but the far inside which cannot be reached 'by uprooting oneself but by plunging deep within towards what is most intimate, where lies desire'.[15] In that sense, Tagore's understanding of education is self-educative, is about being led out of himself, a dependence not on the colonial outside but his Eros inside. Both his nature-education and concepts of institutional building, as discussed in what follows, thus converge on the significance of dissipative learning—a plastic pedagogy that legislates in the liminality of excess, explosion, and law.

---

[13] S. Radhakrishnan, *The Philosophy of Rabindranath Tagore* (Baroda: Good Companions Publishers, 1961), 408.

[14] Jan Masschelein, 'Experimentum Scholae: The World Once More . . . But Not (Yet) Finished', in *Making Sense of Education*, ed. Gert J. J. Biesta (Dordrecht: Springer, 2012), 105.

[15] Jean-François Lyotard, 'Foreword: Spaceship', trans. Rosemary Arnoux, in *Education and the Postmodern Condition*, ed. Michael Peters (Westport, CT: Bergin & Garvey, 1995), xx.

Flashpoint I

Bird, Skin, and Body

'By the bank of the river Padma, in Shilaidaha, I lived a quiet life amidst my literary pursuits,' writes Tagore. 'With a mission to create I came to Santiniketan.'[16] It was a sublime mission in that it endeavoured to realize an 'ambition' which largely knew the immense difficulties it had to encounter and yet which ceaselessly inspired him to turn an ashram into a school woven round with fresh ideals of education and a distinct aesthetics of pedagogy. This sublimity works on the aesthetics of splendid waste, as opposed to the cringing pressures of economic gain, social prosperity, and cultural recognition. The destructive plasticity, non-habitués, which triggers the poet's dislocation, is the delightful 'irresponsibility' of the butterfly. Tagore writes, 'The silkworm seems to have a cash value credited in its favour somewhere in Nature's accounting department . . . but the butterfly is irresponsible. The significance which it may possess has neither weight nor use and is lightly carried on its pair of dancing wings. Perhaps it pleases someone in the heart of the sunlight, the Lord of colours, who has nothing to do with account books and has a perfect mastery in the great art of wastefulness.'[17] The ashram school is set up by courting values which could not have discounted the butterfly (the ideal,

---

[16] See Tagore, 'Siksha', in *Rabindra Rachanabali*, vol. 14 (Kolkata: Government of West Bengal, Saraswati Press Limited, 1992), 477. Tagore arrived at Santiniketan in 1901. He writes: 'Fortunately for me I had a place ready to my hand where I could begin my work. My father, in one of his numerous travels, had selected this lonely spot as the one suitable for his life of communion with God. This place, with a permanent endowment, he dedicated to the use of those who seek penance and seclusion for their meditation and prayer. I had about ten boys with me when I came here and started my new life with no previous experience whatsoever.' Tagore, 'My School', in *Personality* (Kolkata: Rupa, 2002), 141. 'It is against the nature of a genius to be content', writes Rathindranath Tagore, eldest son of the poet, 'with a monotonous existence or be satisfied with a single purpose in life. Father was no exception. Throughout his life he would constantly want to change his living quarters, his surroundings, his food and his clothes and, what mattered most, he needed fresh fields to give scope to his active and a creative mind. It was no wonder that Shilaidaha could not hold him for very long. His next move was to Santiniketan. He had become restless and was eager to find a congenial place where he could experiment with his ideas about education.' *On the Edges of Time* (Visva Bharati, 1958), 41. The formal opening ceremony was performed on 23 December 1901.

[17] Tagore, 'A Poet's School', in *Towards Universal Man* (London: Asia Publishing House, 1961), 285. This essay was written in 1926.

what is conventionally understood as impractical) against the silkworm (*utilitas* and *potentia*). When Tagore brought together a few boys 'one sunny day in winter, among the warm shadows of the tall straight sal trees with their branches of quiet dignity, he started to write a poem in a medium not of words'. Seeking to exorcise the phantom of his boyhood experiences at school where he was briefly enrolled, the poet sought to 'live in the lives of other boys, and to build its missing paradise with ingredients which may not have any orthodox material, prescribed measure, or standard value'.[18] He desires to have a school away from the turmoil of human habitation, aspiring to a site for 'quiet studies and teaching'; here his pupils can 'grow up in the sacred and profound atmosphere of learning'—a school inaugurated with five students and five teachers (interestingly, much to the chagrin of Hindu orthodoxists, among the five teachers Tagore recruited, three were Christians—two of whom were Catholics and the third his son's English teacher from Shilaidaha) with the ambition that 'man could become truly human by responding creatively and sympathetically to his environment'.[19] Tagore commits to building a school that has to be 'situated in a quiet spot far from the crowded city', having the 'natural advantages of open sky, fields, trees and the like', a kind of 'a retreat where teachers and students would live dedicated to learning'.[20] Can the aesthetics of education be configured within the connections built between 'open sky, fields and trees' and a 'profound atmosphere of learning'?

At Tagore's ashram school, Willie Pearson records an incident during one of his class lectures conducted under a tree (that practice continues to this day)[21] when a boy draws his attention to the song of a bird. 'I am quite sure', he commented, 'that my class learnt more from that bird than it had ever done from my teaching and something that they would

---

[18] Ibid., 285, 286.
[19] Uma Das Gupta, *Rabindranath Tagore: A Biography* (New Delhi: Oxford University Press, 2004), 15.
[20] Tagore, 'The Problem of Education', in *Towards Universal Man*, 75.
[21] C. F. Andrews writes, 'We have no classrooms. The boys sit with their teachers, in the open air, under the trees. There are no large classes. A group of eight or ten boys will be seated round the teacher, asking him questions. . . . Like the open air education which Plato loved in Athens, the greater part is carried on through conversation. The boys soon learn to bring all their difficulties to their teachers; and the teachers get keenly interested in the boys' questions and answers. Such living education can never be dull.' 'An Open-Air School', *Visva Bharati News*, Silver Jubilee Number (1957), 2.

never forget in life. For myself, my ears were opened, and for several days I was conscious of the songs of the birds as I had never been before.'[22] What does the class learn from the birdsong? How can learning plasticize beyond formal teaching? Is experience in plastic pedagogy strictly subservient to textual meaning or do experiences outside the domain of ceaseless meaning effects contribute to experiential richness? Thinking non-dualistically through the body and the mind is always an achievement—a mode of being that involves embodied meditation of the world and its consequent intellection. This is about psychophysically knowing a truth of education where, for instance, the act of knowing by the ear (song of the bird) is connected with refigurations of mentalization (achieved through a distinct experience of learning). Here the lived body or the feeling body never becomes the whole because, as Jean-Luc Nancy argues, the parts of the 'corpus do not combine into a whole, are not means to it or ends of it. Each part can suddenly take over the whole, can spread out over it, can become it, the whole—that never takes place. There is no whole, no totality of the body—but its absolute separation and sharing.'[23] As a part of the corpus, the ear takes over the whole of a 'feeling and receptive body', generating a surplus of understanding that is difficult to explicate. The education for life at its fullest cannot be experienced simply within a system because without the surplus—in cogitation, in acts, in cognition—the 'fullest' can never be a realistic telos to achieve. By *listening* to the same event, the body of the boy shares his experiences with other fellow bodies to produce a 'beyond the body' realm of experience. Education in the ashram is built on a complexity inscribed in metapsychics[24]—an intricate non-Cartesian system which ensures that physicality of learning is closely integrated with the development and intervention of the mind. Not disharmonious with each other, this ensemble of the body-mind generates the 'play drive' (in the words of

---

[22] Himangshu Bhushan Mukherjee, *Education for Fullness* (London: Asia Publishing House, 1962), 296.

[23] Bernadette Wegenstein, *Getting Under the Skin: Body and Media Theory* (Cambridge, MA: MIT Press, 2006), 7.

[24] Yasuo Yuasa, *The Body: Toward an Eastern Mind-Body Theory*, ed. Thomas P. Kasulis and trans. Nagatomo Shigenori (Albany, NY: State University of New York Press, 1987), 2. Metapsychics is not metaphysics in the traditional Western sense. Yuasa looks into 'non-dualism' which is central to many Asian traditions undercutting 'such Western dichotomies as spirit matter, subjectivity-objectivity, and theory-praxis'.

Schiller) that challenges the dualist infrastructure of thought and feeling. Education in the ashram encourages a plastic pedagogy where the self of a student becomes a plastic subject, subjected to a variety of forces that are at once somatic and psychic.

It is interesting to record Werther's experiences while walking in the wood where the whir and buzz of the little gnats, tremulous rays of the sun, beetles springing out of the grass, the 'moss wresting its nourishment out of the hard rock' configure an experience that defies all Cartesian modes of analysis.[25] Tagore, who believes that 'imprisonment' is the 'best way of making children confirmed criminals', wanted all education to be peripatetic—an engagement with the physicality of learning by releasing children from the confinement of the 'same benches, chairs, walls, buildings, globes and kinds of games'. Tagore advocates, 'let them know other games'.[26] The psychophysical mode of reading—learning being plastic in its directness of somatic experiences and dialectical ways of intellection—is about, as Hans Ulrich Gumbretch argues, reading books and reading the world and not simply meaning attribution. Gumbretch observes that 'it is the never-ending movement, the both joyful and painful movement between losing and regaining intellectual control and orientation, that can occur in the confrontation with (almost?) any cultural object as long as it occurs under conditions of low time pressure, that is, with no "solution" or "answer" immediately expected. This is exactly the movement that we are referring to when we say that a class or a seminar "broadened" our minds'.[27] Experienced somaesthetically, this helps in the thriving of the mind. Gumbretch argues further that 'rather than having to think, always and endlessly, what else there could be, we sometimes seem to connect with a layer in our existence that simply wants the things of the world close to our skin'.[28] The closeness of the experience of the world to our skin helps us to avoid our compelling status as 'intercourse beings'.[29] The nakedness of skin is textured with deep social insertions that forget the psychophysical experiential directness of things

---

[25] See Johann Wolfgang von Goethe, *The Sorrows of Young Werther and Selected Writings*, trans. Catherine Hutter (New York: New American Library, Inc., 1962), 62.

[26] Tagore, 'Schooling', *The Visva Bharati Quarterly* 29, no. 4 (1963–64): 274, 275, 278.

[27] Hans Ulrich Gumbrecht, *Production of Presence: What Meaning Cannot Convey* (Stanford, CA: Stanford University Press, 2004), 128.

[28] Ibid., 106.

[29] A. Dworkin, *Intercourse* (London: Arrow Books, 1988), 25–26.

under the influence of social encrustations and habitus of being and performing; these are much opposed to the vitality of connection with the world around. The consequent disability leaves one close to being a discursive being and not an embodied individual for whom 'broadening the mind' is not about gathering knowledge but surely about a fullness of experience. In trying then to grow an intense connection with nature and objects, Tagore looks into the possibilities of intense joy generated through efforts to discover a layer of existence beyond the mere cultural and material values of things—experiencing the 'things of the world in their preconceptual thingness.'[30] In his school, Tagore seeks to introduce 'sparks' emerging from the mundane and the ordinary into ways of teaching and understanding—the amazement which moments of surplus bring through a closeness with the everyday. This is Cézanne-like in that Tagore sees pedagogy as drawing upon the experience of a moment much in the same way that Paul Cézanne desires to live in a 'minute' and 'become that minute.'[31] In such 'presences', plastic Tagore wants an alternative atmosphere of aesthetic intensity, such 'spots of time' (in the words of William Wordsworth) within a non-Cartesian and pre-discursive presence pedagogy.

The integration of the laws of nature (both its meaning effects and presence effects) and the laws of humans (in this case the inmates of the school) operates on possibilities (something that Tagore likes to see as surprise, wonder, excitement, mysteries) beyond the exhaustion that technology provides. Indeed, heartless technological dominance and the growing rationalization and intellectualization have taken the wonder and mystery out of our lives and civilizational ways. Tagore sees a rift being opened up between the individual and the world—a Simmelian tragedy of culture—where the subject–object dualism works on an internal logic of development that does not inspire a return to totality or harmonic completeness. The 'disenchantment' that both Georg Simmel and Max Weber talk about is something that also disturbs Tagore.[32]

---

[30] Gumbrecht, *Production of Presence*, 118.

[31] Quoted in Maurice Merleau-Ponty, *The Primacy of Perception*, ed. James M. Edie, trans. William Cobb (Evanston, IL: Northwestern University Press, 1964), 169.

[32] Enchantment (*zauber*) is being destroyed by the advance of rationality in a process of 'Entzauberung der Welt'. See Max Weber, *Political Writings*, ed. Peter Lassman and Ronald Speirs (Cambridge: Cambridge University Press, 1994).

Privileging the 'dispersion of mind' over 'concentration of mind', he commits to prepare the children for a 'real home-coming into this world'.[33]

Liberation in nature is about 'allowing' nature the space to articulate back its values—both intrinsic or extrinsic—and Tagore's ashram accommodates them in its infrastructural bareness, spartan life habits, and remarkably conscious ways of connecting with the 'earth' (for instance, the ashram students walked barefoot on ruddy muddy roads, students sat on the bare earth underneath the tree for their classes, part of the teaching between the teacher and student was conducted while walking between the rows of trees). Ashram education works within a bureaucratic green shot through in an ecological ethics of co-sharing and coexistence. Tagore terms nature's method of discipline as 'freedom cure'. This is similar in essence to the doctrine of discipline by natural consequence as formulated by Rousseau and later developed by Herbert Spencer. But freedom cure is more human in spirit and more plastic in possibilities. Tagore observes that when mind and life are given 'full freedom' they achieve health. The philosophy of freedom cure allows his boys to run about, to climb difficult trees, often to come to grief on their own, get drenched out in the rain, and swim in the pond. This is a freedom, a suffering, a disquiet, that is, however, not without method. Within a kind of green democracy, the 'freedom cure' is fun, a 'letting go'. Freedom cure is crucial to a self-construction that mere textbooks cannot bring—the 'leaps of self-abandon',[34] as Richard Shusterman calls it. It makes plastic pedagogy a fluid dynamic of imagination, wonder, and curiosity.

Unlike Stoic thinkers for whom reason is insulated from affection, and unlike Plato who is sceptical of the soul conjugating with the body

---

[33] Tagore, 'Thoughts on Education', *The Visva Bharati Quarterly* 13 (May–October 1947): 4. Amita Gupta notes that 'rational constructivists, led by Piaget, consider the child as an egocentric self and the construction of knowledge as an individual and cognitive process. The focus of Piaget's research has been on genetic epistemology and its scientific discourse has described the human being in such clinical terms as individual, organism, and biological. Piaget's theory explains cognitive development and learning in the human being in terms of the physical interactions between a biological organism and a physical environment through a process of assimilation and accommodation. This precludes the influence that social, cultural, and historical factors—by way of interactions with people, language, traditions, and rituals—have on children's learning and cognitive development. Piaget's emphasis on logicomathematical reasoning denies the multiple realities of children's worlds and the powerful role that fantasy plays in these realities.' See Amita Gupta, *Early Childhood Education, Postcolonial Theory, and Teaching Practices in India* (New York: Palgrave Macmillan, 2006), 7–8.

[34] Richard Shusterman, *Performing Live: Aesthetic Alternatives for the Ends of Art* (Ithaca, NY: Cornell University Press, 2000), 203.

to produce clarified thinking,[35] Tagore sees imaginative reason as arising from our bodily experiences. Freedom cure, as counter-education, is meant to guide the child to the realm of the variable and the vital, creating 'body emotions'. Learning in the ashram can be seen as not essentially about thinking but also about touch, affect, and dependence on material things. Kinaesthetic education—combining both kinesis and aesthesia—cannot rule out proprioception also. Proprioceptive aspects of body pedagogy demand attunement to the situation and atmosphere, enabling a cluster of skills and modes of accommodation which the ashramites work hard to develop. Tagore, thus, orders a body knowledge, a body behaviour, informed through the principles of *brahmacharya*. The harshness of setting and the compulsive inconvenience of living bring forth a unique *sambandha* (negotiation) between the body that endures and the mind that provides the strength of endurance. The Spartan bareness of *brahmacharya* makes children peg their education on a 'Why'—questions as to what difference (the plasticity, the surplus) this would bring to their learning when thrown against conventional forms of schooling. On such points of flashpoint pedagogy, children become enfleshed learners.

Opposed to spectator theory of knowledge, freedom cure comes to emphasize, in a Deweyian way, an embodied understanding that replaces the Cartesian asomatic type with a post-Darwinian one.[36] Freedom cure, as part of plastic pedagogy, cannot simply submit to the prioritization of sight and hearing for it then would only lead one to objectivity (the act of watching and thus believing), detachment (sans involvement in the phenomena or the reality before man), and passivity (relishing the role as a receptor). Premised in an embodied mode of existence, it works through experiences in a living world that cannot be understood through a pure mind alone. The ashram school behaves like an 'organizing' society, a cooperative, the kind that Émile Durkheim has called 'a small society'.[37]

---

[35] Plato notes: 'when the soul uses the instrumentality of the body for any inquiry, whether through sight or hearing or any other sense—because using the body implies using the senses—it is drawn away by the body into the realm of the variable, and loses its way and becomes confused and dizzy, as though it were fuddled, through contact with things of a similar nature'. Plato, *Phaedo*, in *The Collected Dialogues of Plato*, ed. Edith Hamilton and Huntington Cairns (Princeton, NJ: Princeton University Press, 1963), 62.

[36] See Raymond D. Boisvert, *John Dewey: Rethinking Our Time* (Albany, NY: State University of New York Press, 1998), 97.

[37] Émile Durkheim, *Moral Education: A Study in the Theory and Application of the Sociology of Education* (New York: Free Press, 1961), 150.

The spirit of discipline through *brahmacharya* involves regularity of conduct, obligation to be obedient towards the fulfilment of a moral order of Tagore's small society. Tagore makes possible a system that schools the body into appreciating human dignity and, as Durkheim has argued, the fullest possible development of humanity.[38] The physicality of living (the ritual, the manual, and the formal) generates bodily emotions and desires which, in the process, get connected with the movements of the mind, resulting in education both at the level of carnal sociology and 'lived body' (*Leibkörper*). Durkheim notes that education cannot merely operate both at the level of the intellectual and the emotional to shape the personalities of pupils. This kind of education is not intended or employed to endow the mind with some theoretical ideas or speculative notions; it is designed to usher in a principle of action. The flesh of Tagore's ashram becomes a site or acts as a location for intellectual, emotional, and psychical inscriptions (both the *Körper* and *Lieb*);[39] this results in habitual actions, imagined expressions, and aptitude for sympathy which, as Durkheim notes, is predominantly social—for Dewey it is sociocultural—but for Tagore is both social and aesthetic (*sambandha*). For Durkheim, as much as for Tagore, communal life contributes to schooling and corporeal processes contribute to the moral realization of society whether it be the one that a student grows into or the small society in which a child learns the art of self-development.

Trying to live through the bodily memories of living, Tagore points out in his *Boyhood Reminiscences* how school education affected his mind through the contraction of the body and how he desired to free himself from dogmatic learning and stereotypical systems of instructions. This made possible an 'enselfment' realized through resonant and resistant experiences. Enselfment realizes itself in experiences where the body is continually in *sambandha*—body being always the other. Bodies outside *sambandha* are impossibilities and in such relational realities the mind does find a place to grow and get endowed. Education then is being with others: an alterity which takes into account both the human and its non-human counterpart—a contact where students are made to invest in the

[38] Émile Durkheim, *The Evolution of Educational Thought: Lectures on the Formation and Development of Secondary Education in France* (1938; London: Routledge, 1977), 150.

[39] See Bernard Andrieu, *Le Corps disperse: Histoire du corps au XXe siècle* (Paris: L'Harmattan, 1993).

other, not suppress oneself in the other. By establishing 'other landscapes besides my own',[40] students function to make the life of education in the ashram a contested site, a flesh which Merleau-Ponty has qualified as an elemental medium where the self and world are constructed through mutuality. Education through the body reverses what the body is fundamentally known for and experienced as—not as a mere object simplistically understood as something which when cut renders pain or aches when empty of food. Body is both a material organism and a metaphor as Le Goff has argued—'it is the trunk apart from head and limbs, but also the person [as in "anybody" and "somebody"] ... The body is at once the most solid, the most elusive, illusory, concrete, metaphorical, ever present and ever distant thing—a site, an instrument, an environment, a singularity and a multiplicity.'[41] As a site for subjectivities and consciousness, the body of a student in the ashram becomes a 'locus of sensory-aesthetic appreciation (*aisthesis*) and creative self-fashioning'.[42] This self-stylizing, autopoiesis, works on several factors which Tagore seeks to cultivate in the atmosphere of his ashram: character, integrity, and sensitivity. Within such a frame of experience, students are seen as plastic subjects whose selves are in transition—in varying states of becoming. In a somatic-affective way, education built round books, bird cries, the shrill cry of the kite in the sky, and the touch and smell of bare earth cannot be non-reflectional and non-pragmatist always. The negotiation among forces is deeply plastic.

Tagore sees the nakedness of the child's body interacting with the nakedness of nature, assigning, in the process, a separate dimension to the notion of shame. Education in the ashram is envisaged as a kind of shamelessness—an unclothed, unwrapped state of being encountering randomness and what Tagore qualifies as the infinite. This prepares a separate flashpoint of experience. Book-bound education, Tagore believes, imparts knowledge of the world but not the earth, of our culture but not our nature, of our intellect but not the soul; it requires reinvestments through an intense connection with the circumambient nakedness. Tagore moans, 'We do not touch the world with our mind, we touch

---

[40] Maurice Merleau-Ponty, *The Visible and the Invisible* (Evanston, IL: Northwestern University Press, 1968), 141.

[41] Wegenstein, *Getting Under the Skin*, 2.

[42] Shusterman, *Performing Live*, 138.

it by books.'[43] The logic of books (inductive, agonistic, declarative) and the logic of body-processed (both human and earth, elemental and candid) education are different. This is not to misconstrue Tagore as suggesting a collective disapproval of books. This is about education that connects in vital terms the 'flesh of our body' with the 'flesh of the earth', a lived, animated body-subject processing meanings for the consumption of mind and the industry of intellect. This prepares one for moments of plasticity. He notes that 'children with the freshness of their senses come directly to the intimacy of this world. . . . They must accept it naked and simple and never lose their power of quick communication. For our perfection we have to be at once savage and civilized.'[44] The impersonality of education achieved through books is contrasted through live, gestural talking ('movements of the eyes, modulation of the voice, signs of hands and fingers'[45]) in education which for Tagore has life—speaking lessons, rather than reading lessons; education is lived through the body and then allowed to settle in the intellect, avoiding, thus, 'world-weariness'.[46] Resonating with Merleau-Ponty's words—'I am not the spectator, I am involved'[47]—Tagore's methods of body education can be eclectically interpreted through the interactive processes involving environed/conceiving subject and the environing/conceived objects. Somaesthetically, the politics of embodied learning solicits as much interplay from the agency of the children as it does from the contribution of the dynamic surrounding.[48] This emphasis on being educated at the primary stage through the pores of a body untrammelled by tropes of shame and culture

[43] Tagore, 'Abaran', *Rabindra Rachanabali*, vol. 14 (Kolkata: Government of West Bengal, Saraswati Press Limited, 1992), 383. Tagore laments how we ignore the beautiful unclad body of ours. Our face is uncovered in both the summer and the winter and so our facial skin is the most cultivated. It knows the art to balance itself with the outer world, complete in itself, and does not require any artificial refuge like other parts of the body. See ibid., 381.

[44] Tagore, 'A Poet's School', 291–92.

[45] Tagore, 'Abaran', 343.

[46] Ibid., 344.

[47] Maurice Merleau-Ponty, *Phenomenology of Perception* (London: Routledge & Kegan Paul, 2003), 354–55.

[48] I am tempted to look into the life of the ashram as a totality which Mencius (371–289 BCE) has argued as a developmental continuum and an interpenetration of the sociopolitical and the cosmic—a deep understanding of self and subjectivity, the I–Me dialectic. The ashram school looked in its own way into what Mencius calls qi (氣, vital energies), the allowance for subjectivities and a consequent release of imaginative cohabitation with the natural and the objective world— a mind–body conjugation. Tagore's school ensured that a culture was built across an embodied existence in personal cultivation and psychospiritual transformation. See A. K. L. Chan, ed., *Mencius: Contexts and Interpretations* (Honolulu: University of Hawai'i Press, 2002).

is, for me, Tagore's talking body that creates paths for the emergence of the talking intellect.

Bunyard and Morgan-Grenville argue that 'in modern farming the farm worker is increasingly isolated from the soil he is tilling; he sits encased in his tractor cab, either with ear muffs to shut out the noise or with radio blaring, and what goes on behind the tractor has more to do with the wonders of technology than with the wisdom of countless generations of his predecessors'.[49] The disconnection from the Earth in accumulation of knowledge—life experiences in screened-off glass cubicles of self-contained technological incarceration—creates vacuities which Tagore chooses to refurbish by reclaiming the notion of 'interdependence'. He writes:

> when they are not engaged in study, the students should work in the garden, loosening the soil around the roots of trees, watering plants and training hedges. Their contact with nature would thus be both manual and mental. In favourable weather the classes should be held in the shade of big trees. Part of the teaching should be in the form of discussion between teacher and student while they are walking between the rows of trees. In the evening recess the students should read the stars, cultivate music, and listen to legendary and historical tales.[50]

This mode of intersubjective existence is not born of the tilled earth or the blue sky or the green fields alone but through a life-consciousness—a diffusive sense-generation through deeply invested plastic moments—which is impossibly difficult to explicate substantively. The body in education is a significant part of a plastic subject alive to the powers of transcendence achieved through a changing consciousness—responding to non-human bodies through touch, hearing and seeing and resonating, in the process, with others. As Didier Anzieu points out, 'from before birth, cutaneous sensations introduce the young of the human species into a world of great richness and complexity, a world as yet diffuse, but which awakens the perception-consciousness system, forms

---

[49] P. Bunyard and F. Morgan-Grenville, eds., *The Green Alternative* (London: Methuen, 1987), 71.

[50] Tagore, 'The Problem of Education', 75.

the basis for a general and episodical sense of existence and opens up the possibility of an originary psychic space.[51] Within an evolving perception-consciousness somatic system, the child functioning in the *brahmacharya* system, in psychophysical experiences of being exposed to the heat and dust of an open classroom underneath a tree, in lessons rendered while undertaking long walks down the ashram roads, quite often barefoot, experiences the existential transfigurations that initiate at the level of the skin before it transports its messages, both organic and imaginary, to the skin of the mind. Plastic pedagogy finds its inroads through the skin—the 'skin ego'—which acts both as a barrier and a site of permeability that create experiences, produce psychical differentiation, and engender a surplus of understanding.

Plastic pedagogy, both as communication and communion, cannot do without an excess: a loss of distinction between bodies and minds and yet a coming together in difference (identity-in-difference) that constitutes a force field where separate bodies (teachers, students, natural objects) co-function both tangibly and intangibly, become present and unveil presence. In a delicate art of 'reversibility' (not strictly in the Pontian sense of the term though), the students touch the world with their bodies and are touched back through a chiasmatic nature of involvement. This reversibility is a kind of vulnerability (in the sense of *vulnus*, wound) towards the embodied experiences of learning and knowing or minding the world around. It results in a plasticity of understanding, a kind of learning that is not pressed into shape through a syllabus but allowed to take its own direction and volume both touch-formatively and disembodiedly. Within the flesh of existence, a student, thus, becomes both a subject and an object to oneself. The ashram creates a trans-plastic space for what Merleau-Ponty calls the body schema and motility. Children in the ashram are aware of their bodies in different relational configurations, be that with their teachers, the dietary schedule, the lessons, the leisure hours, the co-curricular activities or other coordinates of its environment. However, motility helps them to exercise agency by incorporating capacities to think and expand the quality and quantity of movements and experiences. So the awareness of the world is actively embodied constituting a

---

[51] Didier Anzieu, *The Skin Ego* (New Haven, CT: Yale University Press, 1989), 12–13.

being towards others; it means that we operate through the body in our functions with the world investing a particular emotional patterning.

Within plastic pedagogy the abstraction from the corporeal world is denied and the perception is structured within an understanding that includes the experience of the world—the Earth—achieved through the body and through things which hide themselves behind other things ('We rob the child of his earth to teach him Geography, of language to teach him grammar. His hunger is for the Epic, but he is supplied with chronicles of facts and dates. He was in the human world, but is banished into the world of living gramophones'[52]). This mode of being makes Tagore and his young students engage with the uninhibited and uncultivated forms of experiences (unpremeditated too) in nature and the world. Such engagements appeal primarily to the body, generating a freedom to choose and realize one's being within a depth that an immersion in culture can rarely help us achieve. Plastic Tagore realizes how this prevalent perceptive mode in the ashram can allow invisible lines of force to influence the becoming of his students—the secret life of the wind, the shadows of the scudding clouds, the rhythm of the cricket-songs, the power of fragrance, the movement of the buds into bloom. (Tagore observes that 'children love the earth with its dust and its dirt, and they love the sun, the wind and the rain. They do not like to be dressed up, they enjoy themselves most when they are discovering the world with their senses, and they are not a bit ashamed to be their natural selves.'[53]) In fact, through the flesh of the ashram the students encounter intersubjectivities which clearly demonstrate secrecies and codes of nakedness, of glances, gestures, and traces whose visibility is unconcealed on them through certain modes of transcendence. This precipitates 'forming', a surrender whose motives are not assessed through determinable categories or intelligible psychophysical paradigms and whose constitution and voice are, most often, irrelevant to the experiential logic of culture and society.

Plastic pedagogy demonstrates a deeply entangled relationship between nature education and body pedagogy; it establishes a surplus and rhythm that leads to a transcendence in learning experiences. The 'heart and body' education is constructed round flashpoints of understanding

---

[52] Tagore, 'Thoughts on Education', 3.
[53] Tagore, 'The Problem of Education', 80–81.

as revealed through 'freedom cure', sensate and sensualization of experiences, refashioning of selves achieved through a complicated nexus between body spaces, somatic submission, enfleshment, reconstructionism in 'mindful awareness',[54] book-boundedness, and touch. Such plasticities in sensualization and mentalization of education manifest the uniqueness of a poet-educator for whom education is a journey in risk, adventure, and romance. Plastic pedagogy, within a distinct rhythmanalytic framework, constructs and complicates a smooth space where interactive and transmissive learning commit to a plexus of instinct, spontaneity, desires, moods, drives, and affect.

Flashpoint II

Counter-Institution

The second flashpoint under discussion in my formulation of plastic pedagogy is the nature of the university—called Visva Bharati—that Tagore established in 1921. He writes:

At first, I had founded the school in Santiniketan and invited children here with the purpose of liberating them in the wide field of Nature. But gradually it occurred to me that the formidable gulf that existed between man and man had to be removed and all men had to be released in the vast Universe of Man. This inner aspiration found expression in the history of the evolution of my institution. For, the institution that bore the name of Visva-Bharati was founded with this call that man had to be set free not only in the field of Nature but also among mankind.[55]

With a profound consciousness of the other, Visva Bharati flourishes as an institution where the West and the East takes close measure of each

---

[54] D. J. Siegel, *The Mindful Brain: Reflection and Attunement in the Cultivation of Well-Being* (New York: W. W. Norton, 2007), 3–28.

[55] Mukherjee, *Education for Fullness*, 98.

other in a cultural and intellectual 'traffic' of varied scope and potential—
Yatra Visvam Bhavatyekanidam—'where the whole world finds one nest'.
Emphasizing the need for cross-traffic, Tagore writes that 'it is the task of
Visva Bharati to invite all the ages and all the peoples to that India which
belongs to all ages and all people'.[56] Citing the cohabitative spaces and
the regulative ideal—among scholars, traditions, knowledge systems—
generated in universities like Nalanda and Vikramshila from ancient
India, Tagore envisions a similar growth in his Visva Bharati: an effort
to understand how the Indian genius expressed itself, the need for integration of diverse streams of thought and the production of knowledge
in the universities that make dissemination a secondary task. By the
time Tagore was born (1861), a colonial system of education had already
found its own permanent settlement—a system that declared the support and proliferation of English language and English studies as against
the consequent denudation of importance and interest in Sanskrit and
Persian language and studies. Vernacular means of education were ignored for colonial educational ideals and patterns of execution. This
strategic segregation effected under impositional colonial structures of
education brought home a backlash—a rebound energy for the restitu-
tion of one's cultural past, making education combative when it ought to
have been synergic and osmotic. Dispirited by such ideological warfare
and institutional superintendency, Tagore wanted a university with a different culture inscribed in individuality, indigeneity, otherness, curiosity,
and desire hitherto unavailable in contemporary universities during his
time—a project in dynamical plasticity. The exemplarity in education is
in knowing the art of 'negotiation'—both a vertical negotiation with one's
tradition, languages, and cultures and a horizontal dialogic familiarity
with a corpus of knowledge that indigeneity would not be able to deliver
but could surely have profited from.

Derrida observes that

Neither in its medieval nor in its modern form has the university dis-
posed freely of its own absolute autonomy and of the rigorous conditions of its own unity. During more than eight centuries, 'university'
has been the name given by a society to a sort of supplementary body

---

[56] Ibid., 106.

that at one and the same time it wanted to project outside itself and keep jealously to itself, to emancipate and to control. And in a certain way it has done so: it has produced society's scenography, its views, conflicts, contradictions, its plays and its differences, and also its desire for organic union in a total body.'[57]

Perhaps, aware of these imprisoning projections that have constituted universities in its medieval and its modern form, Tagore decided to call his university just 'Visva Bharati' and not 'Visva Bharati University', a preference that made allowance for deconstructive claims on spaces and notions that a classical university was expected to celebrate and establish. By naming it 'Visva Bharati', Tagore intended plasticities of understanding, sense, and 'traffic' into his idea of the university as a site for contestation, conflation, and construction; for me, it is 'That plastic supplement'.[58]

The university, with its space distinct from what we usually get in society and other areas of our daily existence, is a world built round certain principles of normativity and isolation. Even within the encompassive traffic, Visva Bharati, as is the case with ashram school, is not without a disciplinizing machine which exacts conformity, a network that makes claims on power and knowledge. It is not a feudalistic hierarchy; rather, a place, as Derrida has argued, where 'people know how to learn and learn how to know'.[59] This space reconfigurates our notions of tradition and questions the rationality and raison d'être of university as a modern-day institution. Its pupils look both ways—inside and outside—and like the Derridean ship our focus changes once we are on-board at the port and then again when on-board at mid-sea. Visva Bharati is conceived as a space for reflection and analytic thinking, a site for Socratic dialecticism, without any collapse into undifferentiated syncretism. As a secular agonistic space, Visva Bharati owes something to Tagore's deep faith in India's cultural past; but the space starts to question the problematic

---

[57] Jacques Derrida, 'The Principle of Reason: The University in the Eyes of Its Pupils', *Diacritics* 13 (Fall 1983): 19.

[58] This is in deliberate imitation of the title of the Chapter 2 of Part 2 ('. . . That Dangerous Supplement . . .') from Derrida's *of Grammatology*, trans. Gayatri Chakravorty Spivak (Baltimore: Johns Hopkins University Press, 1998), 141.

[59] Derrida, 'The Principle of Reason', 4.

of responsibility which attends a vocation or call, non-aporetically—a 'setting-to-work'. As a part of plastic pedagogy Visva Bharati changes the ethical dimension of the idea of the university.

Visva Bharati forms itself round an agonistic solidarity in a multiverse traffic. Mary Parker Follett arguing about unity in diversity seeks unity, and not uniformity, as her aim. She observes that 'differences must be integrated, not annihilated, nor absorbed'. The university is embedded in 'intricate reciprocities', an equilibrium which is not quiescent but shifting, varying and yet compounding, coordinating and harmonizing.[60] Visualizing an ideal commonwealth, Tagore went on to reveal different people to one another, exploring the 'meeting ground' where there could be—albeit ideally—no question of intractable conflicting interests. He pointed out that 'some of us belong to the Brahma Samaj sect and some to other sects of Hinduism; and some of us are Christians. Because we do not deal with creeds and dogmas of sectarianism, therefore this heterogeneity of our religious beliefs does not present us with any difficulty whatever.'[61] Visva Bharati, with its harmonious heterogeneity, is one such territory—a multiversity—where people can work together in a common pursuit of truth, share their common 'human' heritage and realize that artists in all parts of the world have created forms of beauty, scientists have discovered secrets of the universe, philosophers the problems of existence, while saints make the truth of the spiritual organic in their own lives, not merely for some particular race to which they belong but for all mankind. In plastic harmony, Visva Bharati becomes a site for struggle where 'local knowledge' is made to meet 'global knowledge' in a cultural pluralization that represents different worlds in different ways.[62] The indigenous and exogenous are pragmatized into a 'knowledge society' which renegotiates self-definition with self-othering. Visva Bharati, thus, produces 'human knowledge' which does not have the cussedness of 'local' and the imperious recalcitrance of the 'global'; it considers conversation as one of its major paradigms of unfoldment.

---

[60] Mary Parker Follett, *The New State: Group Organization and the Solution of Popular Government* (New York: Longmans, Green and Co., 1918), 35, 76.

[61] Tagore, *Personality* (London: Macmillan & Co., 1970), 136.

[62] Alistair Pennycook, 'English, Universities and Struggles over Culture and Knowledge', in *East–West Dialogue in Knowledge and Higher Education*, ed. Ruth Hayhoe and Julia Pan (New York: M. E. Sharpe, 1996), 64–82.

Within a space that is 'set to work', Tagore, as a prophet of 'free inquiry', calls for sympathy, a connection, a mutuality, which can successfully contribute to a consortium of cultures and constitutions of knowledge. The knowledge inherited at birth is not the gift of any one nation. Knowledge makes us powerful but sympathy helps us to attain fullness. Tagore's transnationalism is a natural and logical manifestation of his humanistic 'plastic' philosophy, his philosophy of 'secular humanism', generated from his distinct and nuanced understanding of the Upanishad. Shocked by the horrors of the world wars, he realizes that calamities in history have always sprung from the 'non-availability' for the other—the 'traffic-deficit'. Tagore's speculative philosophy is committed to a moral dynamics that brings elements of reverence and order into our structures of existence. The university as a space does not qualify as a universal category but is an affirmation in relationality and experience—complex and interdependent. In the words of Whitehead, the ethical dimension of education cannot be 'morally neutral'. Visva Bharati, at some point in its inception, becomes a 'duty' which ascertains a belief in changing prevalent forms of experience with 'attainable knowledge'.[63] In its trials of exfoliation, Visva Bharati speaks at once of a rootedness and rootlessness, working outside the preparedness and value-neutral schematization of a modernist institution and yet not entirely processual in its value radicality. This makes for the experiences in thresholds of plasticity. It works towards an enhancement of value, a humanization of learning and interactive practices, without ethical absolutism or ethical nihilism. However, the affirmative traffic is more postmodernist in nature where its organismic growth, falling out of modernist Eurocentric models, refuses to subscribe to a single universal cultural hegemony but promotes instead an advancement of diverse human systems and affiliations.

Tagore is not aware of any rules about establishing a modern university because he has never been to any institution of such order and has reservations as to its ideology, philosophy, and functional principles. This is not a conceptual opacity but a flashpoint situation where the plastic Tagore inspires himself to invent a rule which comes, in a certain sense, from no-responsibility (from the perspective of a non-affiliation to a stable and

---

[63] Alfred North Whitehead, *The Aims of Education and Other Essays* (New York: Mentor Books, 1929), 26.

established centre of knowledge and authority); this no-responsibility is a responsibility demanding response of a different order, as Derrida argues, to two injunctions, different and incompatible. Derrida points out: 'That's where responsibility starts, when I don't know what to do. If I knew what to do, well, I would apply the rule, and teach my students to apply the rule. But would that be ethical? Ethics start when you don't know what to do, when there is a gap between knowledge and action, and you have to take responsibility for inventing the new rule which doesn't exist.'[64] Within such premises of wilderness, plastic Tagore launches with a responsibility to invent a rule that is born out of an uncanny gap between knowledge and action—a notional uniqueness which becomes his Visva Bharati as against the claims of pragmatism that the imperium of a modern university rigorously imposes. This is positive plasticity that inspires an invention of a rule, a space, a rationality, a judgement, and a reason different from the accredited, well-funded, reified principles of institutionalization.

The poet finds his true inspiration, writes Tagore, 'only when he forgets that he is a schoolmaster.'[65] This forgetting is the encounter with the plastic explosive, unpacking wolves that challenge all forms of unitotality. Visva Bharati is conceived with the responsibility and forgetting of a plastic kavi who invents and supplements and thwarts any dour intent of a schoolmaster who instructs and, bound within rules, validates. This poet-educator inspires the emergence of the plastic Tagore. He has the philosopher's crisis in that he is unable to resolve the tension between theory and practice, his ideals and prospective enactments, in the face of the mounting paradigm conflict generated from outside. This requires getting responsible towards the responsibility that others have for this space. Responsibility and risk conjugate in the dynamics of this plastic space that tries to hold on to the troublous, at times inscrutable, subtlety of this conjugation—the actional aporeticism in conflation with oneiric inexorability.

Tagore spells out the aims of the university and what he sets out to achieve. This doing spells out rules; but a commitment to plastic pedagogy starts to unmake many rules as his project progressed, setting off

---

[64] M. Paine and J. Schad, eds., *Life After Theory* (New York: Continuum, 2003), 31–32.
[65] Tagore, 'An Eastern University', in *Creative Unity* (London: Macmillan and Co., 1922), 179.

a lifelong angst. The ethics of the university works itself out on showing and performing which in a Wittgensteinian sense can be qualified as 'practice', the performative ability. The conduct of the reality and the ideal within the institutional space is not directed to a conscious rule-following but, instead, maintains learning in contexts through observation, communication, emulation, trials, and experiments. Tagorean practices are not aberrative and idiosyncratic because he ensures that enactments in his moral-aesthetic education are both a part of the pedagogical heritage and derivations external to the relentless lockstep certainty of authoritative programmes.

Plastic Tagore's Visva Bharati is the 'everyday', by which Derrida means a phenomenon that does not stop. It is everyday traffic—inauguration of departments, politics of institutional governance, concourse of people from various places in India, international visitors programme, fund-raising trips and ventures, the ineluctable anxiety of staying afloat amidst ideological worries about collapsing into colonial educational machinery, and the pragmatic impulsion to avoid being anachronistic. Visva Bharati does not believe in the erasure of hierarchy but cannot, in its dynamical plasticity, avoid a kind of Derridean opposition to 'a certain stabilizing or stabilized coding of a hierarchy'.[66] This is not anarchism or a provocation to remain stranded between tradition and the neglected and phobic other. It is a way of interrogating the *arché*, the commandment, without being irreverent to certain hierarchical codes required to continue 'negotiations'.

Derrida notes:

in the knot of negotiation there are different rhythms, different forces, different differential vibrations of time and rhythm. The word knot came to me and the image of a rope. A rope with entanglement, a rope made up of several strands knotted together. The rope exists. One imagines computers with little wires, wires where things pass very quickly, wires where things pass very slowly: negotiation is played along all of these wires. . . . Also, cables that pass under the sea and thousands of voices with intonations, that is, with different and entangled tensions.

[66] Jacques Derrida, *Negotiations: Interventions and Interviews 1971–2001*, ed. and trans. with introduction by Elizabeth Rottenberg (Stanford, CA: Stanford University Press, 2002), 21.

Negotiation is like a rope and an interminable number of wires moving or quivering with different speeds and intensities.[67]

Tagore's negotiations—quivering and radiant with different flashpoints—are not uncritical assimilations but a process in entangled tensions that is deeply underwritten by a conflictual syncretism; plastic pedagogy is a complex and uninterrupted engagement, a continual countering—with-against. By seeking such a purchase on the concept of the university, plastic Tagore leaves rigid-framed institutionalists in a state of discomfiture. Visva Bharati becomes a constellative space of 'counter'—redemptive and yet non-inimical—to the totalizing ways of institutionalization. It exists as a problem and plastic Tagore knows the vexed harvest of a 'counter'. Derrida writes:

> In abstract and general terms, what remains constant in my thinking . . . is indeed a critique of institutions, but one that sets out not from a wild and spontaneous pre- or non-institution, but rather from counter institutions. I do not think there is, or should be, the 'non-institutional'. I am always torn between the critique of institutions and the dream of an other institution that, in an interminable process, will come to replace institutions that are oppressive, violent and inoperative.[68]

Tagore choses a counter-path within which the university does not merely include its own institution but builds susceptible trajectories involving the side paths, off the highway and into the with–against mode of appropriation and acknowledgement of the other. Counter here is to encounter, to meet and to engage, to be in contact with an intent to reciprocate—the complicated intimations of hospitality. Visva Bharati's inside is mediated by the outside, and also by something outside the normative teaching machine—institutionalized in counterpoint, in the 'dream of an other' (in the words of Derrida). The other manifested as the presence of a variety of cultures and discourses from across the world is like a dream which is, at once, irreducibly attached to the other and exists as a hunger for the other,

---

[67] Ibid., 29–30.

[68] Derrida, 'I Have a Taste for the Secret', in Jacques Derrida and Maurizio Ferraris, *A Taste for the Secret*, ed. Giacomo Donis and David Webb, trans. Giacomo Donis (London: Polity Press, 2001), 50–51.

an aspiration to think counter. Plastic Tagore's Visva Bharati is a 'dream for an other', enfolding institutions within institutions and, like a dream, does not necessarily promote closure, balance, and resolution. It is the deterritorialization of the familiar space that a university institutionally projects and perpetuates, morphing, thus, into an extraterritorial standpoint which Derrida prefers to see as keeping the institutionality of institution open and having a future (*avenir*).

One must note that Tagore's celebration of one's tradition is conditioned upon its openness to other traditions, a promissory structure that cannot do without the dream and the breath of the other. Acknowledging one's roots is not about forgetting the profit that comes from the counter which is a form of negotiation and not condescension—a solidarity that comes through a sense of the *avenir* and activism across borders. This speaks of a sovereignty that is, however, not in consonance with the notions of a timeless independence of traditional universities. Rather, Visva Bharati's sovereignty as a counter-institution has the logic of an informed and fecund traffic. The exceptionality of this plastic space, distinct from the unified community that the German Idealists propose, anticipates dereferentialization of culture and, in a certain sense, a posthistorical position which has a separate logic of cultural syncretism and performativity. Tagore combines a consciousness of past, the impress of inheritance, and also a critique of a future. Understanding culture is an acknowledgement which does not fail to mark out the exchange, the note of traffic hidden in it. The traffic is not mere economism but an economy of exchange within notions of reciprocity, deference, deferment, debt, and obligation. This entails both the notions of response and responsibility. Visva Bharati is a site under permanent construction, where spaces produced are akin to the writer's rough draft tossed away for another redaction.

With such notions of the other, Tagore's idea of hybridity was probably deeper than what he could express and envisage as a poet-thinker. He admittedly looks into the space where self-essentializing is not self-ghettoization but, rather, a moving out in acts of recognition of the other for greater ways of self-definition. The Hindus need the Buddhist and the Christians to 'define' themselves. And Tagore clearly maintains that in such articulations of hybridity the historical locations are as important as the sense of belonging to a place and community. The consciousness

of difference is the inspiration to negotiation—his unique ways of conjugating the aesthetics with politics. Herein lie the flashpoints of alternative thinking. Jeremy Waldron notes pertinently that 'though we may
drape ourselves in the distinctive costumes of our ethnic heritage and
immure ourselves in an environment designed to minimize our sense
of relation with the outside world, no honest account of our being will
be complete without an account of our dependence on larger social and
political structures that goes far beyond the particular community with
which we pretend to identify.'[69] The man is superstructured to meet the
universal man. Waldron notes further that 'we need to understand our
choices in the contexts in which they make sense, but we do not need
any single context to structure our choices. To put it crudely, we need
culture, but we do not need cultural integrity.'[70] Tagore's Visva Bharati—
interestingly, as time wears on, Visva Bharati struggles in a coeval muta-
tion, becoming an extension of Tagore's utopic ideal and an un-Tagorean
organism whose evolutionary reality gets into conflict with the poet's
sublimic aspirations—defends the minority, the ignored, and their rights
are allowed to surface and circulate in a kind of culture which is proposed
to be adaptive and co-optative. He advocates the necessity to feel entitled
to one's community, the vernacular identity, but the 'potential' which
such entitlements and particular ethnic habitus generate prepares the
grounds for what he envisages as the communal *sanmilan*. Specificities
of this nature are not obdurate determinants of communal behaviour;
but they plasticize the community to make choices out of the power
and confidence that the community feels for transborder openness—
vernacularism and nativism are no hindrance to Tagore's universalism.
The interest in hybridity can easily submit to 'parity' where acknowledging difference is not about engagement with the 'differential' but cultivating a certain compulsive indifference to it. Coco Fusco is right to note
that too often 'the postcolonial celebration of hybridity has been interpreted as the sign that no further concern about the politics of representation and cultural exchange is needed. With ease, we lapse back into the

[69] J. Waldron, 'Minority Cultures and the Cosmopolitan Alternative', in *The Rights of Minority
Cultures*, ed. Will Kymlicka (Oxford: Oxford University Press, 1995), 104.
[70] Ibid., 108.

integrationist rhetoric of the 1960's, and conflate hybridity with parity.'[71] Tagore's search for hybridity has an identitarian character to it, is invested in subjectivities, which, however, does not disable a submission to finding a legitimate political and cultural identity, a constituency that forbids deracination. Gómez Pena captures the concept of postcolonial hybridity through what he calls the New World Border, 'a great trans and intercontinental border zone, a place in which no centres remain. It's all margins, meaning there are no "others," or better said, the only true "others" are those who resist fusion, mestizaje, and cross-cultural dialogue. In this utopian cartography, hybridity is the dominant culture: Spanish, Frangle and Gingonol are linguas francas; and monoculture is a culture of resistance practiced by a stubborn or scared minority.'[72] Tagore is in support of an enactment—a critical responsiveness—that introduces a new logic of justice built on multicultural education and understanding. This concept of diversity is plastic working on the contingent and the relational, rendering a broad side to the frigidity that ontological and transcendental proclamations generate. Tagore sees identity as constellative and coalitional inscribed in strife and freedom. His plastic pedagogy bespeaks historical agency, self-transcendence, and invention.

Democratic listening of Visva Bharati knows that 'when two people understand each other, this does not mean that one person "understands" the other.'[73] Difference, not similarity, determines us. Ethnic and cultural specificities in Visva Bharati then are not allowed to impede the tactical and productive solidarity that syncretism is allowed to build. Becquer and Gatti point out that 'syncretism designates articulation as a politicized and discontinuous mode of becoming. It entails the "formal" coexistence of components whose precarious (i.e., partial as opposed to impartial) identities are mutually modified in their encounter, yet whose distinguishing differences, as such, are not dissolved or elided in these modifications, but strategically reconstituted in an ongoing war of position.'[74] Syncretism thus 'signals, not the preordained telos of a redemptive higher

---

[71] Coco Fusco, *English Is Broken Here: Notes on Cultural Fusion in the Americas* (New York: New Press, 1995). 76; quoted in Peter McLaren, *Multiculturalism: Pedagogies of Dissent for the New Millennium* (Boulder, CO: Westview Press, 1997), 10.

[72] Guillermo Gomez-Pena, *The New World Border* (San Francisco, CA: City Lights Books, 1996), 7.

[73] Hans-Georg Gadamer, *Truth and Method* (New York: Bloomsbury, 2013), 361.

[74] Marcos Becquer and José Gatti, 'Elements of Vogue', *Third Text* 5, no. 16/17 (1991): 69.

unity contained within a diachronic self-unfolding, but the historicized interchange between elements based on the complex play of differences and affinities in a collective will to hegemonize.[75] Tagore's massive and yet vastly intriguing project to syncretize is certainly aware of the ambiguity and participatory complexity of such enactments. The respect for difference makes such an enactment dialectical where pluralization is not merely about coercing submission to certain universals. The university space is bound to be 'smooth' in its inexorable transculturality. Plastic Tagore, to my mind, is aware of the difficulty that such a space might generate. Visva Bharati, in its inception and subsequent ramification, produces this confusion in its engagements with the other which only an unconditioned smooth space is capable of generating.

Plastic Tagore works on deconstructing reified notions of inheritance of knowledge through an astute intertwining that acknowledges a centrality of cultural emission (Tagore writes, 'it is this which makes me urge that all the elements in our own culture have to be strengthened, not to resist the western culture, but truly to accept and assimilate it; to use it for our sustenance, not as our burden; to get mastery over this culture, and not to live on its outskirts as the hewers of texts and drawers of book-learning'[76]) and espacement. For him, this is about thinking outside a university to frame up a university; rather, as Derrida has put it, 'how can we not speak of the university?' By not speaking about the university as it exists—within a discourse that academies usually produce—he is speaking of a creative anarchy that refuses to flinch before the power of axiomatic institutional locations and reductive ideologies. Despite harbouring obvious reservations about bounded discourses that neo-humanist institutions are embedded in, Tagore cannot think of a modern university as a 'ruined institution' and so Visva Bharati is not reactively projected as a redeeming legitimate model to disestablish it. As a topos of possibilities, plastic Tagore works on the notion of community as absence: the yet-to-be-achieved forms of human contact where non-recognition of otherness is a statement of the incompleteness of the self.

Visva Bharati is envisaged within a separate logic of responsibility and hospitality: responsibility seen as going beyond the academic time-tested

---

[75] Ibid., 70.
[76] Tagore, 'An Eastern University', 194.

version and hospitality as not being envisaged to merely absorb and accept differences—both being for and being with. It is never designed to become 'responsible before a non-academic instance' which means that its autonomy contested the superior reason that the state imposes as the founding and functioning principle of an institution. Building its own flashpoint moments, such an approach flexes up the academic freedom and reconceives the 'self-legitimation and self-affirmation of the university'.[77] As a 'constructum', Visva Bharati, rather, is marked by Derrida's phenomenology of the finis[78] that repremises academic topology, investing distinct values into 'academic reason' where finitude is not about drawing up the yeses and the noes but is a dialecticism in disclosures and enclosures, bordering the inside and the outside of the reflexive non-cynical habitus of the university. Visva Bharati becomes a flashpoint commentary on the unquestioned rational idea of a university. It addresses what Derrida qualifies as 'question of man, to a concept of that which is proper to man'[79] through the experience of knowledge and humanization which is both relational and dialogical. Plastic pedagogy does not allow Visva Bharati to be seen as looking into the future of a university; it is an experiment to transcend 'conditional university'—not 'as should be' but 'can possibly be'.

Within such formations, what should be the nature of hospitality that Visva Bharati in its counter-institutionality can afford to provide? It is difficult to accept that Visva Bharati offers unconditional hospitality but it allows a gesture of invitation that provides shelter, recognition, and possibilities of value-laden encounters. In a letter to Kshitimohan Sen, Tagore observes, 'I have taken courage to invite Europe to the fields of Bolpur. There will be a meeting of truths here. I feel confident that they shall accept our invitation. What we have to ensure is that their hearts are not starved when they are with us. As a poet I can merely play the flute at the gate.'[80] The music of the flute is not absolute hospitality. The

---

[77] Derrida, 'Mochlos ou le conflit des facultés', *Du droit à la philosophie* (Paris: Galilée, 1990), 401, 404.

[78] Christian Moraru, 'Fringes, Margins, Diaphragms: The University and Textual Reason after Derrida', *Crossings* 3 (1999): 84.

[79] Derrida, 'The Future of the Profession or the University Without Condition', in *Jacques Derrida and the Humanities: A Critical Reader*, ed. T. Cohen (Cambridge: Cambridge University Press, 2001), 25.

[80] Letter written on 30 November 1920; quoted in Das Gupta, *Rabindranath Tagore: A Biography*, 81.

threshold politics involved in Visva Bharati's potential as a counter-institution grid up three issues: the discursive ethics which Tagore establishes and can never be happy seeing violated in the least; an openness which is deeply tied to a conditioned possibility; and the compelling pressure of throwing up a non-nomadic hospitality different from the one that we encounter in conventional institutes of power and learning. The hospitable space is problematic, hence plastic, for it seduces and yet knows its limits, ambivalent and processual and yet not remorselessly transitive. Identities are not questioned but a correspondence with the quintessential character of Visva Bharati becomes a conditioned token for an entry: passage comes with an ideological similarity in passport. In its apparent open-endedness and unbounded hospitality Tagore, unlike Derrida, encrypted his own password—a shared space with the violence of limits. Plastic pedagogy stands enframed within limits and codified, at some points, purposively.

Though not a believer in 'absolute hospitality', plastic Tagore, to an extent, wants a disquietude in his world by getting people to visit his university—an interval in the lull of repetitive solitude, trials of conceptual accommodation, a 'war embrace' (in the words of Coleridge) with realms of possibility. He is always committed to inventing a present and, thus, constructing a future, which, in the sense of the not-yet, holds incalculable dimensions for him. Hospitality cannot just be timely only. Patterns of negotiation, expected structures of exchanges can be intertwined with untimeliness in the form of effacement and renomenclaturing of identities. Tagore's foreign visitors—Indo-Sinologist Sylvain Levi, Moritz Winternitz of the Oriental Institute in Prague, Sten Konow from Norway, British sociologist Arthur Geddes from France, linguist Fernand Benoit of Switzerland, painter Ju Peon from China, historian Stella Kramrisch from Vienna, Irish poet and writer James Cousin, Indologist Guiseppe Tucci and Carlo Formichi of the University of Rome, Dutch musicologist Arnold Bake, Chinese savant Tan Yun-Chan, and others[81]—bring with them response-ability because foreignness comes as a question, with a note of reflexibility, and does not naturalize but leaves behind further questions—the viable ethics of such moves, efficacies of cultural

---

[81] Uma Das Gupta, *Rabindranath Tagore: An Illustrated Life* (New Delhi: Oxford University Press, 2013), 83.

collusion, and aesthetic transgression of borders of thinking and hosting. Here Tagore's conceiving of hospitality transforms the inmates into becoming guests of foreigners—allowing the visitors to extrapolate in the potency of the host a space which students and teachers inhabited as guests to experience the services of learning and educate themselves through the uniqueness of a homely foreignness. Visva Bharati as utopia in the sense of no-place and out-of-place is inscribed in transcendence— the intriguing dynamics of being transcended by the other, the host transcended by the guests and the hosts staying guests in a perpetual possibility of being transcended. This alludes to 'transcendifferances'.[82] He, in a state of hostage, looks out for the other as a way to unshackle him and also make the other know his own resources. This is the radical processuality of 'is'—'is' as both 'has been' and 'not there'. What this does to Tagore's project is that the spectrality of Bharati comes unfailingly to haunt Visva. Visva and Bharati never blur into each other but transcend one another without discrediting the mutual presence. This problematic of transcendence with its own flashpoints of understanding is interesting because the process subjectivizes Tagore all through his life both as a dwelling host and an indwelling guest.

Coda

We are 'habits' and 'nothing but habits—the habit of saying "I"', as Deleuze argues.[83] It is this 'I' that becomes a habit, fearing a disequilibrium that might scuttle its essentiality. The 'I' finds an easy refuge in unreflectiveness and sedimentation. However, when Malabou says that 'being is nothing but its plasticity',[84] it underlines the vulnerability of being to fluidification of habits, the ever-existing second natures. But in

---

[82] Thomas Claviez, ed., *The Conditions of Hospitality* (New York: Fordham University Press, 2013), 32. Claviez writes: 'If the figure of two legs moving alternately and equally toward some telos adequately captures the teleological movement of dialectical sublation, limping toward a radical concept of hospitality that dispenses with a dialectical economy of reciprocity connotes the fact that we acknowledge multiple transcendances moving and tearing left and right, veering us off a fixed track, and maybe making us go in circles—even in our own homes' (ibid. 40–41).

[83] Gilles Deleuze, *Empiricism and Subjectivity: An Essay on Hume's Theory of Human Nature*, trans. Constantin V. Boundas (New York: Columbia University Press, 1991), x.

[84] Catherine Malabou, *Plasticity at the Dusk of Writing: Dialectic, Destruction, Deconstruction* (New York: Columbia University Press, 2010), 36.

the poesis and praxiality of plasticity everything that happens is not un-expected and random. There is a clear line of historicity, and events are 'never pure events, but reveal a dialectical relationship between antici-pation and chance'. Malabou writes: 'Existence reveals itself as plasticity, as the very material of presence, as marble is the material of sculpture. It is capable of receiving any kind of form, but it also has the power to give form itself. Being the stuff of things, it has the power to both shape and to dissolve.'[85] In that sense, plastic pedagogy is 'anarchic' where anarchy, as Malabou clarifies, is not about a complete absence of models. A model does not necessarily have to be a law or anything definitive; it is like a mask which one can wear for a certain time, in order to find one's iden-tity, and then cast away when one thinks it has outlived its utility. By af-firming that 'education is impossible without this play of masks', Malabou explains the core of plastic pedagogy in that all of Tagore's projects, as invested in Hegel's unhappy consciousness, become commitments to un-masking. The play of mask is a declaration of how form is 'always more than itself'.[86] Habit as form in plastic pedagogy is always on the verge of exceeding itself. And trans-plasticity through contingency, historicity, accidents, and reformation is always a possibility, an active marble that is ever conducive to more and more sculpting. Unlike the habitué who 'does not experience or countenance that the condition of possibility of their world, the one which is made for them, is precisely the condition of impossibility for others',[87] Tagore subjects himself to repeated 'self-forgetting'—a state of trans-plasticity of habit and habit-ability. His in-difference to states of formalized habits creates a steady supply of plastic moments, a world under the plastic passion of ceaseless construction. Plastic Tagore is often the sculptor and the marble exchanging positions, threshold points of malleability and essentiality. This, for me, is the prob-lematic of plastic unity.

In the unfolding praxiality of his institution as a project in plasticity and proposing an enfleshed education with corresponding mentalization (the two plastic moments as discussed in this chapter), Tagore indulges in 'unconditional commandment' which brings him to commit to his own

---

[85] Ibid., 81.
[86] Kjetil Horn Hogstad and Catherine Malabou, 'Plasticity and Education—An Interview with Catherine Malabou', *Educational Philosophy and Theory* 53, no. 10 (2021): 1049–53.
[87] Wormald, 'Habitués', 123–38.

poetic, construct his own moral content, and fix his own principles of right and wrong.[88] The irony in Tagore is the struggle that a life-project of 'hypergoods' (in the words of Charles Taylor[89]) brings, compounded by balancing forces of self-creation with allegiances—rather, filiations to community or greater good—the enormous ironic pain to conjugate the two. Tagore's plastic pedagogical moments as enunciated in the two sections of this chapter are witness to this pain. It is the pain that inspires flashpoints of pedagogical innovations and inventions. Plastic Tagore senses the terror of a reality and allows education to work on a provisional self that encounters the world, the reality, its norms and forms, to develop the agentic individual. This agency is plastic whose commitment is to reinvent what we generically call the 'contemporary'—an invocation of dynamic contemporaneity. More than politico-pedagogical projects, they are aesthetic projections: points to reach but reaching as a form of travel. This is the Tagore Agonistes who is a provocateur, an inciter, and in whom 'the sense of the heroic and saintly can be evoked'. As against the self-actualization motif, we encounter the self-potentiation dynamic where 'the seed itself is not yet formed, that there is unformedness in each soul, and that we must struggle to add new powers to our spiritual base'.[90] Ingrained in an autopoietic system, plastic Tagore's thoughts have an apparent simplicity which hides an entanglement; it is a 'complexity' thinking that involves an ethics of non-linearity, transphenomenal concerns, and an 'always-evolving reality'.[91] The multi-temporalities that contribute to the contemporary make for a plasticity of thinking that is never without a Hermes[92] who is a mediator, a traveller, making unexpected correspondences and serendipitous connections. Closer to the French philosopher Michel Serres, for whom 'the goal of instruction is the end of instruction, that is to say, invention', the flashpoints in Tagorean pedagogy consider invention as a deeply intelligent act. Invention is the

---

[88] Richard Rorty, *Contingency, Irony, Solidarity* (Cambridge: Cambridge University Press, 1989), 37.

[89] Charles Taylor, *Sources of the Self* (Cambridge, MA: Harvard University Press, 1989), 4–5.

[90] See Bert P. Helm, 'Emerson Agonistes: Education as Struggle and Process', *Educational Theory* 42, no. 2 (1992): 171.

[91] Brent Davis, 'Complexity and Education: Vital Simultaneities', *Educational Philosophy and Theory* 40, no. 1 (2008): 60.

[92] See Michel Serres, *Hermes: Literature, Science, Philosophy* (Baltimore, MD: Johns Hopkins University Press, 1982).

only true intellectual act, the only act of intelligence.[93] The troubadour Tagore troubles me by taking upon himself the affective task of producing plastic pedagogy, a counter/flashpoint education, calling for invention, imagination, and experimentation without being prohibitively indulgent.

[93] Michel Serres, *The Troubadour of Knowledge*, trans. S. F. Glaser with W. Paulson (Ann Arbor, MI: University of Michigan Press, 1997), 92–93.

3

The *Plastizität* of Visva Sāhitya

Visva Sāhitya (World Literature) is 'untimely': quite often, caught in
italics. Italicization, for me, is an evocation of cultural boundarization,
a re-marked optic distinction not simply inscribed into the text flow but
also signposted within the flow of our understanding. It is a redrawing
of the consciousness of a usage that demands 'outstanding' and, hence,
outsider attention, questioning the efficacy of translation, inscribing
its distinctiveness within the narrative, and bracketing its status from
the rest of the text flow. As a practice, philosophy, and desire, italicization is mostly about 'closing the circle': circling in the concepts, cultural
understanding, and ideologies, and discretion in acts of representation
and narration. If visva sāhitya is about negotiating the worlds of literature across nations and cultures, every world would come with its own
italicization—specificities of cultural formation and particularities of language, expression, and establishment. Any commitment to question the
italicization of reading sāhitya would make for the opening of interesting
spaces of negotiations. Where, then, do we locate the 'de-italicization dialectic' that makes for transcendence and collapsing of borders of cultural,
literary, and epistemological negotiation?

The word sāhitya[1] retains its Sanskrit origin but is now commonly
understood as literature encompassing poems, plays, poetics, and other

---

[1] V. Raghavan argues that the concept of sāhitya had a grammatical origin. It became a poetic
concept even as early as Rajasekhara (an eminent Sanskrit dramatist, poet, critic); as far as we
can see at present, the Kavyamimamsa (880–920 CE) is the earliest work to mention the name
sāhitya and Sāhitya-vidya as meaning poetry and poetics. Even after Rajasekhara, grammatical
associations were clinging to the term up to Bhoja's time. Kuntaka (950–1050, Sanskrit poetician
and literary theorist), about the time of Bhoja himself, was responsible for divesting sāhitya of
grammatical associations and for defining it as a great quality of the relation between *sabda*
(word) and *artha* (meaning) in poetry. Sometime afterwards, Ruyyaka or Mankhuka wrote a
work called Sāhitya-mimamsa, which was the first work on poetics to have the name Sāhitya.
Afterwards, Sāhitya became more common and we have the notable example of the Sāhitya-
darpana of Visvanatha (a famous Sanskrit poet, scholar, and rhetorician writing between 1378
and 1434).

Plastic Tagore. Ranjan Ghosh, Oxford University Press. © Ranjan Ghosh 2024.
DOI: 10.1093/9780198922995.003.0003

forms of creative writing. Sāhitya comes with *sahit* and *vidya* (knowledge): *sahit* in the sense of 'combination' and also coming together: 'it means "with-ness", "togetherness", "accord"—that is to say, in the terms used by Rabindranath in "Sahityer tatparjya", "closeness" (*naikatya*) or "coming together" (*sammilan*)'. Jayanti Chattopadhyay observes that 'certain classical Sanskrit rhetoricians had defined the sahitatwa of literature in terms of the accord of word and meaning'. But, she says, Tagore changes the bandwidth of meaning to observe that 'it is not only the accord of idea with idea, word with word, work with work. Sāhitya alone can work the profound, intimate accord between one human being and another, between the past and the present, the near and the far.'[2] Although *sahita* means 'united together', this does not point to fusion or intermelding but connection, a kind of being-with. Coming together is about understanding the politics and performative of italicization and figuring ways to de-italicize: sāhitya, understood and interpreted as both coming together and being together and informed with the motor of cosmopolitanism and migrancy, performs the de-italicization in critical-aesthetic thinking. Sāhitya is not simply a linguistic equivalent of the English word 'literature': it is, for Tagore, a plastic performance, an event, and an experience in surplus, aesthetic formations, and geocultural transcendence. What kind of *sahit* does sāhitya create for Tagore? How does this *sahit* matter in helping sāhitya matter meaningfully and creating world(s)? Where does Tagore see sāhitya's *visva* and, what makes for visva sāhitya the being of sāhitya?

Questions remain as to what this world is or worlds are: is the 'world an interior', as Emily Apter questions, 'with a border that marks its difference from an exterior? Is a world constituted by the various perspectives of the individuals who inhabit it or is there something transcendental in a world, invariant and resistant to and even constitutive of multiple perspectives? Are worlds distinct and exclusive, or interpenetrating and inclusive? Is our knowledge limited to and by our historical and geographical situation in a world, or do we have access to truths that link multiple worlds?'[3] Interestingly, for Tagore, the visva(s) of sāhitya are remarkably

[2] Jayanti Chattopadhyay, 'Tagore's Aesthetics', in *The Cambridge Companion to Rabindranath Tagore*, ed. Sukanta Chaudhuri (Cambridge: Cambridge University Press, 2020), 370.
[3] Emily Apter, 'Philosophizing World Literature', *Contemporary French and Francophone Studies* 16, no. 2 (March 2012): 171–86.

encompassive, interpenetrative, and border-crossed and do not speak about mere localism or a simple cosmopolitanism. Such dissipative and disparate worlds lead to 'literatures'. Jean Bessière observes that 'world literature plays upon the unity and diversity of literature(s) by focusing upon some manifest literary routes or the world circulation of some unchanged literary forms such as *pantoum*, world literary histories in one language or many, literary groups and works that have attained world importance but cannot be kept too distant from less recognized ones; whichever prominent literary work or literature world literature quotes, there are always minor counterparts. World literature should, therefore, be put in the plural.'[4] Tagore evinces a strong faith in 'literatures' and does not consider the world as a container that holds the totality of objects and subjects. The visva is not the planetary container where all obvious, discrete, and sensate fall into and exist. Literature written into a culture and nation, builds immediately its own potentially palpable worlds outside cultural and national specificities to produce more intelligible spaces of understanding. These spaces are not immediately understandable for the world of literature constructs its potencies beyond the human-scripted forms of expression as well. Pheng Cheah notes that the world is the 'largest possible spatial extensivity, and we can determine it through geometrical and cartographical coordinates. However, objects and subjects can only appear to us if they are already part of a network of references and relations. For Heidegger, the world is this referential network of meaningfulness that precedes the rational human subject and brings us into relation with other beings. It is that openness that lets us encounter and be together with other beings.'[5] The openness is the worlding that can often exceed the rational subject by building its own reasons. The plasticity of visva sāhitya seeks 'openings' in that its worldling does not necessarily stem from intellection and intelligibility all the time; it can emerge out of a plasticity that lies prior to the constructing and pre-creative subjects—the environing visva.

---

[4] Jean Bessière, 'What Is Left of Comparative Literature and World Literature? Notes on International Literature, Its Concrete Universality and Enigmacity', *Canadian Review of Comparative Literature / Revue Canadienne de Littérature Comparée* 44, no. 3 (September 2017): 407–19.

[5] Pheng Cheah, 'Worlding Literature: Living with Tiger Spirits', *Diacritics* 45, no. 2 (2017): 94.

If being becomes 'a real distress and a real liberation',[6] how can the distress and liberation be effected and explored in the being of visva sāhitya? The question that at once inspires and bemuses me is what constitutes such a being and whether the being is explicable and accessible to enunciation. Heidegger's history of being leads us to rethink the 'obvious', and this 'obviousness rethought' can be the premise to begin thinking about visva sāhitya. If finding a text in a remote recess of a culture and rescripting its presence within the predominant circulation of the literary marketplace becomes an agenda that 'world literature' is usually seen to promote, there is manifest profit in working through the obvious; this allows the unconcealment of truth that contributes to our thinking of the literary. How can visva sāhitya work through the obvious? What would it be or be with? The obvious carries a 'presence' with it, a kind of attainment that does not always pitch on the methodologies or protocols of reading. It has a pervading and pervasive history that most thinking on/around visva sāhitya has failed to acknowledge. The obvious 'is' and, again, 'is not'; the obvious loses its potency, its world-forming possibilities, in its obviousness. So visva sāhitya formations are not always conditioned and calculative and obvious; the obvious, rather, corresponds with the meditative, the truth of the unconditioned and the undogmatic. The obvious in visva sāhitya is what I see as the real stand-off with the status quo of reception and inheritance of understanding. What, then, can we interrogate in sāhitya when there is a world prefixed to it? How does that *open* the world of literature, the being of sāhitya?

The plastic event of sāhitya is a case in point. Following Sandra Lee Bartky, we see two formations: one is the 'horizontal' being-event that 'refers to the meaning of what has heretofore happened, to the way in which Being, which is historical "in its essence", has given birth to the epochs of metaphysics', and the other is the 'vertical' being-event that 'refers to the ways in which within any epoch beings (*das Seiende*) come to be the beings they are'. On that note of explanation, horizontal being-event is about the 'varieties of world-disclosure' and the vertical being-event is committed to the 'modes of world-disclosure'.[7] The world of sāhitya is 'there';

---

[6] See Ranjan Ghosh, 'Jugalbandi', *Comparative Literature Studies* 55, no. 4 (2018): 954.
[7] Sandra Lee Bartky, 'Heidegger and the Modes of World-Disclosure', *Philosophy and Phenomenological Research* 40, no. 2 (1979): 212–36.

so before we see a text as belonging to a culture, a particular background, a relational context, and a timescape, the world of sāhitya precedes our reductive experience counter-intuitively. This, for me, contributes to how we see visva sāhitya, presenting and 'presencing' its formation not in isolation or apartness but by living holistically; this is the 'opening forth'. If the pre-reflective and pre-discursive experiences are pressed into play, then the *dasein* of sāhitya works around a 'poetic' where mattering and presencing oppose the tyranny of the theoretical (the structured). What kind of truth are we exposed to? This brings us to the 'imperative' to understand the experience and truth of 'uncoveredness'—the disclosures we effect and sāhitya's own world-disclosures, its worldings; for instance, more than what Tagore as a creative writer says or represents, we vector towards what unconceals Tagore, the world of Tagore, the 'obvious' Tagore, his being in the world: this is not what Tagore does or can be theorized about and, hence, reduced to explanatory parts and his own constructivism but the Tagore as an existing being that has always been on attendance upon alethic potencies—the uncovering of Tagore beyond our worldly understanding of him within his obvious literary, cultural, and political and existential circulations. Tagore within the flow and directions of world literature is an italicized entity, 'obviously' regional in comparison to global English. But the visva of sāhitya puts him under the anxiety and eros of being de-italicized. We, thus, uncover Tagore (technized) as much as Tagore is always attending an unconcealment and 'openedness'.

What I mean is that all understanding is not theory; some understandings happen, not necessarily waiting to be theoreticized and technologized. Understandings can be potentials, 'out-of-condition' thinking, and mere empathetic responses as well. This, however, need not be confused with the aesthetics of excess and lack, the surplus and suture. Working through Heidegger's idea of the world, we encounter a space that is 'unintended' and present in an unprominent way, somewhat outside the conscious formalization of understanding and thought. What stares back at us is the articulative difference between visva sāhitya and what is 'out there' in the visva of sāhitya: representation and constructivism need not always find their way in the ways of the visva of sāhitya. Is visva sāhitya both being in the world and attunement (*Stimmung*)? It is interesting to note, following on Heidegger's notion of the 'being-complex', that a text written within *desh-kāl-pātra* (place-time-pot) is meaningful only within a *sambandha* with others (*sahit*): the being of a text is in the complexity that it builds with others—'a formal or transcendental notion in that it refers to the structure of any possible experience of being-in-a-world'.[8]

Words change; concepts morph; expressions and meanings begin to vary. And with time, contexts conspire to produce new sets of circumstances and manifestations—circumstances include cultural locations, biographical indexes, the transmissive potency of subjects, the generative interest that language creates through translation, the cross-cultural intent and intensity. Circumstance, as Michel Serres notes, creates a productive 'local' and a kind of metastability that inspires fluctuations and fragility on forms of understanding and meaning. Charles Phillips writes that,

> Critically, for Serres, circumstance is not a spatial container or surround. It is an unformed spatiotemporal envelope whose shape is open. The time or temps of circumstances is therefore meteorological: it is a cloud of conditions that can precipitate as a shape of change. World in this sense is a circumstantial metastability, or what following Serres, we might call a circumstability: a spacetime always being tensed by the pressure of incalculable changes in the cloud of variations from which it emerges. In this sense, the circumstantial is the particular configuration of elements and forces transversal to scale, from elemental energies to the molecular economies of a body, that provide the conditional constraints within which a sense of something happening emerges.[9]

Visva sāhitya is a product of circumstability; it is an 'exscription'—that which scripts and scripting as excess—embedding a variety of circumstances in what it is, how it came to be, and what might happen to it. So once written into a system, sāhitya becomes plastic in a variety of ways. As the philosophers Jean-Luc Nancy and Aurelien Barrau have argued, world 'is entering into a movement of indefinite expansion, both on a

---

[8] Ibid., 214.

[9] Charles Phillips, 'Bend, Engage, Wait, and Watch: Rethinking Political Agency in a World of Flows', PhD diss., Johns Hopkins University, 2014.

"cosmic" scale and in our methods of knowing and acting on it and within it', becoming, in the process 'the crucial point where all of the aspects and stakes of sense' in general are 'tied together'.[10] Sense-making, rather sensing, ensures our being in the world, authentically and engagingly, and also securing and driving us into a point above such world-embeddedness to create a different world-meaning. Coexistence signaturizes world literature: but co-existence arises through the elements questioning their status of relation among themselves. Intimacy cannot always be in stability; intimacy is profoundly operative through fragility. There is, in the words of Nancy and Barrau, an 'uncoordinated simultaneity': a kind of 'continuous creation where what is constantly rekindled and renewed is the very possibility of the world'.[11] There is a 'becoming aesthetic' or a post-aesthetic to world literature comprehensions. This is an affective and aesthetic attunement to a world or worlds that reveals in a plastic moment, something that grows with time, eludes our conservative understanding, and becomes powerfully disclosive.

Plastic Sāhitya

Tagore points out in his essay 'Visva Sāhitya' (1907) how man expresses his joy in literature, how and in what form the human soul chooses to manifest its diverse, variegated, multiple images of self-expression; he considers this as 'the only thing worth considering in world literature'. Literature must

> actually *enter the world*—whether it pleases to express itself in the form of the diseased, the accomplished, or the ascetic person—to know how far man can find his *kinship* in the world, and to what extent he can realize truth. It will not do to know it as an artificial construct; it is a world in itself. Its essence exceeds the individual's grasp. It is in continuous creation, like the material universe itself, but in the innermost

---

[10] Jean-Luc Nancy and Aurelien Barrau, *What's These Worlds Coming To?* (New York: Fordham University Press, 2015), 2, 1.

[11] Ibid., 49, 52.

core of that unfinished creation is a perfected ideal that remains unmoving.[12]

If sāhitya *enters* (sensed out of the Old French *entrer* meaning 'enter', 'go in'; 'enter upon', 'assume'; 'initiate') into the world, then it must be coming from a world of its own or worlds affiliated to the writer, his times, context, tradition, and, finally, a world beyond his own comprehension and construal. Sāhitya's entering is about worlds coming together, initiated, assumed, and getting into negotiation and play, into forms of expression and aesthetic matterings challenging the notion of the universal milieu. Here is the life world that sāhitya builds with the world-being: the patterns of disclosures, or the levels of unconcealment that the self and the other in their complex turnings and returnings construct and inhere: 'in the world,' writes Tagore, 'we witness two things—the expression of work and the expression of emotion. But that which is being expressed through work we cannot witness in its *totality* or understand fully.'[13] Not that such a life world denies the essence of history or historical world-making; rather, world-making operates and is made to happen as forms of entering—an ingress that unfixes worlds of understanding and performs its own disclosive acts of expressions.

What kind of meaning can sāhitya generate when Tagore notes that we can connect through 'joy', *hṛdaya-rasa*, self-expression and the dharma of our heart? Tagore observes that this dharma of our heart 'wants to disseminate its emotions into the world. It is not complete in its self. It always wants to make its own truths the truths of the world. The house it inhabits is not merely a structure of bricks and mortar—it attempts to make it a home and colours it in its own hues. The country in which the heart lives does not remain as earth, water and sky—instead, only when that country manifests itself as the mother-image of God's life giving force, then it finds joy.'[14] Sāhitya connects with the dharma of the heart to create 'dwellings' initiating and possibilizing a 'coming into being': sāhitya as 'setting up' of worlds, building 'openness' among things both human and non-human. The plasticity of sāhitya is in realizing that visva often precedes 'opening',

[12] See Tagore, 'Visva Sāhitya', trans. Rijula Das and Makarand R. Paranjape, *Journal of Contemporary Thought* 34 (2011): 289; my italics.

[13] Ibid., 284.

[14] Ibid., 282.

constructing a negative totality of thoughts, ideas, emotions, and many other things. This athwartness of critical thinking leaves us with an access to excess; for Tagore, it can be interpreted as joy. It is the failure to know how we manifest in the 'other' and how the flow of *hṛdaya rasa* can generate 'joy' in the being-in-the-world that creates an interruption between what we understand and what stands outside us to be understood. Not all understandings are directed at us, to the core of our rationality and reason; this can preclude, in the process, a breadth of openings. The plenitude of self is at odds with what Tagore calls 'self-interest'; it prevents the joy to find *sambandha* where every system of understanding is never without its own failings.

Where do we connect the joy and the world, joy as world-making, the joy as the manifestation of sāhitya-being? The joy in visva sāhitya comes from three identifiable sources—travel, estrangement, and nexus. This is sāhitya in its encompassive solidarity—in *comradeship* as Tagore has redoubtedly emphasized. Sāhitya exists in being comparative where its plenitude, plan, and power is caught in *trans* (ferrying across, momentum across traditions and genres and sites) and nexus (relationality)—both scalar and planetary. Uniquely, Tagore brings us before World-Comparative Poetics. However, the problem of creating such a discursive-performative space is in the vexatious mix of imagination, a totalizing impulse and pattern, and a plan that finds difficulty in negotiating with the invisible factors that create both the global and literary capital. The difficulty of enframing the local and the global in understanding the visva of sāhitya complicates the nature of 'joy' further. Our aesthetic mappings enable *rasa*-generation (emotion) and also *rasa* that was never predetermined or preconceived. Here is the *more* in the disclosures of sāhitya: always unworlded, worldized. The more has an undertow of joy. This is a joy that does not make us, as Tagore argues, 'limited by the power of the intellect or the power of work', but makes us experience ourselves without any 'cover or calculation in between'.[15] Tagore observes,

> The son is dear not because we long for the son, but because we long for the *atma*, our true self. Property is dear not because we desire the

[15] Ibid., 213.

property but because we desire the *atma*, or the self. This means that in whatever we experience ourselves *more* fully, we desire that. The son eliminates my shortcomings; I find myself all the *more* in my son. In him, I become *more* of myself. This is why he is my dearest kin; he is a manifestation of my self outside of me. It is the truth I experience so certainly within myself that makes me experience love; that very same truth I know in my son and therefore my love for him expands. That is why to be close to someone is to know what they love. It is thus that we understand where, in this wide world, they have located themselves and how far they have spread their souls. Where my *affection* does not lie, my soul only skirts the rim of its own boundary.[16]

It is a profound desire that dwells in the joy emerging out of being local and global at the same time—the father (the global, as it were) finding himself in the son (our assumed local). This enables the son to become dear to the father. In turn, the father comes to know himself more in the affective momentum, leading him to reach out to the son. This is his desire to locate himself in his son. That desire, again, is developed paradoxically, through a reaching-in, in modes of inner immigration, leading the father to find himself; so, finding oneself more in others is to become more of oneself. This is integral to the visva of sāhitya. The dharma of the local global as a part of the sāhitya being is the *sambandha*, the astute listening where the father (global) and son (local) address each other in a resonant relationality. In *sambandha*, the global finds itself in the local, enabling a knowledge that helps the global to discover its globality, as when the father finds more of himself in his son. Here lies the *more* that produces joy when one's own truths become the truths of the world. Compared to a house, a home in its affective and aesthetic configurations is more fluid, less constricted, and knows the art of accommodativeness where the father and the son can live and learn and make greater senses out of their living (*sambandha*) at different points of time. I would like to argue that the house of the local and the global built out of the bricks and mortar of ideology, principles, traditions, and cultural individualities becomes the home of the 'more of the global' where the local and the global,

---

[16] Ibid., 214.

like the son and the father, exceed themselves in the joy of discovering and reaching out for each other. The flow of knowledge in such continued disequilibria is not between the local's reaching for the global and the global's reaching down to meet the local. Instead, it becomes a moment, a now, that is both achronic and cross-chronic.

The *more* defies the calculative and formal categories of separating the global and the local; instead, the local–global assemblage is an affection that leads one to experience the other outside oneself and eventually to know oneself better. Tagore's essay builds in its own *rasa* within the confines of a local rendering both in its particular context and experience but stays unworlded in its own *rasa* even if it is not translated into a dominant global language. This is because the event of sāhitya as revealed through the essay has always formed its world-disclosures both vertically and horizontally. Tagore's essay is 'local global': affirmative and active sāhitya-being. Tagore considers the 'local' as holding on to the demotic rhythm that builds a thought in particles—dispersed and spread out—before they hive in to form a narrative whether the Arthur Legends or the Ramayana–Mahabharata. It is the powerful local that thought-quantum springs up from and disseminates through, something that may not find a place in the final text that history has come to offer us as an accepted form of reading. Here Tagore implies a plastic figurality of movement which leads to a totality of thought-formation—a common and justified desire—with a kind of universality attached to it. This speaks of the worlding of the local. Tagore argues that anything that is stable and is considered as not having any possibility of alteration is difficult to believe and accept as existing. Writing and the writer's mind are touched and impacted by other cultures, traditions, and thoughts flowing across borders and affiliations and allegiances.[17] Writing from a local context—*sthaan-patra-kaal*—is not ignoring the *rasa* that connects literary effort with the currents that are circumambient to all literary forms: I call this the 'greater form' that the world-disclosures are informed by. This form, this potential to accept the locality and yet transcend it through its *rasa* experience, brings us to question the national, cultural, and ethnic borders of sāhitya, as also, the ideologies of

---

[17] Tagore, 'Sāhitya Shristi', in *Rabindra Rachanabali*, vol. 10 (Kolkata: Government of West Bengal, Saraswati Press Limited, 1989), 350; translations are mine unless otherwise stated.

feminism, race, and body studies. This is close to *littérature-monde* that 'signifies a literature open to the world or, in other words, a literature which speaks of the real and the lived rather than turning in on itself in a state of narcissistic self-consciousness'.[18] Speaking of Goethe and *littérature-monde*, Typhaine Lesevot argues that 'despite his initial desire to break up the fixed canon of the classics by daring to suggest that it was possible to admire contemporary authors, Goethe's world literature remains an elitist concept which favours the literary production of certain nations over that of others (France over Germany), of certain periods over others (the ancient world over the modern), of certain genres (poetry rather than the novel) and of certain readers (those from the elite classes rather than from the lower classes)'.[19] For Tagore, sāhitya is certainly not hierarchical as he admits to 'interference' in all forms of sāhitya—interference in forms that are cultural, rhetorical, political, linguistic, epistemic, and national. It is not a cluster of texts predetermined through certain protocols and patterns but a meaning-making process, a high entropy event where the singularity of literature speaks of a world 'in which there is room for everyone'; Nancy likes to see this as a 'genuine place one in which things can genuinely take place (in this world). Otherwise, this is not a "world": it is a "globe" or a "glome," it is a "land of exile" and a "vale of tears"'.[20]

Sharing the world is world-forming for Tagore and not globalization with its limiting enclosures of understanding. Raffoul and Pettigrew explain that this understanding of world-forming, for Nancy, 'maintains a crucial reference to the world's horizon, as a space of human relations, as a space of meaning held in common, a space of significations or of possible significance'.[21] Within such world-forming, Visva Sāhitya refuses to align with globality for such an orientation denies the opening of

---

[18] See Michel Le Bris and Jean Rouaud, eds., *Pour une littérature-monde* (Paris: Gallimard, 2007), 25; quoted in Typhaine Leservot, 'From *Weltliteratur* to World Literature to *Littérature-monde*: The History of a Controversial Concept', in *Postcolonialism and Littérature-monde*, ed. Alec G. Hargreaves, Charles Forsdick, and David Murphy (Liverpool: Liverpool University Press, 2010), 36–48.

[19] Leservot, 'From *Weltliteratur* to World Literature to *Littérature-monde*', 41.

[20] Jean-Luc Nancy, *The Creation of the World or Globalization*, trans. and with introduction by François Raffoul and David Pettigrew (Albany, NY: State University of New York Press, 2007), 42.

[21] Ibid., 2.

sense and possibility by proposing a direction over the capacity to form a world. In line with Nancy, Visva Sāhitya opens up the antinomy between worldly and the global where the inherent world-forming potencies of Visva Sāhitya are thwarted at the doors of the 'unitotality' of globalization. In its immanent construction, Visva Sāhitya becomes the space for Nancy's event of 'taking-place', a world-space that has room for all. Plastic sāhitya is the 'opening forth', acts in the 'opening of space-time', a 'spatio-temporal dis-positing dispersion', where everything can take-place.[22] Sāhitya's world-formations believe in what Tagore calls 'comradeship' where possibilities of cohabitation and coexistence are built incessantly. Hinged on unpredictability that exceeds representation, chance that escapes the 'horizons of calculability', direction that is not merely a choice between fixed possibilities, orientation that is more than a method and excess, it is, thus, 'a place for a proper taking-place and dwelling, because to take-place is not to simply occur but to properly arrive and happen'.[23] Interestingly, meeting the *other* is turning away from the *self* but not to flee as part of renouncing action and responsibilities. This fleeing is freeing one from the reservations of the self to 'enter into another life'.[24] Visva sāhitya enables such sharing where being in a world is entering into another world, another life.

Visva sāhitya finds its home in world-disclosures that qualify as a kind of expenditure that hardly thinks of losses. It expends and enjoys its bankruptcy: therein lies the joy of expression, argues Tagore, something he ascribes to the plenitude of sāhitya. Expenditure of this nature re-endows the self, brings the self back to thinking about itself, where staying within is reaching out for the world(s) without. This expenditure is 'living' in the sāhitya-being—its truths (the historical and political), happenings (sociocultural), event as happening, and the disclosive power (meaning formation). So visva sāhitya embeds in 'incommensurabilities'—impediments and challenges to think out the *sambandha* between the self and the other and the kinship with the world. Tagore points out that 'to recognize the dharma that is natural to us, to know it as such, to realize its full powers, we need to encounter impediments in its way. It is only thus that

---

[22] Ibid., 73.
[23] Ibid., 10.
[24] Gilles Deleuze and Claire Parnet, *Dialogues* II, trans. Hugh Tomlinson, Barbara Habberjam, and Eliot Ross Albert (New York: Columbia University Press, 2007), 36.

it realizes itself consciously, and the more its consciousness deepens, the more profound its joy is. Everything follows a similar pattern.'[25] Tagore argues the importance of the struggle of failing when one learns to ride the cycle, for the whole effort is not to learn the falling but the ride—the impediments before one finds a way, the incommensurabilities before one gets to build the relation with the cycle. It is an expansion of the circle, the desire to manifest one's self in the other, the pleasure of connecting historically with the world 'when we see our own character manifest in many people, many nations, many eras, many incidents, many varieties, and many shapes.'[26] In fact, it is the regime of *swadharma* that commits to configure experiences between the self (*sva*) and the other. And the challenges to the understanding of plastic sāhitya are both in the *sva* and the other: 'It wants to disseminate its emotions into the world. It is not complete in its self. It always wants to make its own truths the truths of the world. The house it inhabits is not merely a structure of bricks and mortar—it attempts to make it a home and colours it in its own hues. This is the cosmopolitanization of love, understanding of the self, the image of the other, the networks of existence, our *svadharma*.'[27] In such forming, plastic sāhitya has its own dharma, and the unwordlings it generates and enters into have their dharma too.

For Tagore, knowing sāhitya is often about knowing the limits of questioning sāhitya, which does not mean knowing the points of exhaustion; rather, it becomes a reminder of our inability to question further. The aesthetic of Tagore's visva sāhitya can be found in sāhitya illumination—the truth establishing system, the bringing-forth as an activity that is both translational and transcultural. The world-being of his sāhitya is to question the conditions of knowledge-generation; it tries to see literature as 'existing', as a phenomenon whose truths await to be discovered and are not always imputed and constructed. The truths of such findings lead us to see the 'fundamental' of visva sāhitya where the fundamental is not merely about what 'is there' but about what essentially survives our investigation—Tagore's unexpended quotient of the 'literary'. This brings us to question the finitude of sāhitya as performance and act: if

---

[25] Tagore, 'Visva Sāhitya', 289.
[26] Ibid., 281.
[27] Ibid., 282.

Heidegger has inspired us to question the very role and dynamic of metaphysics in our thinking and understanding of life, I prefer to extend this to our thinking of both the visva and Tagore's visva of sāhitya. If every move, gesture, act, and performance come with historicity, as has been the idealized narrative of expectation and fulfilment in Western cultures, we are missing some part of the world that sāhitya ungrounds and something that visva sāhitya, as I see it, has not been able to realize. If visva sāhitya, through a technology of thinking, permits and promotes certain protocols and procedures of doing and performing, it can also make allowance for certain unmapped categories and experiences. Here visva sāhitya for Tagore confronts its own 'poetic'; this is not merely the uncanny but a non-appropriative relation to the being of sāhitya. Isn't there a way to understand sāhitya non-theoretically, a different vein of plasticization in thinking? Admittedly, this builds an across-factor that escapes a method and obviates a method after one has built a connection with the text. Thinking with Heidegger, I call this the 'unconditioned across', the across that is more fundamental than we could ever think out and about; it has its own tribunal of reason. I claim the power of the ordinary and the obvious in a text and extend the notion of the 'across' through terms that are more fundamental, associative, preconditioned, pre-reflective, and, hence, less settled in the said than in the saying. This qualifies as the plastic literary that reinvests Tagore's essential and performative relationship with sāhitya.

In 'Saundarya and Sāhitya' (Beauty and Literature) Tagore refuses to distinguish between the ugly and the beautiful, attributing all to a totality whose experience and milieu is incomplete. This totality is the other name of 'truth' that inspires a desire to reach, know, connect, and conquer realms of understanding across cultures and modes of being and existence. The incompletion in *rasa* experience is the rhythm that Tagore considers as 'beauty': how the manifestation and constriction, the release and restriction make for the 'beauty'. Discriminative judgement as to what is beautiful and what is not segregates and, consequently, enervates understanding. Sāhitya does not discriminate between the good and bad; it allows itself to be a flow and not hedged by restrictions as to what it must be; it cannot be a river that stands to be embanked for then it becomes a pond. Cultural thought-tradition or conceptual identities—be it geoculturally East or West, North or South—are donative and relational.

Jean Luc-Nancy observes that 'the difference between East and West is a difference impossible to pin down in terms which are—shall we say—geocultural, geophilosophical or geotheological. One could say that these terms refer to certain valencies or tendencies which move across and accentuate each formation of thought in various ways, depending on the circumstance.'[28] The finitude and comparability of 'what is East' and 'what belongs to the West' evoke frangibility and fragility and, consequently, transcultural mobilities. This is not identity-dissolution or conceptual dilution or paradigm compromise but a plasticity and, later, a faith, to see how what is 'me' today can be 'us' tomorrow and stay 'with' others in the future. In 'Sāhitya Shristi' (The Creation of Literature) Tagore talks about 'formation', the coming into being, of ideas and thoughts around a subject—a plasticization of the literary. This, as Tagore qualifies, is a ceaseless process. Fruits coming to the branches do not stay quiet: the hog plum ripens, fills up in juices, puts on colour, grows aromatic, hard in its interior, the stone, and exceeds the tree it is a part of.[29] Thoughts flow and follow such a figuration: it forms and its formation exceeds the forming source. If an object or a thought settles into a site, building a context of its own, it speaks about itself and the milieu that contributes to the forming and existence. Togetherness is enmeshed, entangled, and entropic. It is here that a plasticity of literary growth can be located—plasticity both in the sense of malleability and diffusion, seepage and materialization.

Plastic Visva Sāhitya

Elaborating on *plastizität* Catherine Malabou explains how plastic can mean ' "susceptible to changes of form" or malleable (clay is a "plastic" material); and on the other hand, "having the power to bestow form, the power to mould", as in the expressions, "plastic surgeon" and "plastic arts" '.[30] Tagore's visva sāhitya is form, giving form and form-ability. The

---

[28] Jean-Luc Nancy, ' "Our World": An Interview', *Angelaki* 8, no. 2 (2003): 47.

[29] Tagore, 'Saundarya and Sāhitya', *Rabindra Rachanabali* 10 (Kolkata: Government of West Bengal, Saraswati Press Limited, 1989): 382.

[30] Catherine Malabou, *The Future of Hegel: Plasticity, Temporality and Dialectic*, trans. Lisabeth During (New York: Routledge, 2005), 8.

function of a form is about forming through exceptions, incorporations, and modelization. This elaboration and extension of form is not simply accidental; it is gradually transformative as well by giving something the function of a form, a kind of donational plasticity by which connections and networks are made increasingly intelligible.[31] Staying as sāhitya is being in a continued state of plasticity which is a state of change and exchange. It is a reality that becomes its own alterity. Tagore's understanding of visva of sāhitya is *wandlung* (transformation) and *verwandlung* (metamorphosis) in that sāhitya performs as a 'scheme' in motion: it is difficult to imagine a source point of its emergence. Malabou would see sāhitya here as not a change from A to B but as a changing A forming into a changing B. Change is not initiated like a button pressed; change comes as changed. Surplus is not always A to B and then B+; if 'change invents what it changes' then B+ was always a component of B and most often did not need A to make that happen. Malabou's deep interest in form becomes a point of engagement for me. Form is not always referential to forms that precede its beings; coming into being is not always coming through a development with a genetic originary source point. Sometimes form forms in a kind of emergence where change is seen as immanent and not an evolutionary development or a follow-up. Form is rest, is restive; it arrests and wrests; it is arresting. Form in-forms itself. Sāhitya is such an (in)form-ation.

Tagore's idea of 'totality' as form is plastic which is both 'self-engendering and self-destruction'.[32] Visva sāhitya, through its inherent failings, keeps demonstrating 'forms' that 'cross the line'—keeping, receiving, and exploding at the same time. Malabou evinces her faith in the future 'not of the other of form but of the other form, a form that no longer corresponds to its traditional concept'.[33] Sāhitya seeks other forms not in the sense of mere alterity and tradition that lack flow (tradition for Tagore 'is helpful is like a channel that helps the current to flow'[34]). There

---

[31] See Alexander Hope, 'The Future is Plastic: Refiguring Malabou's Plasticity', *Journal for Cultural Research* 18, no. 4 (2014): 329–49.

[32] Malabou, *Future of Hegel*, 293.

[33] See Brenda Bhandar and Jonathan Goldberg-Hiller, eds., *Politics, Legality, and Metamorphosis in the Work of Catherine Malabou* (Durham, NC: Duke University Press, 2015), 5.

[34] See Tagore, 'Art and Tradition', in *Angel of Surplus*, ed. Sisirkumar Ghose (Kolkata: Visva Bharati, 1978), 50–51.

is the transubstantiation that is at once 'the condition and the result of change'. And the form of visva sāhitya owes to minds giving 'form to the line; the form of a life that is from here out revolutionized, reversed, and opened in its middle'[35]—form as flow.

Visva sāhitya re-forms and trans-forms: it comes both with schema and donation of form. The forms of world-making trigger the flow and vortices of sāhitya-*rasa* which can be both pre-national and post-national constellations. The visva(s) of sāhitya declare(s) an allegiance to nationalist traditions but is(are) also a celebration of a return to the philological home in earth that can 'no longer be the nation'.[36] The *Geist* of doing sāhitya has its own forms of supercession. The flows and figures, laminar and entropic, implicate post-national approaches and unmapped worlds that have their constellative manifestations, certain forms of incompletions and inevitable failings. The plastic figuralization of Tagorean sāhitya-formations is informed by a Serrean 'flow'; nothing is outside flow and so everything is not without finitude, the principle of transience, transitoriness, and impermanence. Michel Serres explains that the 'world is a multiplicity of flows, each inclined in relation to the others, and every stream runs its slope. The ensemble of fluencies forms a cycle, by a generalized inclination to the global state of the materials of nature. These circulations are not circles, precisely on account of inclination. A circumference plus an angle, however small it may be, produces a spiral'.[37] The worlding and the collapse of worlds in Tagore's visva of sāhitya become interactions between vortices in the flow, possibilizing creative emergence. Thoughts across cultures and traditions can be Lucretian *clinamen*—imperceptible atomic swerves—having their swerves, bends, angles, and gradients. This visva of sāhitya is a system that hardly moves straight or in a mere predictable orbit but in a vortex or in the intermingling of the vortices *forming* fresh plasticities of understanding.

Visva sāhitya is inherently anachronistic. Tagore notes,

---

[35] Malabou, *The Heidegger Change: On the Fantastic in Philosophy*. trans. Peter Skafish (Albany, NY: State University of New York Press, 2011), 279.

[36] Erich Auerbach, 'Philology and *Weltliteratur*', trans. Maire Said and Edward Said, *Centennial Review* 13, no. 1 (Winter 1969): 16–17.

[37] Michel Serres, *The Birth of Physics*, trans. Jack Hawkes (Manchester: Clinamen Press, 2001), 58.

All I have wanted to say is that just as the world is not merely the sum of your plough field, plus my plough field, plus his plough field—because to know the world that way is only to know it with a yokel—like parochialism—similarly world literature is not merely the sum of your writings, plus my writing, plus his writings. We generally see literature in this limited, provincial manner. To free oneself of that regional narrowness and resolve to see the universal being in world literature, to apprehend such *totality* in every writer's work, and to see its interconnectedness with every man's attempt at self-expression—that is the objective we need to pledge ourselves to.[38]

It is interesting to observe the 'estrangement' that world-comparative literature builds: writing and expression is one's own and yet the greater currents take one's work outside what one intended to establish and formalize. The very idea of visva sāhitya is a mode of estrangement—attachment to *sthaan-kaal-patra* is the italicization and the de-italicization is the estrangement from its origins of culture and context; it is an affect form that exceeds every text's being in the world. Estrangement and attachment are caught in simultaneous order. This is the text's life world that is always an unintended victim of disclosive release. This is, most often, responsible for the joy that Tagore talks about; it articulates the 'plenitude' of sāhitya beyond enframed anticipations and prenominations. Sāhitya, in promoting *sahit*, paradoxically believes in losing *sahit*, for disjunctures are the realities for transcendence and world-forming. So, Cheah notes,

structurally detached from its putative origin and that permits and even solicits an infinite number of interpretations, literature is an exemplary modality of the undecidability that opens a world. It is not merely a product of the human imagination or something that is derived from, represents, or duplicates material reality. Literature is the force of a passage, an experience, through which we are given and receive any determinable reality. The issue of receptibility is fundamental here. It does not refer to the reception of a piece of literature but to the structure of

---

[38] Tagore, 'Visva Sāhitya', 288; my italics.

opening through which one receives a world and through which another world can appear.[39]

Here *sahit* is in the nature of a disjuncture–conjuncture *sambandha*: the phenomenon of cutting-together-apart. This, again, brings me to the being-event of sāhitya—the *sahit* as not mere combinations but incommensurabilities that await transcendence and where the going beyond is networkism and world-formation.

Tagore argues that

> in this world, whatever we see, we see in a scattered way; we see it a little here and there, a little now and then; we see it mixed up with ten other things. But in literature those gaps, those adulterations do not exist. There all the light shines upon that which is being expressed. For that time being nothing else is allowed to be seen. Through many contrivances such a place is created that allows only that to be luminous. That is why one places nothing that cannot withstand such stark individuality and luminosity in the space of literature. Because, to place the undeserving in such a location is to humiliate it.[40]

Sāhitya has this ability to bring things together—not leave in isolation—build connections among things that look apparently scattered, here and there; this is the power of the comparative, the power of visva sāhitya as an 'ethical project'; this makes for the cosmopolitan force that creates its own *rasa* of 'coming together'. Bruce Robbins argues that

> set against 'other times and eras,' as it is here, being oneself also signifies occupying the present tense. And being a self-in-the-present-tense signifies two quite different things. On the one hand, it signifies the burden of a provinciality or partiality or self-interestedness from which one may need and even want to be released. On the other hand, however, it also signifies the opportunity for an action that will produce change, an opportunity that the past by definition cannot offer and from which we should

---

[39] Pheng Cheah, 'What Is a World? On World Literature as World-Making Activity', *Daedalus* 137, no. 3 (Summer 2008): 35.

[40] Tagore, 'Visva Sāhitya', 287.

fear to wander too far away. The study of world literature, however cosmopolitan, can never be the most efficient or momentous of actions, yet action remains a criterion that permits a discrimination of better and worse cosmopolitanisms.[41]

Visva sāhitya needs to look into promoting good and effective cosmopolitanism and also 'estrangement as interconnectedness' through informed and productive ways of understanding and judgement. The estrangement is, at a certain level, translational: a work written within the confines of a nation, a community, builds its own *rasa* outside the intentions and commitments of the writer. If a work relates to the circulation of writing outside oneself, the *rasa* of the work is relational. All expressions are relational-translational; 'everything is translated,' notes Bruno Latour, 'we may be understood, that is, surrounded, diverted, betrayed, displaced, transmitted, but we are never understood *well*. If a message is transported, then it is transformed'.[42] So the travel in world literature through translation is also the travel through trans-formation; for me, besides worldiness, there is a world outside the text that *forms* the worlding, the ambiguity of its reception and reading, the politics of its global and transcultural flow, and the power politics of language and dissemination. The intensity of this subject deepens through a correspondence with how Jean-Luc Nancy takes this self and the expression further through what he argues as the singular plural where the self is much more than mere I and You, the same and the other, in that a *singulus* does not exist and the self (*soi*), an 'each one' is always already in relation. For me this is where Tagore's notion of sāhitya as *sahit* is always already in motion—a 'taking place'[43] where 'selves ("les soi"), are not in relation ("en rapport"), but "together" ("ensemble"), where being-together is characterized by mutuality and sharing, not by the strict reciprocity of a same/other relation with its cycle of debt and credit'.[44] The self-sāhitya dynamic owes

---

[41] Bruce Robbins, 'Uses of World Literature', in *The Routledge Companion to World Literature*, ed. Theo D'haen, David Damrosch, and Djelal Kadir (Abingdon: Routledge, 2012), 383–92.

[42] Bruno Latour, *The Pasteurization of France*, trans. Alan Sheridan (Cambridge, MA: Harvard University Press, 1993), 181.

[43] Jean-Luc Nancy, *Being Singular Plural*, trans. Robert D. Richardson and Anne E. O'Byrne (Stanford, CA: Stanford University Press, 2000), 119.

[44] Christopher Watkin, 'A Different Alterity: Jean-Luc Nancy's "Singular Plural"' *Paragraph* 30, no. 2 (July 2007): 50–64.

less to the self-in-relation and more to a 'self-as-relation' and, hence, the dichotomy of the same and the other does not exist.

The sharedness—the self-as relation—is coterminous with the phenomenon of co-appearing (*la comparution*) in Tagorean transpoesis. Thinking and writing are always about co-appearing; if the logic of thought is escaping thought,[45] reading Tagore, in transpoesis, is escaping Tagore. Tagore's viśva of sāhitya becomes an 'ensemble' where everything holds together: and interestingly, 'even if we held everything in "one" ensemble, that ensemble would be joined by the thought that holds it, making two ensembles. Every appearing being harkens to the ensemble of being and appearing with which (and only with which) something can appear and be, as though it were harkening to its ultimate condition for appearing and to its deepest origin. In short, everything that is or appears, co-appears.'[46] Thinking and doing sāhitya for Tagore is an event of co-occurrence and co-appearing. Juan Garrido is right to observe that 'co-appearing cannot be reduced to any single figure. Nor can it be reduced to the figure of a simple plural, a pure multiplicity. Co-appearing must consist each time of a plurality of units, whether those units can be listed one by one or whether they form distinct groups. Without one, there cannot be many, for a many (*un divers*) without numerous unit, without the "ones" that can be distinguished, compared, or contrasted, is not many.'[47] The transpoetical understanding of sāhitya cannot be a phenomenon of 'simple unity' or 'simple plurality' or 'simple totality'. It is about the forms and norms of 'address' which, for me, is Tagore's 'connection of joy', the 'experience of ourselves in another', and the phenomenon of 'finding myself more in my son'. This 'address', as Jean Luc-Nancy notes, is a kind of thinking that 'addresses itself to "me" and to "us" at the same time; that is, thinking addresses itself to the world, to history, to people, to things: to "us"'.[48] On that line, Tagore's transcultural understanding of sāhitya is our 'curious "being-with one- another," [*être-les-uns-avec-les-autres*], toward our addressing one-another'.[49] There is,

[45] Juan Manuel Garrido and Vanessa Doriott Anderson, 'The Poetry of the World', *Diacritics* 43, no. 4 (2015): 54.

[46] Ibid.

[47] Ibid., 55.

[48] Nancy, *Being Singular Plural*, xv.

[49] Ibid.

hence, a singularity in Tagore's idea of visva sāhitya which inspires efforts to diminish apparent differences and, consequently, generate meaningful interference in cross-conceptual and cross-cultural negotiations. We are dynamically settled in the 'us'—the singularity which is the other name for a singular–plural coexistence. Nancy observes:

> If one can put it like this, there is no other meaning than the meaning of circulation. But this circulation goes in all directions at once, in all the directions of all the space-times [*les espace-temps*] opened by presence to presence: all things, all beings, all entities, everything past and fu-ture, alive, dead, inanimate, stones, plants, nails, gods – and 'humans', that is, those who expose sharing and circulation as such by saying 'we', by *saying we to themselves* in all possible senses of that expression, and by saying we for the totality of all being.[50]

Tagore sees such a 'circulation' as a singular–plural entanglement—a to-tality in motion. He observes that 'everything from a particle of dust to the Sun, Moon, and stars thus encounters my intellect. In this way endless secrets of the universe are bringing out man's intellect and expressing it in a magnified way to him; after this meeting with the universe, man's in-tellect returns to him once again, augmented. This confluence of intellect with outer objects is intelligence. And in this confluence is the joy of our capacity to understand.'[51] The intelligence underwrites an entanglement to produce a plurality of operative nows.

The visva of sāhitya has and builds these nows; and not always that these nows are 'discretely or uniformly slotted; they do not all line up on the same synchronic place'.[52] Tagore notes that 'writers have come from all times and all nations to work as labourers' to build a totality (the *visva-manav* as a project of coming together to accomplish a plan) whose plan is not available to us'; 'every labourer has to use his natural compe-tence to integrate his own composition into the whole and thereby com-plete the invisible plan'.[53] Importantly, the plan exists but is touched by incompletion—a fragility that keeps the plan somewhat unplanned and

---

[50] Ibid., 3.
[51] Tagore, 'Visva Sāhitya', 281.
[52] Wai Chee Dimock, 'Literature for the Planet', *PMLA* 116, no. 1 (2001): 174.
[53] Tagore, 'Visva Sāhitya', 287.

under construction. This is another version of circulation and coming-together that the visva of sāhitya generates outside the 'regulative power of clock and calendar'.[54] This idea of supranational time keeps sāhitya in transit and *sahit* in continual operation through integration, incomple-tion, and invisibility. The 'extra-territoriality' and anachronistic reading are deeply beholden to singular–plural entanglements with which all texts grow and continue to survive and thrive—a deep investment in what I have called elsewhere 'intra-active transculturality'.[55] Texts across continents and borders have 'travelling frequencies': 'frequencies re-ceived and amplified across time, moving farther and farther from their points of origin, causing unexpected vibrations in unexpected places'.[56] These create 'unstable ontology' and 'planetary time' that evolve an 'un-expected web of allegiance'.[57] What Tagore calls intelligence (something that I interpret as entangled circulation) submits to the 'more than global' context of visva sāhitya where the 'more' is experienced through the con-nective power generated among diverse traditions of thought and con-cepts, travelling theories and experiments conducted in cross-border and cross disciplinary thinking.

Plastic visva sāhitya *continues* to get built through the entangled aes-thetic of distance and desire—'kinship in the world', as Tagore has em-phasized. Tagore manifests his apparent anxieties over the rupture and separation between two interacting thought and cultural paradigms which, again, through the power of self-expression—the *visva-manav* as a moving and encompassive power—are replaced by communication and correspondence; it is the desire as kinship that collapses historical distances, overcomes difference in time zones, and inflects concepts from one tradition with a different momentum to 'travel' across other cultural zones. There is much more to read in the metaphor of the Sun that Tagore writes about:

---

[54] Dimock, 'Nonbiological Clock: Literary History against Newtonian Mechanics', *South Atlantic Quarterly* 102, no. 1 (2003): 158.

[55] See Ranjan Ghosh, 'Intra-active Transculturality', *Modern Language Notes* 130 (December 2015): 1198–220.

[56] Dimock, 'A Theory of Resonance', *PMLA* 112, no. 5 (1997): 1061.

[57] Dimock, 'Nonbiological Clock', 489.

The substance of the Sun's core is recreating itself in many liquid and solid forms that we cannot see, but the corona of light that surrounds the sun ceaselessly proclaims its existence to the world. Thus it constantly bestows itself and unites itself with everyone. If we could perceive the totality of humanity in a visual metaphor, we would see it as a vision of the Sun. We would see its matter slowly arranging itself in many layers within itself, surrounding itself in a halo of joyful expression, shedding its light in every direction. Regard literature for once as that halo of expression composed in language and enfolding humanity. Here is a tempest of light, the source of radiance, here are clashes of brilliant spray.[58]

The ever permeative and encompassive light of the visva(s) of sāhitya informs the invisible plan of 'thinking' literature which is ever active and singular plural. It 'constantly bestows itself and unites itself with everyone'. The figure in plasticity that it constructs is not, in words of Derek Attridge, 'pre-programmed by a culture's norms, the norms with which its members are familiar and through which most cultural products are understood'. When singularity is understood in such intricate and profoundly fraught ways—through intra-active entanglement, resonance, transcultural now, singular plural—it cannot stay 'pure'. Attridge argues that 'it is constitutively impure, always open to contamination, grafting, accidents, reinterpretation, and recontextualization. Nor is it inimitable: on the contrary, it is eminently imitable, and may give rise to a host of imitations.'[59] The totality of plastic visva sāhitya involves an 'impurity' in its formation—an eroticism in construction that refuses to stay immured in particularity, specificity, culture-boundedness, and conceptual autonomy, 'arranging itself in many layers within itself, surrounding itself in a halo of joyful expression, shedding its light in every direction'. If sāhitya is meant to generate 'clashes of brilliant spray' it announces networks of contacts and diffractive strength of expression.

Through these complicated matrices of assemblage literature that Tagore implicates—the openings and entries—we encounter the problematic of 'milieu'. Developing a poetics of relation, a relational poesis,

---

[58] Tagore, 'Visva Sāhitya', 288.
[59] Derek Attridge, *The Singularity of Literature* (London: Routledge, 2017), 63.

through his entangled understanding of the milieu, Georges Canguilhem observes that 'the milieu proper to man is the world of his perception—in other words, the field of his pragmatic experience, the field in which his actions, oriented and regulated by the values immanent to his tendencies, pick out quality-bearing objects and situate them in relation to each other and to him. Thus the environment to which he is supposed to react is originally centered on him and by him.'[60] The relational relief is not merely with the existent only, not with that merely precedes our understanding and thinking; it is both with what pre-exists us and a constitutive relationality which comprises 'sens': 'the milieu proper to men is not situated within the universal milieu as contents in a container. A center does not resolve into its environment. A living being is not reducible to a crossroads of influences'.[61] Sens is functionality, a system of reference; and for William James sens is argued as a kind of biological entity and entitization but not without its relational potencies; sens individuates out of the relations that it constructs and projects. It is time that we argued about the 'sens' that Tagore's visva of sāhitya makes or generates. This sense transmission and articulation in Tagore come from both the grounded and the ungrounded relational thesis and aesthesis. One looks into the fantastical character of a fragile totality where 'originary being only shows itself in and as a series of masks, each succeeding the other, but nowhere in this succession does anything lie behind or beneath the mask itself. Originary exchangeability, change and transformation are as such only in and through this primordial absence or void of essence, substance or ground.'[62] The issue of cultural grounding in the reading and experience of literature or any other subject of discourse stays no less ungrounded and exposed to a shudder—cultural ontology of reading always already within ontological explosion, the *reissen*. Hence, the transplasticity of sāhitya is the ontological unease in cultural, political, and social readings of literature.

How much of the world of literature as against world literature can be conceived through destructive plasticity? A concept or thought in

---

[60] Quoted in Carlo Caduff, 'Canguilhem's Vital Social Medicine', *History of Anthropology Review* 4 (February 2019), https://histanthro.org/notes/vital-social-medicine/.

[61] Shaun Gamboa, *Canguilhem Notes: Normal and Pathological* (self-published, Academica, 2013), 5.

[62] See Ian James, '(Neuro)plasticity, Epigenesis and the Void', *parrhesia* 25 (2016): 9.

a culture and tradition can be vulnerable to a 'new wound': the *vulnus*, the fragility, that most thoughts for me are exposed to. This is not absolute biodegradability of thought; it is mostly impossible to have such distinctive and decimative biodegradation. If plastic degrades only to stay plastic, then plasticity is about changing form to reach a form whose shape and status are indefinite and indeterminate. Staying plastic is in being amidst plasticities. Being in a thought is about being in thought-differentiations: the future of a thought is mostly about existing in untimely temporalities. Identities are formed but this does not call for a complete breakdown of *the* identity. So destructive plasticity in understanding world literature vagarizes thinking, resists easy assimilativeness, forms continents of thought without losing touch with an identity that provoked and initiated such formations. The world in visva sāhitya is powerfully subjective and extra-subjective too: the extra-subjectivism coming from one's helpless submission to invisible forces of textual transmission, the inability of the subject to control the forces that determine the future of a work—the text's own world-disclosures. The world of vishwa sāhitya builds its resources and expanse through a new order of production both through its writers and the writing, as every writing becomes its own rewriting—a kind of co-occurrence and co-performance—through its transference and transmission in the global circulation of literary and market capital. Caught in symmetrical–asymmetrical translation, geo-critical spatialization, itinerancy, and transcultural semiosis, plastic visva sāhitya spells out a *totality*. Tagore sees this totality in an inexhaustible plenitude—the 'universal being' of sāhitya—that expends itself to regenerate; he sees this in the connectedness that visva sāhitya constructs and sponsors; he finds it in the 'comradeship' that visva sāhitya builds working through the disjunctures and differences among literature across cultures and nations. Works across cultures and continents are 'compatriots', which means ploughing a land here is connecting, albeit unaware, with the ploughing elsewhere—the 'joy' and inevitability of connect. However, this totality is not totalitarian; it speaks of a formation that does not allow interpretarive conquering but has its own ways of manifestation and reordering. Totality forms additively with the worlds of a variety of literatures emerging from a variety of cultures, times, and places. But this aggregatory formation challenges itself every time one tries to conceptualize its existence. It is where 'desire is mobilized and set into circulation, and where our "projections" about others are ne-gotiated.[63] Totality is in the *across* and lubricates the idea of space and place in Tagore's visva of sāhitya. This disfavours canonicity and elitism which is strategically and preferentially inclusive of works across na-tional/regional literatures: it also refuses to be daunted by the immensity that informs the 'quantitative approach' to reading world literature and sets itself up as a 'happening' across cultures and times, questioning the fluid roots and rootings of a work. Christian Godin notes that 'we see a monkey in the tree, whereas we only see part of a monkey in a fragment of tree'[64] and every investigation results in fragmentation and every explan-ation leads to additional fragmentation. This promises and actualizes the anxiety of the 'unfinished', the recurrence and remanifestation. There is a *śeṣa* which means the residue, the remaining, the remainder. Visva sāhitya has its remainders that are not inert—'it has nothing to do with leftovers', rather, 'it is on the basis of this remainder that everything can begin again.'[65] The totality, thus, declares immanental reading, a literary semiosis; it ensures that visva sāhitya and the visva of sāhitya remain as unfinished projects and through such incompletion and failing Tagore's visva sāhitya continues to stay plastic.

[63] Sanja Bahun, 'Politics of World Literature', in *The Routledge Companion to World Literature*, ed. Theo D'haen, David Damrosch, and Djelal Kadir (Abingdon: Routledge, 2012), 373.

[64] Christian Godin, 'The Notion of Totality in Indian Thought', *Diogenes* 48, no. 189 (2000): 59.

[65] Ibid., 61.

4

Plastic Moment: *Kavi-Aitihāsik*

History enlarges itself through 'listening'. Comparative historiography builds the plastic moments around 'listening', allowing discourses to speak to each other and plasticizing a communication where conversation is not always coincidence and coming together is not always fusing into each other. Historical discourses across cultures have their own hidden structures, forms, and formations that call for 'attentive' listening. Reading history on the street, through community interactions, in molar revolutions, cultures across borders, comes with 'listening out' and 'listening in': deliberative spaces are plastic experiences in disagreement, dissent, and doubt. Transhistoricality is underpinned by 'apophatic' and exotelic listening where historical understanding demands a principle of suspension: suspending one's bias and expectations to allow the other to be heard, suspending the differences between self and the other to make room for critical understanding through comportment and not always compartments. Andrew Dobson's 'apophatic listening' involves temporary suspension of one's own categories, frames, and expectations 'with a view (a) to listening to what is "actually being said", and (b) to listening out for the unexpected and surprising'.[1] Apophatic listening underpins his conception of dialogue as 'structured disagreement' and of 'dialogic democracy' which 'takes its time, it engineers silence, it makes sure all voices have been heard—and then it listens again'.[2] Listening in historical consciousness and historicality is a plastic event that does not simply privilege a sovereign subject but considers, as Jeffrey Librett argues, 'a

---

[1] Andrew Dobson, *Listening for Democracy: Recognition, Representation, Reconciliation* (New York: Oxford University Press, 2014), 173.
[2] Leah Bassel, *The Politics of Listening: Possibilities and Challenges for Democratic Life* (London: Palgrave Macmillan, 2017), 5.

Plastic Tagore. Ranjan Ghosh, Oxford University Press. © Ranjan Ghosh 2024.
DOI: 10.1093/9780198922995.003.0004

subject conceived as always also radically other than, and external to, itself. Listening pertains to the character of the subject not (alone) as a process of being or coinciding with itself but (also) as a process of seeking itself across the deferrals and referrals of otherness, and thus to the character of the "presence" of the subject as one that is pervaded by representations, in the (ab)sense of other selves and signs in search of their own meanings, values, and proper presentations.[3] Transhistoricality calls for an 'ear'—giving an ear in humility, possibility, non-hegemonic arguments, and communicative praxis.

To explore this paradigm in our understanding and theorization of transhistoricality, Rabindranath Tagore's philosophy of history as a distinct mode of historical thinking both as *itihasa*,[4] with its indisputable allegiance to his cultural and historical background, and as a way of life (*theoria*), a life view, encompassing the history of the quotidian, the habitual, the everyday (*pratyohik*), is a good place to begin. The transhistoricity here repremises the concept of the historian and provides a configurative proximity to what we call the *kavi-aitihāsik* (poet-historian). Plastic Tagore's historical sense does not merely produce a 'unified sensibility', a nationalist agenda of one form of history drawn from the nativist past and the values of a particular heritage. His understanding of history turns out to be the point of contact with a past, an instant, a much-needed continuity in discontinuity between the past and the present. The overlapping temporalities call for plastic moments. He is for representational history and de-disciplinization of historical thought where the past is a reservoir measured not in recorded experiences alone, but through a philosophical-aesthetic interest that is not bound to the

---

[3] Jeffrey S. Librett, 'On an Intermittent Subject in Jean-Luc Nancy', *Diacritics* 42, no. 2 (2014): 36–58.

[4] Ranjan Ghosh, 'India, *itihasa* and Inter-historiographical Discourse', *History and Theory* 46, no. 2 (2007): 210–17. Jitendra Nath Mohanty writes: 'The dictionary Vācaspatyam gives the following definition of itihāsa (the closest, but not exact, equivalent of "history"): itihāsa means "arranged in the form of stories and past happenings, conveying instruction in dharma, artha, kāma, and mokṣa, i.e. in [the goals of] righteousness, wealth, sensuous love, and spiritual freedom." Kautilya writes that itihāsa includes the purāṇas (tales of past ages), itivṛtta (dynastic chronicles; also accounts of men and times that are past), ākhyāyikā (short tales), udāharaṇa (exemplary stories), dharmaśāsrta (laws), and arthaśāstra (political economy). Itihāsa and purāṇa seem to be identified or at least closely juxtaposed as early as *Bṛhadāraṇyaka Upaniṣad.* An old etymology of the word itihāsa is given by Durga's commentary on Nirukta ii. 10: it lets us know "thus it was." The *aitihāsikas* or historians were the traditional storytellers.' See Jitendra Nath Mohanty, *Reason and Tradition in Indian Thought* (New Delhi: Oxford University Press, 1992), 188.

consequences it brings. History is not a rigorous form, a system of narrative, symbolic patterns, and representations; it finds a home in 'inconsequentiality' and processes of worlding. Transhistorical listening begins here.

Evincing a strong taste of *itihasa*, Tagore's historical attitude places its trust in facts and yet stays a bit shy of keeping history under the obdurate protective custody of evidence and the heft of verifiability. Tagore argues that our tryst with *itihasa* finds its life in investigating the innermost truth and intention of India's consciousness, of human consciousness, building on a philosophy of *itihasa* where truth and intention (will) are never sundered categories—the listening-in. He shared the urge and vision with many alert and active minds writing during the colonial period—primarily the late nineteenth- and early twentieth-century littérateurs and historians, such as Bankimchandra Chatterjee, R. G. Bhandarkar, Romesh Chunder Dutt, Rajendralal Mitra, and Akshay Kumar Maitreya—about *itihasa* being acknowledged as different from the imperialist version of looking at the past. This homes in on constructing an identity of one's own without being oblivious to a much-critiqued epistemological vacuum that India is said to have suffered from for not having a formalized sense of history. I find it difficult to concur with the argument that sees Tagore as doing history in a spirit of trenchant cultural revivalism with the singular intention of writing back from the colony, challenging the representational politics and methodological praxis of the British Raj. There is certainly some truth in this. However, Tagore was more interested in premising historical experiences in ways that are peculiar to his plastic sensibility, his own culture and times, and the conditions of the present. His views on historicality and historical experience mediate between the pulls of a strong non-Western sensibility and an informed access to certain paradigms of Western models of historical thinking, resulting in Tagore's individual way of according a global accent to his vision of history—the listening-out.[5]

---

[5] Raimundo Panikkar notes that 'adverbs of time, such as yesterday and tomorrow, the day before yesterday and the day after tomorrow, three days before and three days later, are in each case the same word in Hindi, the essential point being the distance from the center without giving priority to an orientation toward the past or the future'. See Raimundo Panikkar, 'Toward a Typology of Time and Temporality in the Ancient Indian Tradition', *Philosophy East and West* 24, no. 2 (1974): 162–63.

Kal

To develop my critique of Tagore's theory of history and notions of transhistorical listening I have built my arguments in three parts: *kal* (past), *kaal* (time), and *aaj-kal* (present/now-past)—*itihasa* in its dialectical and fictive incarnation, in intricate temporality, and as presence and presentification.

In the operative ways of the world, Tagore saw a continuous inhaling and exhaling, a state of sleep and waking, a rhythm of ascent and descent, and a halting and a restart.[6] He explains that in absence and presence, in dark and light, in concealment and manifestation, such a rhythm is maintained. This speaks of a continuity: the yes and the no, the positive and the negative, the attraction and repulsion that become a part of the creative rhythm essential to our understanding of historical situatedness, our ever-rhythmic connections with past and present. Tagore observes that the 'perfect balance in these opposing forces would lead to deadlock in creation. Life moves in the cadence of constant adjustment of opposites; it is a perpetual process of reconciliation of contradictions.'[7] Historical consciousness, he elaborates, builds on the rhythm of opposition, in adjustments between polarities, not through a linear onrush of energy but a circularity that keeps the rhythm of life going. Linearity is not the character of life, writes Tagore.[8] Energy and force built in singular unifocal velocity are destined to create division; life becomes bare, barren, and banal with no music, creativity, and play. When opposite forces meet and multiple forces come together, Tagore argues, the rhythm of creation constructs its own steps and stages. India's *itihasa*, he implies, is built in opposition and agonism, which her consciousness has learned to accept and find a settlement in—a poise in conflict, in turmoil, in exchanges that are not always non-aggressive. This is the rhythm of *itihasa*.

---

[6] Tagore, 'Bharatvarsher itihaser dhara' (The Tradition of Indian History), in *Rabindra Rachanabali*, vol. 13 (Kolkata: Government of West Bengal, Saraswati Press Limited, 1990), 491. All translations are mine unless otherwise stated.

[7] Tagore, *A Vision of India's History* (Kolkata: Visva Bharati Bookshop, 1951), 13. In his book *Sadhana*, Tagore points out that 'the world in its essence is a reconciliation of pairs of opposing forces. These forces, like the left and the right hands of the creator, are acting in absolute harmony, yet acting from opposite directions.' See Tagore, *Sadhana* (New York: The Macmillan Co., 1914), 9.

[8] Tagore, 'Bharatvarsher itihaser dhara', 491.

Tagore knows that finding this rhythm is difficult because man is born not to balance but to flourish in the extremes. The rhythm is synonymous with forming plastic moments.

In the history of the West, he notes, imperialism is the unidirectional force— belligerent and pugnacious—that overpowered all that came in its way to establish sovereignty. But *itihasa* is about learning the dynamics of this rhythm and not merely about recording the tumult of times and documenting the din of events; it is, as Tagore notes, about finding the energy, the power that lies within. Configuring *itihasa* is *tapasya*,[9] Tagore observes:

> It would be wrong for us, when we judge the historical career of India, to put all the stress upon the accumulated heap of refuse, gross, and grotesque, that has not yet been assimilated in one consistent cultural body. Our great hope lies there, where we realize that something positively precious in our achievements still persists in spite of circumstances that are inclement. The best of us still have our aspiration for the supreme end of life, which is so often mocked at by the prosperous people who hold their sway over the present-day world. We still believe that the world has a deeper meaning than what is apparent, and that therein the human soul finds its ultimate harmony and peace. We still know that only in this spiritual wealth and welfare does civilization attain its end, and not in a prolific production of materials, not in the competition of intemperate power with power.[10]

The sense of *itihasa* struggles to work itself out through a recognitive reciprocity between the spirit of the soul that India's deep past has been able to evoke and the pragmatics of the machine (what Matthew Arnold would lament as the 'faith in machinery' in his *Culture and Anarchy*) that the West has obsessively celebrated. The exclusionist scope of the Hegelian notion of history causes further restrictions on the ramifications and dynamics of *itihasa*. The Hegelian historical consciousness is surprisingly anachronic as

---

[9] Ibid., 508.
[10] Tagore, *A Vision of India's History*, 38–39.

Hegel theorizes the exclusion from history of cosmology, Darwinian biology (Hegel's nature has no evolution, only self reproduction), the astonishing new finds of historical linguistics (excluded because the changes of language are unconsciously made), the family (which Hegel thinks is natural and changeless), the working class (because it merely reproduces itself), gender and women, India and even China which, though it has many and extensive histories, lacks the sense of developmental change, according to Hegel, straining every nerve to find a way to exclude the non-West.[11]

Tagore, by contrast, advocates for an inclusivist notion of history—the intra-listening—where the rhythm of life and values in *itihasa* are found to be immanent and imminent. Constructing a historical consciousness that is 'curatorial'[12] and not exoticist and magisterial, Tagore's sense of *itihasa* works between the principles and politics of identity, differentiality, and discrimination which enables better appropriation of his tradition and habitations in modernity. This comes close to the Martinican poet-thinker Édouard Glissant's speculative philosophy of history that in its exposition of what he calls 'nonhistory' (a different form of historical listening) argues against the hierarchical vision of single History. Anti-Hegelians both, Tagore and Glissant overlap in their expectations from history—Tagore's acknowledgement of the latency of history and Glissant's 'submarine' history—in the form of surprise, power, and the creative energy of a dialectic between nature and culture.[13]

Tagore regrets that the history of India we learn textually and institutionally is a history of carnage and catastrophe, a vortex where we are confused by a legion of invaders, infiltrators, acts of settlement, dispossession, and overpowerment—a saga of confused armies, mostly ignoble, clashing and clamoring for power and sovereignty.[14] But in such a welter of facts, hard and bloody, Tagore misses the 'man'—the *Bharatvashi*, the

---

[11] Thomas R. Trautmann, 'Does India Have History? Does History Have India?', *Comparative Studies in Society and History* 54, no. 1 (2012): 195.

[12] Amartya Sen, 'Indian Traditions & the Western Imagination', *Daedalus* 134, no. 4 (2005): 170.

[13] See Édouard Glissant, 'History-Histories-Stories', in *Carribean Discourse: Selected Essays*, trans. J. Michael Dash (Charlottesville: University Press of Virginia, 1989), 61–62, 66.

[14] Tagore, 'Bharatvarsher *Itihasa*' (The History of India), in *Rabindra Rachanabali*, 13:121.

Indian, as he would like to qualify him—his life and the everyday. Ralph Waldo Emerson notes that 'Time stills the loud noise of opinions' and 'sinks the small, raises the great, so that the true emerges without effort and in perfect harmony to all eyes; but the truth of the present hour, except in particulars and single relations, is unattainable'.[15] Working on the small, the particular, and the poetics of relationality that this generates, Tagore narrates that on a blustery day, the storm, despite its ululation and intensity, cannot be the most important event because somewhere under the dusty, squally sky there would be narratives of pain and cheer, of happiness and frustration, in several homes in the village. Should transhistoricality be only about comparative historiography of big-time history? Where is the particular, the obvious, the 'micro' in our historical listening across borders of our existence, the nation, the culture, and the sociopolitical background? How does that redefine our ways of thinking the trans-force in historical formations? The storm, in its might and measure, succeeds in concealing those narratives because the interest and drama shift to the raging phenomenon of the storm. But the acts and play of humanity—the *pratyohik jibon*—sink but do not stop throbbing. To the foreigner walking along the village street, the storm is the great story, the fact and the focus, because, as Tagore notes, 'he is not inside the house, but exists outside'.[16] The plasticity of rhythm in historical consciousness changes. Imperialist history can give us the dust, the eddy, the swirl, the energy of the storm—the consequential and big-league—but misses the 'story' of the home, the hearth, the vibrant nest of daily life and thought and its delicate correspondence with the world at large. Tagore laments that such an approach to historical thinking misses the 'man', his community, emotion, pain, suffering, mirth, tension, failures, crests, crises, and how these congeal into a *bharatvarsha*. He does not mount an attack to dismantle the extant historical periodization—the handmaid of colonial historiographical methodology (for example, ancient Indian history as segregated from the medieval or Afghan history distinguished from the Mughal period). Instead, he demonstrates a taste of *itihasa*, which must focus attention on the insignificant, inconsequential, the

---

[15] Quoted in Mark Salber Phillips, *On Historical Distance* (New Haven, CT: Yale University Press, 2013), xi.

[16] Tagore, 'Bharatvarsher *Itihasa*', 122.

non-textual, the unrecordable, the unworthy—the life current that has helped find and provide support to *bharatvarsha*.

In such transhistorical worldings, Tagore makes no bones about the impossibility of having an overarching world history. Is there a world outside what we conventionally discursivize as world history? He argues that when people get thwarted by the deficit and scarcity of departmental and classified documents that might have provided political, military, and socio-economic information about a country's past, they, in haste and despondence, jump to the conclusion that the country has no history; the common understanding being that without politics there cannot be history.[17] But such investigation, as Tagore animadverts, is tantamount to looking for brinjals (aubergines/eggplants) in a rice paddy; the consequent frustration makes one deny the paddy as a part of agricultural crop production. History is brinjals, paddy, and the rest.

Learning and knowing one's history is a process that has influenced us since our childhood, creating a consciousness that is very difficult to express and an emotion whose trajectory is, most often, impossible to predict and chart. Tagore points out that the essence of a nation enters our consciousness in childhood, enjoying a near unhindered seepage through our affection, imagination, and other related imperceptible sources.[18] It is a strange power: it has a decisive impact, potent and profound, that generates substantial contact between the past and the present. What kind of historical sense does this power produce through its rare energy, possibility, and immanence? India, notes Tagore, has always tried to find a synthesis in pluralism, a solidarity in networks of diversity. It did not seek to negate the differences that history imprints and hands down to us; rather, it manifests as a realization that tries to settle on the 'deepest connection'[19] that every kind of difference, dialectic, and divergence possesses. The politics of such historical consciousness is in opening up to the negotiations of the other (*sambandhas*) and the self (*swadharma*, which is not nativist totalitarianism) through a 'political unity' (rarely effected under a hegemonic dispensation) that honours the capacious character of *itihasa*. People who cannot be united, argues Tagore, should

---

[17] Ibid., 123. Also see Tagore, 'Bharat-*Itihasa*-Charcha', in *Rabindra Rachanabali*, vol. 15 (Kolkata: Government of West Bengal, Saraswati Press Limited, 1994), 528.

[18] Tagore, 'Bharatvarsher *Itihasa*', 123.

[19] Ibid., 124.

be left to their situation and individual right to exist. Hegemonic efforts to bring them under the same sky can produce fragmentation and fractious consequences because the 'dissimilar' cannot forget their dissimilarity and might rebound to avenge all effort to quash it. Historical listening is embedded in *sambandha*. The essence of India's historical sense, Tagore explains, lives with such a truth. Tagore's sense of *itihasa* finds a life in the dialectic—the co-optative and collateral character of historical thought, which is not a Hegelian sublation or conciliation—with the spirit of acceptance, acknowledgement, and approval. He considers this as the 'talent' of *itihasa*: the latency of an energy to create *sambandhas*. This is a continuum, as it were, an envelope holding our belief, intelligence, our life, ways, manners, and even the afterlife—a different vein of transhistoricality. Just as the life of the hands, legs, head, and stomach are not different from one another, or rather cannot be indifferent to one another's existence and functions, this form of *itihasa* does not ignore the 'politics' of pluralist solidarity. Tagore observes that the dharma of India's *itihasa* is a continuity, a non-sectarian way of seeing and believing, the life spirit that knows where its roots are and the head is.

Tagore's *aitihāsik* (historian) makes us believe in a transhistorical listening that has its ownness, a depository and reserve with the potential to communicate even with colonial historiographical ways and certain modes of Western historical thinking. He demonstrates the dignity and validity of native historical consciousness—the *itihasa* of our own living—and builds a historical consciousness that is global not in its overcoming of the local but in a cohabitation that is collaborative and conversational. Through this plastic moment, he teaches us the consciousness of *itihasa*, which finds its succour in 'listening'—the *swadeshi* reserves of learning and wisdom opening up with dignity and depth the lines of communication with the *videshi* ways of historical thinking and knowledge-formation. Dialectical *itihasa* thrives in composure and not in compulsive syncretism where release is richness, confinement is credence, liberty is love, and self-consciousness is often wisdom. This is the plasticity that *itihasa* produces: being born in history needs to complement being born into history.

Tagore does not consider Western colonial historiography to be successful in communicating the *lila* of human nature.[20] In its obsession

---

[20] Tagore, 'Sirajud-Daulah', in *Rabindra Rachanabali*, 15:511.

with the 'historical turn of events', the politics of state and society, and being immured within a particular mode of expression and form, colonial historical discourses miss the 'heart' in historical writing: 'the *lila* of the heart'.[21] It is here that another version of the plastic rhythm starts to emerge. But this does not render his *aitihāsik* tendentious and emotional at the cost of truth and objectivity. The 'peace of truth'[22] is formed around historical objectivity, the impulse and inconstancy of human nature and the *pratyohik* (everyday). Words or stories proliferate like active and living matter spreading by mouth and through changing times. Man's creativity lends a structure to his 'storied' and factual inheritance in ways that he finds truthful and legitimate.[23] Tagore argues that situations in the past cannot have their sole reflectors in events only—brute but not mute facts.[24] Historical truth is an intricate compound—the molecularization of history—of the reality of events and their dissemination and dispersal over time through people and situations. Truth is in details and facts, is of the body and the heart, the mind, and its moods.

Tagore's firm belief in renewing the past creatively, removed from 'academic historiography with its insistence on keeping its narratives tied strictly to public affairs', evinces a power and plasticity. Ranajit Guha observes:

It is wisdom born of the experience of living dangerously close to the limit of language as one must to be a truly creative writer. For it is the latter's vocation to exhaust language and push it to the brink. Which

---

[21] Ibid.

[22] Ibid., 512.

[23] Tagore, 'Itihasa', in *Rabindra Rachanabali*, vol. 14 (Kolkata: Government of West Bengal, Saraswati Press Limited, 1992), 447. Historical truth stands perpetually embedded in curiosity and educative lesson. Tagore evinces his faith in a history that respects private belief and the character of the recipient and the narrator. Does historical truth have anything to do with the orientation of the agent and his customs, mores, and modes of living and experiences? The Englishmen think they never speak untruth; much as they might think so, Indians in colonial India, Tagore points out, know how truth can be ordered and witnesses and evidence can be staged. So reading history is also about personalization of truth and narrative—the mind of the historian, as Tagore points out—redoing experiences that might, at times, be opposed to the originary enactment. It is difficult to have a final word on every confusion bred over source and text. So believing with blindness and submissiveness the history written by the British can be as fragile and delusive as the belief that all history written by Indians is immune from taints of falsity (ibid., 447–48).

[24] See Mary Poovey, *A History of the Modern Fact* (Chicago, IL: University of Chicago Press, 1998).

is why Tagore had learned to recognize a limit when he saw one, and the limit of World-history could hardly escape so keen a poet's eye. However, his reproach about the poverty of historiography is not only a comment on the failure of the genre but also a call to historians for a creative engagement with the past as a story of man's being in the everyday world. It is, in short, a call for historicality to be rescued from its containment in World-history.[25]

Acts of rescue from the containment of world history can come through popular mediums like *yatra* and *kothokatha*[26]—the forms of transhistoricality. Tagore observes that education or schooling in history has its own importance; in school, students, through acts of tutoring and memorialization, master with relative efficiency their lessons in history written out in formal discourses of narration. Historical knowledge, Tagore argues, is not a mere documented knowing of the past: it is a plasticity of realization, a consciousness, an understanding about community, man and his world, his works and means, his dreams and ruin, his survival and prosperity.[27] Tagore believes that *yatra* and *kothokatha* could be used as alternate (say, plastic) forms of teaching history and are helpful in validating the currency of history in the untrained public sphere.[28] He implicates the 'entertainment' that history can provide, the fun that our different means of unspooling the past can generate. It is not public history but about trying to find the 'public', the 'man', in our historical experiences—less book-bound and more life-bound. R. Radhakrishnan is right to note that Tagore's poetic vision is a deconstruction of the binary between 'the alien' (British imperialist historiography) and the indigenous (nationalist and nativist historiography and historical consciousness): 'thinking the unthought would have to be both against the local and against the general economy of historical meaning, against a

[25] Ranajit Guha, *History at the Limit of World-History* (New Delhi: Oxford University Press, 2003), 7.
[26] *Jatra* (journey) is a popular folk form of Bengali theatre: see https://en.wikipedia.org/wiki/Jatra_(theatre). *Kothokatha* is another popular medium of entertainment where history is narrated in a storytelling manner.
[27] See Tagore, 'Itihashik Chitra' (The Historical Portrait), in *Rabindra Rachanabali*, 15:519–20.
[28] Tagore, '*Itihasa-katha*' (The Narration of History), in *Rabindra Rachanabali*, 14:453.

specific history and against history as such.[29] Tagore's reading of historical figures like Laxmi Bai, Guru Govind Singh, Vir Guru, Shivaji, and Sirajud-Daulah is performed through an intersection of two voices: the voice of emotion and everyday existence and the voice of epistemology. This discloses a different historicality not available to historiography, and 'under the auspices of such a historicality,' as Radhakrishnan argues, 'the worlding of the world is simultaneously ontological and epistemological. It takes place in a time alien to historiography: a time that is neither stranded in immanence nor interpellated by any regime of transcendence.'[30] *Itihasa* promotes a worlding of these historical figures who are 'poetized into their authentic historicality';[31] here we have a historical poesis that mediates between the kavi and the *aitihāsik* to create a life world.

Tagore's essay 'Jhanshir Rani' (The Queen of Jhanshi) throws us into the negotiating points of historicality. More than a close scrutiny of colonial narrative history, which Tagore finds prejudicial and insidious, this engagement becomes a kind of negotiation with a factual past, with ingredients of *kothokatha*, some essentialism, non-rigorous assumptions, imagination, poetic emotions, and 'seeing': a non-pedantic historical approach with its own drama, emotion, and rhetoric. Tagore transports us to a theatre of history that is close to being a private space —his workshop of history—lived away from the public attestation of transcendent paradigms of history. Observations like—

if the English were less self-serving in their ways, if they had faith in sublime intrepidity, they probably would not have allowed the heroes in colonial history to die in such ignominy and insult. Why could not such magnanimity that Alexander exhibited toward Purus be shown to people like Tantiya Tope? Would that not have brought more dignity and admiration to the colonial establishment?[32]

---

[29] R. Radhakrishnan, *History, the Human, and the World Between* (Durham, NC: Duke University Press, 2008), 223.
[30] Ibid., 230–31.
[31] Ibid.
[32] Tagore, 'Laxmi Bai', in *Rabindra Rachanabali*, 15:499.

—are emanations derived from a mix of emotion, poetic sensibility, and reflective judgement that is strictly not the rhetoric and argument of a trained historian. Tagore provides us with a precise procession of details: his reference to Lord Clive and Lord Dalhousie, Laxmi Bai's ascension to the throne in 1857 and her reign till 1858 before the war with the British resumed, interactions of Laxmi Bai with Tantiya Tope, and other such historical information. But Tagore's narration of Laxmi Bai's encounters with the British—her military and moral resistance, intrepidity, and tragic denouement—come through with dramatic power that has a novelistic charm to it, an involved penetration into moments that produce an auratic past that only the poet's imagination can muster. It also has a discursive structure—an affective structuring, in particular—that generates a vivid enactment of facts, such as: Laxmi Bai was a very beautiful woman, her indignity and agony under the British military mission forced her 'beautiful body'[33] to wear military attire; in the aftermath of the British army entering her fort, the queen's forty bodyguards kept fighting a pitched battle until all fell wounded on the ground; but that did not bring them down as they continued to fight, lying bloodstained on the floor of the fort, and gradually thirty-nine of them were killed before the last guard was blown up.[34] Here a diffracted reading of *itihasa* compels the repremising of our sense of time, site, context, and cultural domains. Firmly poised in his position to envisage history as experience and creativity, emotion and epistemology, Tagore reaffirms that no history has ever been above judgement and beyond interrogation. He hopes that one day we shall be able to investigate our own understanding of history distinct from what we have been made to learn through colonial textbook historiography.[35] This is another vindication and vein of 'owning' history, making history speak stories not by nativizing or domesticating facts through strategic incorporation and elision, but in relishing the connection with our culture, agency, traditions, myths, faith, and land.

On the subject of figuring the *kavi-aitihāsik*—the plastic moment of transhistoricality—a brief consideration of John Keats's historical sense and consciousness will be worthwhile. Both Tagore and Keats, humanist

---

[33] Ibid., 500.
[34] Ibid., 501.
[35] Ibid., 503.

historians in spirit, were genuinely interested in historical literature and expressed their own love for the past, a romantic longing translated, sometimes, into historical desire: a curiosity about the past with the head of a historian and then a historical vision alchemized through the heart of a poet. J. Philip Eggers brilliantly demonstrates how the force of Keats's historical imagination worked through many of his poems—'Sleep and Poetry', 'Endymion', 'Isabella', 'The Eve of St Agnes', 'Ode on a Grecian Urn', 'Hyperion', and others—and how he, like Tagore, exhibited his faithfulness to historical sources and guided his historical orientation preponderantly towards appreciating ordinary men in historical settings. The truth of human life, the value of senses, a profundity of understanding of our dailyness and everyday came to plasticize his historical consciousness. In 'Isabella' his sense of the past 'comes forth occasionally in references to ancient Greece, the Druids, and the Indians',[36] and 'The Eve of St Agnes' gains 'its historicity through fact assimilated into memory—from Keats's love of Gothic architecture at Chichester, the carvings of Grinlings Gibbons, French romances, Malory's Morte D'Arthur, Spenser, ballad tradition and Enlightenment history':[37] 'history no longer seems exclusively a monument by which heroic individuals gain immortal names',[38] no longer existing as 'pageant history', something that Tagore never wanted to depict. This is about taking the mind away from the prominent externalities of history—the heroes, heroic passions, the upheavals, and other overwhelming events to the exclusion of the ordinary—but not from historical knowledge. Keats and Tagore function as *kavi-aitihāsik*, not pedants, but chroniclers of life for whom history combines a new sense and horizon. Such 'lessons of history', as Rosinka Chaudhuri argues, 'were lessons to be learned by the creative writer in the matter of how his writing should engage with history, not by historians in the writing of historiography'.[39] In the understanding of historical fiction,[40] Tagore brings the *kavi-aitihāsik* into play for whom lessons of

---

[36] J. Philip Eggers, 'Memory in Mankind: Keats's Historical Imagination', *PMLA* 86, no. 5 (1971): 993.

[37] Ibid.

[38] Ibid., 992.

[39] Rosinka Chaudhuri, 'The Flute, Gerontion, and Subaltern Misreadings of Tagore', *Social Text* 22, no. 1 (78) (Spring 2004): 110.

[40] Tagore, 'Aitihāsika kathāsāhitya' (Historical Fiction), in *Rabindra Rachanabali*, vol. 10 (Kolkata: Government of West Bengal, Saraswati Press Limited, 1989), 371–74.

history involve both the factual and affective life. Page Smith points out that historical fiction 'trains us to extend our sympathies so as to include the alien and the unfamiliar and thus reproduces in the historical arena the most painful and exemplary of exercises—the enlargement of our capacity for participation in the needs, hopes, anxieties, and expectations of others'. This is the restoration of a 'sense of the dramatic in history' constructing the plastic moments.[41] For Tagore, historical fiction generates a kind of affective connection; it restores history to our individual crises, emotion, trials, and values. Maria Margaronis's questions are relevant: What responsibility does a novelist have to the historical record? How much—and what kinds of things—is it permissible to invent? For the purposes of fiction, what counts as evidence? What are the moral implications of taking someone else's experience, especially the experience of suffering and pain, and giving it the gloss of form? Can imaginative language discover truths about the past that are unavailable to more discursive writing?[42] Tagore believes in retelling history, bringing both the dramatic and the poetic into the disclosures of transhistoricality.

Tagore, quoting modern British historian Edward Freeman who tried to dissuade readers from reading Walter Scott's *Ivanhoe* while trying to understand the age of the Crusades, argues that *Ivanhoe* may not be the repository of hard-tested facts of the period, but there are certain eternal truths of human civilization that the novel foregrounds—irresistible and enticing—that make one read conjuncturally the history of the Crusades and *Ivanhoe*. James Simmons observes,

> the nineteenth century was a time of increased historical consciousness when men for the first time became aware of the past as being profoundly different from the present. And in England this developing awareness was nurtured and encouraged by the profusion of historical romances which provided many Victorian readers with their sense of the historic past. The volumes of Turner, Hallam, Palgrave, Grote, and

---

[41] See Page Smith, *The Historian and History* (New York: Vintage, 1964), 245.
[42] Maria Margaronis, 'The Anxiety of Authenticity: Writing Historical Fiction at the End of the Twentieth Century', *History Workshop Journal* 65 (2008): 138.

Thirlwall, unread, collected dust on the library shelves, while readers turned with interest to the latest historical romance.[43]

Walter Scott's novels attracted extraordinary readerly attention; in them, romance and fiction threatened to outflank historical research. Simmons points out:

> Even as late as 1876 the prominent historian Edward A. Freeman noted that a chief error which any historian of the twelfth century had to contend against was 'the notion that for many generations . . . after the Norman Conquest, there was a broadly marked line, recognized on both sides, between "Normans" and "Saxons." ' He traced this misconception back to Scott's *Ivanhoe* and admitted that no amount of argument by prominent historians to the contrary had been successful in putting down this popular belief, indicating the extent to which the general reader derived his impressions of a past epoch from the historical romances rather than the histories.[44]

Novelizing history is not to romance with the past devoid of scruples of conscience; facts hold their place as much as truths of human existence and our being in the world. Pointing to a transhistorical rhythm, Tagore writes: 'If we learn something wrong through poetry, history will rectify it. But the person who does not get the opportunity to read history and continues reading poetry alone is hapless. However, worse is the fortune of the man who would read history but never finds the leisure to read poetry.'[45] Tagore is not debating the value of sober historical research over the importance of romance and insights into human life and times.[46]

---

[43] James C. Simmons, 'The Novelist as Historian: An Unexplored Tract of Victorian Historiography', *Victorian Studies* 14, no. 3 (1971): 294.

[44] Ibid.

[45] Tagore, 'Aitihāsika kathāsāhitya', 374.

[46] John Demos's observations are pertinent: 'Was this perhaps because we do not, as historians, usually claim "human nature" as part of our professional territory? And if so, must we rest content with such self-imposed limitations? Should we continue to leave the most basic, universal, and personally significant parts of all our lives to novelists, poets, philosophers, religious leaders, and their like? I hope not.' See John Demos, 'In Search of Reasons for Historians to Read Novels . . .', *American Historical Review* 103, no. 5 (1998): 1529. Lessons of history can reach through the creative writer to the historian too: John E. Wills argues: 'Like many historians, I have also learned from and enjoyed historical novels about times and places of which I know little or nothing. I noticed the extravagant (and enormously influential) romanticizing of the English Middle Ages in Scott's *Ivanhoe*. I was impressed, however, by Scott's skill in leading the

The *kavi-aitihāsik* is trying to forge the plastic rhythm between Scott and Freeman, suggesting the intermingling of *rasas*—the poetic and historical (*kavya* and *itihasa*).

On similar lines, Tagore sees the truth of the *pratyohik* and the vital unfolding of life and emotions in Shakespeare's *Antony and Cleopatra*. A substantialization of *itihasa* owes as much to the revolutions in the arena of politics, in the domains of love, in the momentous trials of separation and destiny as to the emotional unrest and intensity of the human heart played out in the epic theatre of history.[47] It is here that Tagore finds the intermixture of *rasas* coming into potent play—*aadi* and *karuna rasa* flowing into historical *rasa*—generating a heart-wrenching immensity and distance. Theodor Mommsen, Tagore notes, would see factual inaccuracy and historical blindness in such writing and depiction.[48] But Shakespeare, the *kavi-aitihāsik* that he was, has successfully evoked an enigmatic sense of admiration in the minds of readers and a flush of historical *rasa* that data analysis and verificatory reading cannot diminish. There is no reason to believe that Shakespeare was not conscious of the distinction between poetry and history.[49] Armed with a similar sense of a divide between the two, Tagore admits the pure inalterability of certain sets of data. Shakespeare, Tagore observes, gets the plastic rhythm of history and poetry going where the commitment is not to resolve the quarrel between the two but to amplify the tension emerging therefrom. Shakespeare, as David Quint rightly argues, chose to inhabit the middle ground between historicism and humanism, and in many of his plays, be it *Macbeth* or *Henry V* or *Julius Caesar*, demonstrates what Hans-Georg Gadamer terms the 'effective historical consciousness', where the past and the present put their affect and inputs in collaborative consolidation within a continuum of historical tradition.[50] The intrusion—compulsive

---

reader to a vivid understanding of how different the medieval sense of space and geography was from that of later times, and by his descriptions of the vast forests with only dim tracks through them, and of the holy men in their isolated hermitages.' See John E. Wills, 'Taking Historical Novels Seriously', *The Public Historian* 6, no. 1 (1984): 42.

[47] Tagore, 'Aitihāsika kathāsāhitya', 373.
[48] Ibid.
[49] John P. Sisk, 'The Literary Imagination and the Sense of the Past', *Salmagundi* 68/69 (Fall 1985–Winter 1986): 76.
[50] David Quint, '"Alexander the Pig": Shakespeare on History and Poetry', *boundary 2* 10, no. 3 (1982): 49.

and fractious—of the 'literary' into history problematizes the predicament of the *kavi-aitihāsik*, and Tagore's essays on historical figures vindicate his position. The issue of verisimilitude—the dialectic of historical and poetic truth—is what throws Tagore's historicality against the normative modes of a strict historiographer. Although Tagore does not make such claims as Philip Sidney does about poetry being more philosophical than history, he recommends opening up a possibility in historical thinking that does not limit itself strictly to verisimilitude and does not 'consist in a series of prescriptive models which the past may hand down and impose upon a passive present age' but turns out to be 'the product of an active process of interpretation by which the present may also define itself in relationship to the past.'[51] Within a transhistorical dynamic, Tagore recommends the poet's use of history in parts or as a whole but not without the introduction of historical *rasa*—the essential ingredient that prepares the appropriate diet in the blend of literature and history.

Pursuing a similar line of argument, Tagore is keen to interpret the Indian epics the Ramayana and the Mahabharata as *itihasa*.[52] On the issue of how historical the story of Rama and the great battle of Bharatas is, one can put forth carbon-14 examinations to determine that Rama's story took place between 2850 and 1950 BCE and the battle in 1416 BCE. However, such periodization does not make these epic narratives worthy of our historical attention. Battle lines are drawn between the archaeological truth in such findings and the mythic strength of the stories that tilts them closer to poetic genre than to the discipline of history.[53] Romila Thapar reminds us that '*itihasa* is *smriti* or remembered tradition—and not *sruti* or revelation, as are the *Vedas*. . . . The Ramayana is referred to more often as *Kavya* (poem), or even *adi-kavya* (the first poem). Both texts grew out of narrating stories, the *katha*, and in their earliest and

[51] Ibid., 64.
[52] See Tagore, 'Aitihāsika kathāsāhitya'; see also P. L. Bhargava, 'A Fresh Appraisal of the Historicity of Indian Epics', *Annals of the Bhandarkar Oriental Research Institute* 63, no. 1/4 (1982): 15–28; for more on this line of discussion, see I. Proudfoot, 'Interpreting Mahabharata Episodes as Sources for the History of Ideas', *Annals of the Bhandarkar Oriental Research Institute* 60, no. 1/4 (1979): 41–63; also interesting is H. D. Sankalia, 'Ayodhya of the Ramayana in a Historical Perspective,' *Annals of the Bhandarkar Oriental Research Institute* 58/59 (1977): 893–919.
[53] Sharad Patil, 'Myth and Reality of Ramayana and Mahabharata', *Social Scientist* 4, no. 8 (1976): 69.

shorter forms were referred to as the *Bharata* and the *Rama-katha*.[54] Tagore calls this 'bhavagothoh *itihasa*' or 'yuga' which can be loosely translated as emotional and contemplative thought. Within such functional domains the narrative may not bear out strict evidential testimony but exists as a testament of life truths with the 'hunger of history'.[55] The Mahabharata does not qualify as history under the Westminster paradigms of historical writing; but Tagore's philosophy of *itihasa*, as exemplified in 'Bharatvarsher *itihasa* dhara', cannot endorse a historian's authoritative and autonomous establishment alone through a heuristic commitment buttressed by documentation. James Fitzgerald observes:

> both *itihasa* and *purana* have their first clearly designated, extended attestations in the Mahabharata which was committed to writing around the beginning of the Common Era, and what we see there of *itihasa* is the same kind of application of recorded knowledge of the past in the service of a previously established discourse that we saw in the Brahmana texts, but now with the label *itihasa* attached. The Mahabharata developed from one or more bardic narrative traditions and was recast and amplified by some elements of Brahmin society, and this amplification and reinforcement often took the form of cited *itihasas*, some of them contained purana matter. Both *itihasas* and *puranas*, as we see them in the Mahabharata, are narratives dealing with things that 'happened before'.[56]

Itihasa of the Mahabharata in particular is a natural and candid self-generated discourse of a nation and its community—a canvas of facts, some hidden, some transparent, some vanquished, some conflicting, some coherent, some capricious, a texture or patina of *itihasa* difficult to subjugate to a fixed period of time in the past. Thapar gets a fine grip

---

[54] Romila Thapar, *The Past Before Us* (New Delhi: Permanent Black, 2013), 146–47; this is a fine book of excellent scholarship but surprisingly does not mention Tagore and his visions of history in any detail.

[55] Tagore, 'Itihashik Chitra', 516.

[56] See James L. Fitzgerald, 'History and Primordium in Ancient Indian Historical Writing: *Itihasa* and Purana in the Mahabharata and Beyond', in *Thinking, Recording, and Writing History in the Ancient World*, ed. Kurt A. Raaflaub (Malden, MA: John Wiley and Sons, 2013), 47. I thank Ulrich Timme Kragh, an eminent scholar in Buddhist and Tibetan studies, for bringing this article to my notice.

on the Tagorean spirit when she points out that the function of *itihasa* is not necessarily to provide what we would today call authentic history but 'to project an earlier age and its ideals, as well as to introduce the different context of the later time when the composition was re-edited ... Thus, the archaeological search for material culture as the counterpart of the epic becomes something of a chimera. The manipulation of time in the epic is too complex for there to be a correlation with archaeological periodization. At most, artefacts may provide tangible forms to some descriptions in the epic.'[57] Can the philosophy of *itihasa* be both allegorical and verificatory? Can it be 'literary analogs'[58] of our deepest emotional, social, and civilizational truths? In the workshop of the *kavi-aitihāsik*, *itihasa* is unveiled through these epics in a deeply entangled and diffracted configuration of myth and literary affect. The *kavi-aitihāsik* constructs his *viraha* (longing) with history[59]—a deep plastic moment—not in the sense of *viccheda* (sundering) but as yearning, a desire to know and experience the emotion that *viraha* generates in its unfulfilment: the enticement, allure, and intangibilities of the past disabling the rigorously complete domination of the historian. Simon Schama finds a different kind of charm in the type of history that Herodotus practises or offers, in contrast to Thucydides, who is fiercely obligated to verificatory and fact-based history—Herodotus' 'relish for gossip, his intuitive understanding of the idiosyncrasies of climate and geography, his primitive ethnography, his unabashed subjectivities, the winning mishmash of hearsay and record, real and fantastic'.[60] Not that one is wrong and the other is right. Transhistorical narration has its plasticity in fabula, tropology, emplotting, encodation, rigour, acts of recounting, well-grounded evidential discourses, and surely some romance. *Itihasa* for Tagore is poesis, having at once the ability to legitimize and move its readers, and not just about 'feigning' or counterfeit. The *kavi-aitihāsik* has his own plastic critique of epic history—being at once a humanist, teleologist, narratologist, and an experimenter.

[57] Thapar, *The Past Before Us*, 163.
[58] Robert P. Goldman, 'Historicising the Ramakatha: Valmiki's Ramayana and Its Medieval Commentators', *India International Centre Quarterly* 31, no. 4 (2005): 85.
[59] See Ananya Vajpayi, *Righteous Republic* (Cambridge, MA: Harvard University Press, 2012), chap. 2, entitled 'Rabindranath Tagore: Viraha, the Self's Longing'.
[60] Simon Schama, *Citizens: A Chronicle of the French Revolution* (London: Viking, 1989), 325.

Kaal

Elaborating Johann Herder's *Ideen zur Philosophie der Menschengeschichte* (1784–91) as a notable expression of the modern historical attitude towards the past, W. von Leyden writes that Herder recognized 'the variations of human nature within one and the same period and from one age to another', calling for separate investigations of each stage in history. He had in mind here what to us has become an obvious truth, namely, that just as two moments may be said to differ, so too neither the ancient Egyptians nor the Greeks were at all times the same; and that, for instance, the art of ancient Egypt should not be judged, as in the hands of Winckelmann, by criteria derived from the consideration of art in ancient Greece.[61] History is not predominantly about imposing absolutes or universals or a general idea to explain humanity, events, and times. Every kind of history, historical thought, and historicality will have a separate measure of time rather 'the measure of its own time'. Tagore's plasticity of historical consciousness has its own measure and metre and is not essentially a linear variable of time; it is not a Euclidean perspective that pins down historical understanding to fixed coordinates of time-progression. He did not choose to emphasize a strong non-Western bias and an entrenched opposition to models of Western time. He is not Mircea Eliade's history-fleeing archaic man. *Itihasa* as a narration or tale of human progress has its own world views (encompassing both the non-teleological and the domain of political action), an intelligible understanding of situations, events, emotions, and development without a kind of inscrutable mystique that prejudicially becomes attached to this word. Absolutes cohabit the synchronic; the defined and directed are simultaneous with the unpredictable and serendipitous. This makes for plastic moments and *itihasa* for Tagore creates a delicate interpenetration, producing its own forms of 'listening'. Kenneth Inada explains:

> for the most part, we uncritically accept the condition that the mind, the conscious mind, can only function from the standpoint of temporal parallelism, that is, a parallelism that exists between a mental

[61] W. von Leyden, 'History and the Concept of Relative Time', *History and Theory* 2, no. 3 (1963): 279.

phenomenon and a perceptual phenomenon. An extension of this is, perhaps, the isomorphic theory of perception. When we become conscious of an object we tend to conclude that perception had been a simple and singular event. We normally do not consider the nature of continuity of the experiential process in ways which do justice to the manifold of overt as well as covert factors in function. The life process, after all, goes on incessantly whether or not we are conscious of an object. The process never takes a holiday although consciousness does.[62]

Tagore saw life as something perceptible and comprehensible and also as a process, interminable and immanent. He, like the Buddhists, did not have any problem dividing the time into its past, present, and future segments (*atita, paccuppanna, anagata*). *Itihasa* is not always clock time but a construction of the mind, the sense of the mind of space, time, and situations; hence, *itihasa* is destined to build its own abstract attributes. *Itihasa* is not mere understanding of strict forms and lines of interaction and engagements ranging across society, politics, and nation; it is about making sense of the splits and disruptions of our existence (*khana-vada*). However, Tagore, in line with Buddhism, does not believe in time that is exclusively relational, relative, unpredictable, and completely non-objectifiable. His philosophy of *itihasa* is not predominantly transitive and relative. Inada points out:

> To use an old metaphor, events are taking place like waves in the vast ocean. In mid-ocean the myriad waves are appearing and disappearing as if each is independent of each other but in truth there are many factors and conditions at play which make it possible for each wave to appear and disappear thus and so. Such is also the nature of the rise and subsidence of consciousness. All this goes to show that relational-origination is a conditioning or compounding phenomenon; it is exhibiting the complex but unique way in which an experiential event transpires.[63]

---

[62] Kenneth K. Inada, 'Time and Temporality: A Buddhist Approach', *Philosophy East and West* 24, no. 2 (1974): 172.

[63] Ibid., 176.

Tagore knew this compoundness well enough and realized *itihasa* as conditioned on such relational origination. *Itihasa* takes its own *samay* or has its *kaal* to come to fruition: its emergence is a process involving at once a rational analytic and a 'play'. It is hard to accept that time is without any ultimate ontological status.

Tagore is not looking into a nirvana through *itihasa*. Temporality chains but historicality has its own ways of release. The truth of Tagore's philosophy of *itihasa* is not illusory and unreal. It has its operative connection with *anubhava* (experience) which is distinguished from what we understand simply as experience. It is not about directing one's life through the agency of history but activating the historicality of our existence—living and doing history together through *aparoksha* (direct experience), *anubhava*, *dhristi* (vision), and *kalpana* (imagination). Tagore observes that 'viewed from the standpoint of intervening space, the distance between the earth and the moon may loom large, and tend to obscure the fact of their relationship. There are many double stars in the firmament of history, whose distance from each other does not affect the truth of their brotherhood. We know, from the suggestion thrown out by the poet of Ramayana, that Janaka, Visvamitra and Rama, even if actually separated by time, were nevertheless members of such a triple system.'[64] Here Tagore's philosophy of *itihasa* demands being elucidated through time's vexing relationship with historical distance. Distance (disjuncture and detachment) from the past is a delicate and complex axis on which 'retrospectiveness' (to use Eric Hobsbawm's word) can be rethought.[65] A commitment to *itihasa* and historical intimacy is not a submission to universals of reading; commitment is better realized through 'distancing' and alienation, where the present provides multiple ways of configuring our relations to the past—the vagaries of *viraha*. Tagore sees an opening in historical knowledge through such means of distancing provided by values that one's present culture and tradition generate and an alienation that is triggered by imagination, alterity, affect, and sensibilities. *Itihasa* mediates with our cultural past as much as it participates with the world outside our culture and tradition. The point from which history is required to be viewed stands questioned: is it the point that world history

---

[64] Tagore, *A Vision of India's History*, 4.
[65] Phillips, *On Historical Distance*, 3.

formulates? Should it be the optimum methodological point that rationalizes the clash of historical positions or the organic point that views
historical experience as an intricate mix of rhetoric, emotion, affective
viewing, and intelligibility?

The debate, perhaps, centres on how 'ownness' and *itihasa* are connected. For Tagore, *katha* or *yatra* demonstrates their owning of *itihasa*
by working out this delicate problematic of historical distance: narrative time, context, rhetoric, the sense of fact and fiction coming into a
compound play. *Yatra* demonstrates the repetition that history generates: the same content being presented in a variety of retellings, resulting
in different forms of historical affect, alienation, and kinaesthesia. *Itihasa*
comes with a connotation of *yatra*, the journey, produced through
pramanas (means of evidence/knowledge), perception, testimony, and
inference in both the past and the present. To this, *yatra*, with its own
means of knowledge-production, Tagore added memory (*smriti*). *Itihasa*
is both presentative and representative— a *racanashalay*, a room for creation where *pramanas* come both veridically and affectively. Distance and
desire in *itihasa* plasticize to build their own creativity (*srishtikartritva*).
Tagore and one of his contemporaries, the historian Jadunath Sarkar,
differ in their ideas about historical thinking: one being the poet-seer
historian and the other a rigorous, systematic, trained historian drawing
deeply on the Rankean school of historical meaning-making. Tagore lo-
cates a kind of divine directedness, complemented by a rhythm of *jeevan-
devata* (life spirit) in the unfolding of *itihasa*.[66] Despite falling out with
Tagore on several issues of historical understanding, Sarkar sees the poet
as a philosopher in a first-rate historian, accenting the importance of
finding a philosophy of history. This is closer in spirit to Tagore's *itihasa-
darshana*. Not pledged to a historical thinking that believes in writing,
evidence, and inference alone, Sarkar, like Tagore, finds the divine creative urges in history: an inclusive and binding force that has been a
kind of moral principle, generative of poetic justice and historical judge-
ments in a variety of periods and contexts.[67] The longing for history is

---

[66] For instance, one may look to Tagore's 'Swadeshi Samaj' (31–32) for such references.
Tagore, *Swadeshi Samaj* (Kolkata: Visva Bharati, 1962). In fact, Tagore has made numerous references to this divine or fateful thrust of history in many of his essays.

[67] See Bikash Chakraborty, *Byahato Shawkhyo: Rabindranath o Jadunath Sarkar*
(Kolkata: Visva Bharati, 2011), 102–3.

a desire for the visible in the form of the documented and the present and a counter-energy emerging from negotiations with the unanalysable and the unapprehensible. Is Tagore's notion of *itihasa* sinusoidal[68] and the 'rhythm' that Tagore describes in his 'Bharatvarshar *Itihasa*' indicative of a new sense of tradition where rise and fall, decline and emergence, disruption and continuity are all part of an oppositional progress, the dialectical *yatra* of *itihasa*? Tagore's historical sense, as W. B. Yeats saw it, connects with the unbroken past, and the flow and fluidity of his culture. Yeats pointed out how 'a whole people, a whole civilization immeasurably strange to us, seems to have been taken up into this imagination; and yet we are not moved because of its strangeness, but because we have met our own image . . . our voice as in a dream.'[69] The Irish poet aspired to bring two halves of Ireland together—seeking a 'unity of life', an idea of a unified culture, a piece of beautiful memory. History, Yeats argues, is formed in the mind of the poet: 'literature has tried to express everybody's thought, history being considered merely as a chronicle of facts, but now at the instant of revelation [the fifteenth Phase of *A Vision*] writers think the world is but their palette, and if history amuses them it is but, as Goethe says, because they would do its personages the honor of naming after them their own thoughts.'[70] It is not the segmenting of the past from the present or reading the past in the unfolding of the present that matters; it is the consciousness of the past with which one lives in the present: both a continuity and contiguity.

Aaj-Kal

In 'Sahityer Itihasikatha' (The Historicality of Literature) Tagore writes:

---

[68] Louise Blakeney Williams, 'Overcoming the "Contagion of Mimicry"': The Cosmopolitan Nationalism and Modernist History of Rabindranath Tagore and W. B. Yeats', *American Historical Review* 112, no. 1 (2007): 90–91; see also her *Modernism and the Ideology of History* (Cambridge: Cambridge University Press, 2002), 120–35.

[69] Gitanjali, Introduction, xvi–xvii; quoted in Harold M. Hurwitz, 'Yeats and Tagore', *Comparative Literature* 16, no. 1 (1964): 58.

[70] Thomas R. Whitaker, 'The Dialectic of Yeats's Vision of History', *Modern Philology* 57, no. 2 (1959): 107.

One day I had just come back from school at about four-thirty and found a dark blue cumulus suspended high above the third storey of our house. What a marvelous sight that was. Even now I remember that day. But in the history of that day there was no one other than myself who saw those clouds in quite the same way as I did or was similarly thrilled. *Rabindranath happened to be all by himself in that instance.* Once after school I saw a most amazing spectacle from our western verandah. A donkey—not one of those donkeys manufactured by British imperial policy but the animal that had always belonged to our own society and has not changed in its ways since the beginning of time—one such donkey had come up from the washermen's quarters and was grazing on the grass while a cow fondly licked its body. The attraction of one living being for another that then caught my eye has remained unforgettable for me until today. *In the entire history of that day it was Rabindranath alone who witnessed the scene with enchanted eyes.* This I know for certain. No one else was instructed by the history of that day in the profound significance of the sight as was Rabindranath. *In his own field of creativity Rabindranath has been entirely alone and tied to no public by history.*[71]

History, for Tagore, forms around four points of engagement: a history of the day, the enchantment and thrill, the *pratyohik*, and Rabindranath existing in his own independence as a seer and meaning-maker. What value and inevitability does 'being alone' have in the construction of a historical experience? Is not being connected to the public—the public gaze, the public approval of an event— another mode of doing history, a transhistoricality achieved through a different contact and impact? What is this connection that manifests history in a rare vitalism and immanence?

It is a kind of dissociative-associative historical consciousness where 'being alone' is also 'being with' and where 'being-for' is also about 'being-without'. The 'being with' is the power that historical sense generates—the historicality built with a cow, donkey, cumulus, the light on the trembling coconut fronds. Rabindranath's seeing and being in history contributes

---

[71] I have used Ranajit Guha's excellent translation of Tagore's 'Sahityer Itihasikatha'; see Guha, *History at the Limit of World-History*, 97; my italics.

to Rabindranath Tagore's reflections on *itihasa*, constructing a compelling mix of presentness of the past, past and its pastness, presentness and presentification. The investments of historical consciousness in figurations (not mere constructivism) of life experiences are sublime. This is close to Michael Oakeshott saying that 'experience proper is thought: therefore, all experience is a world of ideas, or imaginings'.[72] Tagore, in the sense in which Frank Ankersmit has argued, would prefer to see Rabindranath as 'consubstantial with history'. Rabindranath builds his own historical moment removed from the public gaze and the herd understanding of historicality and knows that history is in us and we are in it. We are part of a continuum called *itihasa* where collective attestation of events helps in the concretization of history and where history also remains as an abstraction of our self.[73] Tagore's involvement in consubstantial understanding of history makes him see the poetic moment and the moments of history as a unifying strength, which, however, does not blur their distinctions completely within the continuity and synthesis. For Tagore the past does not stay external to him; history is about an intimacy with the past as recreated in the present. This 'intimate' moment in history—like watching the donkey being affectionately licked by the cow—is the disruption that conventional history would find in the continuity between the past and the present. For Tagore, however, it is the kavi who produces the modality of experience where continuity comes to be maintained in ruptures and in broken bits of communication.

Rabindranath lives his 'own' history away from the history of his situatedness in a particular society and community. He is witness to his own history. This plastic rhythm of *itihasa* is formed through a world that exists outside the world that obligates and obtains to the public (*sadharon*), the collective. This world—the plasticities of drama and enactments—is almost always lost to 'pedantic' historiographical thinking. History demonstrates a desperation to vindicate its alternative existence by living through the familiar (the glitter of the dewdrops, the coconut trees, the cow fondly licking the body of the donkey) into a world whose alethic disclosures are not for all: history outside

---

[72] Quoted in David Boucher, 'The Creation of the Past: British Idealism and Michael Oakeshott's Philosophy of History', *History and Theory* 23, no. 2 (1984): 196.

[73] See F. Ankersmit, *Sublime Historical Experience* (Stanford, CA: Stanford University Press, 2005), 257–58.

history comes with its own *nirmiti* (creation) and *bhava* (emotion). The transhistoricality here is 'sublime'; it dissolves the conventional formal public ways of vindicating and discoursing about our experiences and opens on to a world 'without the protective mediation of the cognitive and psychological apparatus that normally processes our experience'.[74] This mediation of history with poetic recreativity is much more complex than it seems. Rabindranath has lived in and out of history and has realized it in both separate moments and in simultaneity.

How do Rabindranath and Tagore interact and negotiate their experience of history? It is a moment that in its 'quasi-noumenal nakedness' and 'its unusual directness and immediacy'[75] creates alienation and wonder, estrangement and uniqueness, perception and prison, and dissolution of public history into other forms of experiences. It is through Rabindranath that history reinvents itself, unforms its pedagogical and pedantic character to transform into finer forms of narration and elaboration—revisionary, rejuvenating, and reconstructive. Ankersmit observes:

> history comes to us in wholes, in totalities, and this is how we primarily experience both the past itself and what it has left us—as is the case in the arts and in the aesthetic experience. The explanation is that history does not rise up before our minds from data found in the archives in the way that a detective may infer from the relevant data who committed a murder: It is, instead, a 'displacement' of the present as dictated by these data, and, as such, it is experienced as a totality no less than is the case with the present.[76]

Rabindranath is the product of a displacement. Experiencing history here becomes nostalgic, a turning-loose of passion and curiosity for a moment; historical distance is built not between what we feel in the present and what happened in the past but between two experiences of history: one about the *sadharon* day when Tagore was getting back from school and the other where Rabindranath was born out of the *pratyohik*.

---

[74] Ibid., 336.
[75] Ibid., 125.
[76] Ibid., 119.

This relates both to the different veins of poeticality and historicality, the manifestation of separate modes of realization and divisions enacted and found in the subject and the object.

Rabindranath stands for a new aesthetic of *itihasa* where knowing, unlike the empiricism of the natural sciences, is an active projection that makes moments act as reservoirs of experience and *eo ipso* auratic by themselves, unconceals a latent history of the everyday, and unhinges the banality of the habits of historical understanding. Here is Rabindranath who stands as a reminder of the impoverishment of history brought about by the occlusion of the individual and the *kavimanush* by the surfeit and dominance of the average and the public. Caught in a deep plastic rhythm, Rabindranath is in his *srishtikshetra* (field of creativity) where his self is non-colonial, non-Hegelian, non-finite, non-public, and yet not unhistorical or ahistorical. He is *osadharon* (outside average, extraordinary) by being tied to himself, his emotions, imagination, and aesthetics of understanding and effectuates a homecoming through the greater enclosures of Tagore. *Itihasa* declares its distinct place through intense moments of worlding and the infinitization of the finite, and both Tagore and Rabindranath find their home at the limits of world history.

The meaningful and strategic cleft between Tagore and Rabindranath imports a host of issues from our contemporary understanding of history and historical writing that involves agency, historical writing as performance and literary act, historical imagination, recreative aesthetics of the past, microhistorical narration, and rethinking of historical truth and objectivity. As an illustration of these different ways of doing history—not the strictly 'pedantic' mode that Rabindranath Tagore had serious problems with—we see Natalie Zemon Davis telling us a fascinating story in *The Return of Martin Guerre* based on her research on records of a 'bizarre court case that occurred in 16th-century France'—a story of a missing soldier and how that disappearance puts his life on existential trials, which by extension, interestingly, investigates complex social issues. Davis mixes the *pratyohik* and the *sadharon* with an exemplary deftness that 'reconstructs the lives of ordinary people revealing hidden attachments and sensibilities of nonliterate sixteenth-century villagers'.[77]

---

[77] Natalie Zemon Davis, *The Return of Martin Guerre* (Cambridge, MA: Harvard University Press, 1984).

Carlo Ginzburg's *The Cheese and the Worms* puts into prominence the miller known as Menocchio and it is through him (his trials and death in the aftermath of heresy) that Ginzburg provides a microhistorical reading of the popular culture in the sixteenth century. In the footsteps of Georg Simmel, Walter Benjamin, and Siegfried Kracauer, he invests his historical explorations in everyday life, in particulars of daily events and life habits with a serious emphasis on ephemera, anecdotes, notes, some insignificant narrations, and apparently unimportant observations.[78] Such ways of approaching history of thought and action enliven the workshop of history with a creativity that cannot overlook a performative historical imagination and a novelty in engaging with the past. The *kavi* wakes up both in Ginsburg and Davis: Tagore observes that the creator 'gathers some of the material for his creation from historical narratives and some from his social environment. But the material by itself does not make him a creator. It is only by *putting it to use* that he expresses himself as the creator.'[79] This art and novelty of 'putting it to use' has opened us on to the creative critical dynamic (the plastic moment) within the 'mold of history'. Robert Rosenstone points out that

> Greg Dening's *Mr. Bligh's Bad Language* not only gives equal voice to Tahitian and European in their South Sea encounter, but exemplifies a case for history as a performative art . . . James Goodman's *Stories of Scottsboro* retells stories that provide a variety of perspectives on that famed 1930s rape case against a group of African American youths without ever insisting that a single one of the versions is the Truth. Elinor Langer's *Josephine Herbst* has the author wrestling in the first person with the shifting meaning of novelist Herbst's life, not simply during her subject's days but also for the period during which the biography itself is being researched and composed. . . . Richard Price's *Alabi's World* creates a past in four distinct voices—including one from an oral tradition that blends 'fact' and 'fantasy'—that contest the telling of the history of the run away slave colonies of Guiana in the 17th century. Simon Schama's *The Many Deaths of General Wolfe* is a history framed

---

[78] John Brewer, 'Microhistory and the Histories of Everyday Life', *Cultural and Social History* 7, no. 1 (2010): 87–109.

[79] Tagore, 'Sahityer Itihasikatha', translated in Guha, *History at the Limit of World-History*, 98.

by a fictional moment and that uses a shifting temporal sense that portrays the past as not linear but circular.[80]

Historical reconstructionism—the putting it to use—can and must vary. Tagore and Rabindranath are committed to different forms of historical writing which, in fact, are integral parts of the 'mold of history'. Both are intellectual constructions despite Rabindranath seeing himself in a moment of excess and intensity through an engagement with a slice of everyday history. It is a different ordering of time and dialogic mediation with realities. If Tagore has dominantly historicized the past, Rabindranath is held at the crossing point of a historicizing present. Rabindranath Tagore's calling for an attack on 'pedantic' historians cannot surely be a commentary on what history is and can be envisaged as. We do history and live in history and so thinking about the past is living in the present to negotiate the past. The 'mold of history' is fragile and rigid at the same time: the plasticities of historical consciousness inform the history workshop.

Hayden White sees creativity in the historian's art of arranging materials, in the ways in which she interprets them. White argues that

on the one hand, there are always more facts in the record than the historian can possibly include in his narrative representation of a given segment of the historical process. And so the historian must 'interpret' his data by excluding certain facts from his account as irrelevant to his narrative purpose. On the other hand, in his efforts to reconstruct 'what happened' in any given period of history, the historian inevitably must include in his narrative an account of some event or complex of events for which the facts that would permit a plausible explanation of its occurrence are lacking. And this means that the historian must 'interpret' his materials by filling in the gaps in his information on inferential or speculative grounds.[81]

---

[80] Robert A. Rosenstone, 'Rethinking History: Theory, Practice, and New Ways of Telling the Past', *Perspectives on History*, 1 April 1998, https://www.historians.org/research-and-publications/perspectives-on-history/april-1998/rethinking-history-theory-practice-and-new-ways-of-telling-the-past.

[81] Hayden White, 'Interpretation in History', *New Literary History* 4, no. 2 (1973): 281.

The poetics of reconstruction and interpretation—the dynamic of making sense of history by being Romantic, Idealist, Positivist, and Critical—inform both the *kavi* and the *aitihāsik* (like Hegel, Droysen, Nietzsche, and Croce). Historians do much more than objectivity and criticality: their labour is invested in ingenuous understanding of facts and deep reflection on the available discourse. This calls for a philosophical-aesthetic approach and often a fresh 'poetic' of understanding that bald reportage and documentation cannot produce. Historical representation and making sense of history can come with what White argues as 'making (an inventio)' with inevitable inputs of imagination and insight. The notion of the 'mold of history' misses these dimensions of historical understanding. There are ways to engage with facts whether that be a donkey that had 'come up from the washermen's quarters and was grazing on the grass while a cow fondly licked its body'[82] or a struggling band of peasants or the aesthetic moment over the glistening coconut frond. The *kavi* transfiguralizes the facts before her; the *aitihāsik* (in this case meta-historians) objectifies, interprets, and speculates at the same time; the *kavi-aitihāsik* realizes the inescapability of the synergic impact that goes into the shaping of her historical consciousness.

Tagore observes, 'Once when I used to travel by boat along the rivers of Bengal and came to sense its playful vitality, my inner soul delighted in gathering those wonderful impressions of weal and woe in my heart which were composed into sketches of country life month after month in a way nobody had done before.'[83] He watched the unfolding of life and its vagaries through the sketches of country life that he composed: these included microhistories, snatches of daily life, and the truths and trials of existence. Tagore likes to claim that, although those rural scenes that he surveyed as a poet were affected by the conflicts of political history, his *Galpaguccha* (the book of short stories) 'was not the image of a feudal order indeed any political order at all'; it was, he claims, in a kind of transcendence from a dour history to *sāhitya aitihasikata*, the resonant history of the 'weal and woe of human life which, with its everyday contentment and misery, has always been there in the peasants' fields and

---

[82] Tagore, 'Sahityer Itihasikatha', translated in Guha, *History at the Limit of World-History*, 97.
[83] Ibid., 98.

village festivals, manifesting their simple and abiding humanity across all of history—sometimes under Mughal rule, sometimes under British rule'.[84] Here Tagore, as the *kavi-aitihāsik*, is doing a form of microhistory and 'putting into use' the little narratives aesthetically and in concentrated intensity to construct the greater web of life. The creative critical in microhistories explores the 'otherness' constituted through the lives and ways of people and events that, most often, don't enter the mainstream of historical discourse. This otherness is outside the pedantism that Tagore vociferously denounces. In the preface to Davis's *Women on the Margins* we see:

The Historian: I asked what advantages you had by being on the margins.
The first person: Margins are where I read comments in my Yiddish books.
The second person: In my Christian books.
The third person: River margins are the dwelling place of frogs.
The Historian: You found things on margins.[85]

The frogs as the otherness in our understanding of margins tell us a different story of agency, specificity, and subjectivity, something that reminds us again of the kavi who saw the gleaming sunlight on the coconut frond that the rest ignored or could not see or considered too much in the margin to be noticed. It is the margin that comes alive through a perception and personality. Antonis Liakos argues that paradigmatic history, in line with Aristotle's understanding of history and philosophy, appreciates the 'particular'. The seeking and exploring of the local and the specific (in short, the micro) give rise to a historical syntax that open up the 'possibilities for communication among historians of various specialization and orientations, working on a great variety of topics, scattered over place and time'.[86] The creative critical inspires 'a proliferation of loci of studies',[87] and through a 'transition from syntagmatic to paradigmatic

---

[84] Ibid., 99.
[85] Natalie Zemon Davis, *Women on the Margins* (Cambridge, MA: Harvard University Press, 1997), 4.
[86] Antonis Liakos, 'The Transformation of Historical Writing from Syntagmatic to Paradigmatic Syntax', *Historein* 2 (2000): 52.
[87] Ibid.

syntax of historical writing, the whole plane of academic historical communication'[88] has come to change in the last quarter of the twentieth century. Did the *Galpaguccha* have its emergence from the dynamic and vibrant margins? The event of writing a short story related to the life of the peasant is a form of historical narration, extending and reorienting the character of historical consciousness; importantly, it cannot be outside the reality of a social history that historians investigate and craft. The *kavi-aitihāsik* is critical without realizing it; his creativity soaks within a critical consciousness that does not necessarily have to throw the objective and archival narratives of social and economic history out of reckoning. Building history out of documents is a deeply plastic act.

The everyday (*pratyohik*) is far more complicated than Tagore makes it out to be. It comes down to 'distance effects'[89] where historical writing chooses its subjects and points of identification and expression. With *Alltagsgeschichte, microstoria,* and post-*Annales* cultural history, the notion of the *pratyohik* has come in for some refiguration. Rabindranath Tagore's journey in historical-literary synthesis from the life and activities of the peasants to his *Galpaguccha* is a form of literarization of history; the insights and reworkings from daily slices of life in the works of Robert Darnton, Natalie Zemon Davis, Le Roy Ladurie, Carlo Ginzburg, Hans Medick, David Sabean, and others speak of a different *pratyohik*. This is not bare academic writing about everyday life and not a unilinear and unilateral form of writing and understanding, either; rather, it is a disruption in progressive, analytic, information-dependent, and predictive understanding of history. A kavi is not merely a practitioner in certain forms of stylistic and performative exercises; a kavi speaks of a distinctive synthetic mind with an extraordinary perception and powers of assimilation about finding rare points of connect. The workshop of history has re-established the kavi in a fresh self-awareness and performativity. The *pratyohik* hides a certain form of history and again has its own ways of historical expression, which are most often drowned out by big-time history. However, the everyday emerging out of Henri Lefebvre's writings and, for instance, Maurice Blanchot's densely ruminative essay 'Everyday Speech' speaks about a process, a history in the making and demanding

---

[88] Ibid., 52–53.
[89] Brewer, 'Microhistory and the Histories of Everyday Life', 2.

of attention that it, most often, does not receive. 'The everyday', writes Blanchot, 'is no longer the average, statistically established existence of a given society at a given moment; it is a category, a utopia and an Idea, without which one would not know how to get at either the hidden present or the discoverable future of manifest beings.'[90] This everyday that is unmarked, often unremarkable, considered often as 'unhistorical', needs a separate kind of attention that can acknowledge the silent corridors and interruptions within the unfolding everyday. It makes for a moment that attunes with delight and surprise to a kavi and can also be a moment that inspires a historian to explore the nuances and hiatus that a daily event and momentary occurrence might leave. In both cases there is a rupture that demands a specific form of attention that ordinary minds miss out on. The *kavi-aitihāsik* is attentive, sharp, insightful, imaginative, and sensitive—a delicate combination of virtues and values that render the segregation of the creative and the critical fallacious.

The historian and the kavi have their 'poetic'. Not that we can equate history and fiction; both have a narrative to it, a method of representation and processuality that come from a few identical matrices of emergence: imagination, choice, perception, insight, and the art of expression. The *kavi-aitihāsik* is not abandoning the distinctions; they draw on each other, flourish at the points of intersection, without forgetting that creativity and criticality are integral to both. What Rabindranath Tagore says about *Galpaguccha* and the trial and test in the lives of people on the banks of Padma corresponds with George Eliot's *Middlemarch* and a historian's study of the provincial society in early nineteenth-century England. This distinction does not call for a stilted and dreary conversation over what a historian does with facts and a novelist performs with fiction. History has often suffered, ironically, at the hands of historians who could not see it beyond a ponderous methodology and pedagogy and heavy-footed social discourse, with arid piling of facts and document layering. Historians in good numbers have started to reflesh the discipline by working out and respecting the 'literary' that history owns and can be endowed with. There is an essence of humanity in it, very close to what the *kavi-aitihāsik* thinks and feels. It is the imagination that,

---

[90] Maurice Blanchot, 'Everyday Speech', *Yale French Studies*, no. 73 (1987): 13.

surprisingly to most, can be a good connector between history as a discipline and history as required to be an art. James Axtell observes that

> perfectly respectable historians have been known to scrounge for 'facts' such as lost landscapes in Tahiti, the color of a dead queen's underwear, the death rate of cats in a French working-class parish, the changing price of peasants' bread, gun barrel and pipe stem bores, the salt content of roily river water and the shell content of native pottery, the forgotten meaning of familiar words, and that most elusive of all quests, the motivations behind human behavior, normal and abnormal, individual and collective.[91]

However, this search for and curiosity about facts do not come with indiscrimination and careless indulgence. Like Rabindranath's commitment to a moment, this is also an investment in a certain kind of specificity about past that is never 'a three-dimensional reproduction of all that transpired in the lives of all people from the beginning of human time; that's the past'.[92] These moments solicit the execution of imagination as it evokes a critical-poetic understanding of the facts and the possibilities and silences that they conceal. Axtell notes that 'it is no coincidence that the historian's penetration of the foreignness of the past bears an uncanny resemblance to the anthropologist's imaginative entry into other cultures and to the novelist's forging of historically plausible though ultimately imaginary worlds and populations. All must find, fashion and re-create alien presences in their imaginations before attempting to share them with their readers.'[93] *Kavi* and the *aitihāsik* make their imaginative entry into certain moments from the present or the past—'once the historian acquires through his research what John Updike calls the "fundamental feasibilities" of a specific place-in-time, he can, like the novelist, "imagine freely there" and close the gaps in his understanding'.[94]

Facts can be overwhelmingly abundant and fleeting, demanding an assumptive and projective mode of understanding. But, interestingly, for both Tagore and Rabindranath, facts matter with a different measure,

[91] James Axtell, 'History as Imagination', *Historian* 49, no. 4 (1987): 453.
[92] Ibid., 454.
[93] Ibid., 456.
[94] Ibid.

relative importance, and principle of reason. Watching an event in our everyday web of life, turning events into a literary narrative, and making a credible story out of microhistorical observations have their own reason, métier, and insight. These are separate in their modalities and character but come together to (un)form the 'mold of history'. Through a unique plastic rhythm, *kavi-aitihāsik* is a scientist and an artist: he tells a story well, deeply informed by criticism and interpretation, and reveals his engagement with facts through reason, sensitivity, and a poetic that lets him know that all facts are not hard metal. Isaiah Berlin sees 'inevitable' facts as owing both to reason and to possibility. Being in a historical process is about admitting the freedom and acknowledging the participation of historical agency to influence the course of events through one's choice and decision. Berlin's idea of 'historical inevitability' makes us believe in the existence of historical events that are inevitable and significant; but the question remains as to the kind of events the *kavi* would consider to be 'inevitable'. Historical reconstructionism considers certain sets of events to be inevitable, for they are causally impossible to ignore and easier to comprehend and accept. In short, a necessity emerges from a chain of events that reads as causally compulsive. Berlin, as Nathan Rotenstreich, notes,

> does not believe there can be any pat formula to steer us away from the Scylla of peopling the world with great imaginary forces such as the historical forces posited by the comprehensive views of history. Nor, on the other hand, can we find a neat prescription telling us how to steer clear of the Charybdis of confinement to the factual, observable occurrences of this world, that is, to empirical conduct determinable by empirical persons at a specific time and place. In other words, the danger is from two directions. On the one side lies the possibility of obviating the reality of the human beings acting in history and of attributing everything to an impersonal course of events; on the other side lies the possibility that we get too involved in the reality of human beings and therefore ignore the broader historical processes in which they play their part. The task of a critical analysis, Berlin adds, is to face these

dangers and to navigate its way through the Scylla and the Charybdis to the best of its ability.[95]

The dangers lie with both Tagore and Rabindranath. And, in fact, the *kavi-aitihāsik* is deeply invested in these dangers. What might be a fact to a *kavi* might not find similar factual importance to the *aitihāsik*, yet facts for both are stated and constructed, reasoned and imagined. Their order may be different, and constructing a relationship with the narrative can be different, too. Both the *kavi* and *aitihāsik* look into the 'dramatic' in history that builds a connective poetics with both these identities; it is a creative-critical imagination that connects the two. The *kavi-aitihāsik* performs within an imaginary that is deeply wired into the creative critical. It is the dramatic that is historical; it is poetic, too. What Rabindranath faces through the events in the morning or the everyday incidents that have a sort of passive languor to them builds a singularity that contributes to the imaginary of a life experience. This waking up to a historical moment survives in a possibility and story that does not have an ostensible significance to it. It is a mystification of a moment that is more about a 'secret index' and emergence than about contingency and historical concatenation. Walter Alvarez sees both continuities and contingencies in the unfolding of history.[96] It is regularity as continuity that informs our lives, but it is the contingencies that make us fall in love or fall off the stairs or make Rabindranath catch a glimpse of the light shimmering on the coconut frond. Contingencies disrupt a monotonous narration into fresh directions of thinking, triggering a separate flush of emotions and ideas.

Albert Bushnell is right to observe that

the ultimate material of history is neither books nor records but mind. We are dealing with the manifold manifestations of human nature; we are trying to decipher triple and quadruple palimpsests of human character; to understand and expound the actions of men who did not understand themselves; to find analogies between historical

[95] Nathan Rotenstreich, 'Historical Inevitability and Human Responsibility', *Philosophy and Phenomenological Research* 23, no. 3 (1963): 395–96.

[96] Walter Alvarez, 'Laws or Comets', *Aeon*, 3 November 2016, https://aeon.co/essays/how-chance-and-probability-affect-the-path-of-big-history.

occurrences without being able to discover the causes of those slight divergences of race, of national characteristics, and of personal bent which upset all calculations.[97]

Thinking history is also about knowing the unpredictabilities that patternize its ways. It is the mind that matters for both the *kavi* and *aitihāsik*, and quite rightly, 'historical consciousness is inward, in that it is created by the inquirer; but also external, in recognizing, in the presence of artefacts, the limits of imagination and therefore the otherness of the objects it has raised in itself'.[98] Tagore's observation that 'there are many events that are there waiting to be known, and it is only by chance that we get to know them'[99] can unconceal the moot issue of chance in historical narration and representation. The *kavi-aitihāsik* cannot be E. H. Carr, for whom counterfactuality is an anathema and the 'might-have-been' school is a 'parlour game'.[100] Unlike Carr, the *kavi-aitihāsik* believes in the accidental, the indeterminate, and the sudden emergence of a historic moment that appeals to the emotion and imagination in a different way. History got its form not merely through an inflexible confinement to facts and empiricism; there are the accidents, discrepancies, and aberrations that lend a form to history as well. The inevitability of facts cannot overlook the accidental facts; there is an inevitable process that feeds on contingencies and fortuitousness contributing to the 'mold of history'.

What explains the hyphen in *kavi-aitihāsik* is the acceptance of a failing in 'total history'. All histories, whether the one that Tagore endorses or the one that Rabindranath envisages, come with an incompletion, as it becomes near impossible to construct and represent the full spectrum of everyday experiences and every strand and shift from the documented and archived past. Is history only about viewing the frog's skin cells under the microscope revealing their physiology, which suggests 'nothing of the frog's place in its ecosystem'?[101] Making sense of history includes

---

[97] Albert Bushnell, 'Imagination in History', *American Historical Review* 15, no. 2 (1910): 234.
[98] Karl Figlio, 'Historical Imagination/Psychoanalytic Imagination', *History Workshop Journal* 45 (1998): 200.
[99] Tagore, 'Sahityer Itihasikatha', translated in Guha, *History at the Limit of World-History*, 98.
[100] Ann Talbot, 'Chance and Necessity in History: E. H. Carr and Leon Trotsky Compared', *Historical Social Research / Historische Sozialforschung* 34, no. 2 (2009): 88.
[101] Brad S. Gregory, 'Is Small Beautiful? Microhistory and the History of Everyday Life', *History and Theory* 38, no. 1 (1999): 100.

focusing both on the cellular moment of the frog's skin and on the greater ecosystem that influences, shapes, and sustains such moments. We may ask: is all historical thinking regulatively bound to the dictates of discursive representations, images, iconography, and material relics? Are the gathered and the aggregated symptoms of history as an idea a manifest or document of truth and conceptual unity? In fact, the problem with our past rolling into the present is not in unity and not always regulated under a conceptual and representational law; it is not a narrative devoid of discrimination. The past as constellation is, for Tagore, composed in discontinuous configuration—Tagore seeing history through inference and causality and Rabindranath experiencing history outside successivity and objectivity—within a plasticity where history exists as an unfinished project. *Itihasa* has an unfinishedness to it, and within the plastic rhythm this incompletion marks the endless dialogue between the *aitihāsik* and the *kavi*. This makes Tagore settle into the objectivity of a supposedly finished history and Rabindranath connect with an unfulfilled history— one with a sense of apparent completion and the other in a roll of excess as both try to make *itihasa* a combinatric experience.

The *srishtikshetra* in which Rabindranath revels is not to be misconstrued as a withdrawal from the chains of proper history that cannot look beyond the perimeters of facts and data. Facts of the everyday are minted in solitude; experiences for Rabindranath do not turn phantasmatic. History is built in the tumult of 'moments of intensity' (in the words of Hans Ulrich Gumbrecht),[102] in one's enclosures of seeing; *itihasa* is a 'presence' that 'can produce effects and radiate energy while escaping efforts to identify and apprehend it.'[103] History tied to the *sadharon* (public) misses this kinesis, this unapprehensible flicker of the surplus. Writing or narrating the everyday is not what usually happens in the creative workshop of history. But here, through the intervention of the *pratyohik*, we find the dissolution of the big-time dimension that we attach to historical events, differentiating what is important from what is not. There is a voice behind the weaving of a historical narrative that determines the gods of big and small things. But such dissolution disrupts

---

[102] Hans Ulrich Gumbrecht, *Production of Presence: What Meaning Cannot Convey* (Stanford, CA: Stanford University Press, 2004), 99.

[103] Hans Ulrich Gumbrecht, *Our Broad Present: Time and Contemporary Culture* (New York: Columbia University Press, 2014), xi.

the continuity of a settled pattern of argument importing digression and detours. Rabindranath is a consequence of a historical detour. History for Tagore is not romantic outbounding, not a relentless splitting of truth: neither a permanent closure on ideological ossification nor postmodern deferral of signification. We are in the midst of Walter Benjamin's 'chronicler' who 'narrates events without distinguishing between major and minor ones acts in accord with the following truth: nothing that has ever happened should be regarded as lost to history'.[104] The *pratyohik* may be lost to the public but not to the hunger of *itihasa*. Seeing a connection among everyday things builds a design in the mind, waking up the imagination, rousing the sensibilities usually deemed dormant in the daily grind of living. *Pratyohik* then is not about today but a 'today' infused with the sense of the yesterday (*aaj-kal*), a continuous investment in missed historical encounters. Rabindranath, in a monadic intensity, 'touches' history through an event seen today but that has its recurrence from the past, in times he was not conscious of, when the outside stayed as outside without its inherent drama, play, imagination, emotion, and whatever else that composed and intensified its unrealized historicality. *Itihasa* makes its demands on creativity always and not, as wrongly supposed, in its chosen moments. Rabindranath connected with the today (*aaj*) and relished the history of the present, but in such connections reindicated our interminable, always embodied, ligatures with the past (*kal*)—the *aaj-kal* in duet, in dialogue, preparing the scripts of *itihasa*.[105]

Historical thinking is both a movement and an 'arrest of thoughts',[106] hustling amid a finitude of thinking, a totality of experience, and the fragmentation of image and idea. Benjamin writes, 'in order for a part

---

[104] Walter Benjamin, *Selected Writings of Walter Benjamin*, vol. 4, *1938–1940*, ed. Howard Eiland and Michael W. Jennings (Cambridge, MA: Harvard University Press, 2003), 390.

[105] An insight into Nishitani's 'Sunyata and History' explains how Zen notions of history approximate to Tagorean ideas of looking into the instant of history as a synthesis of creativity and historical present. Tagore, with the undertow of Zen views on transhistoricality, has not been supportive of the demythologizing, teleological view of history, looking instead into the innocence of the emergence of things and emotions with a strong understanding of rhythm that human life provides and hides. This is not 'pseudohistory'. For Tagore, all history is not interpretation, not eternal recurrence either; there are experiences that demand being left to the realm of imagination, emotion, and sensibility. See Steven Heine, 'History, Transhistory, and Narrative History: A Postmodern View of Nishitani's Philosophy of Zen', *Philosophy East and West* 44, no. 2 (1994): 251–78.

[106] Walter Benjamin, *The Arcades Project*, trans. Howard Eiland and Kevin McLaughlin (Cambridge, MA: Harvard University Press, 1999), 475.

of the past to be touched by the present instant there must be no continuity between them'.[107] Rabindranath leaps out of the unattainability
of historical continuity. Tagore reflects on history and history refracts
on Rabindranath. The moment that distinguishes Rabindranath from
Tagore is the non-actualized possibility that Benjamin sees as generating
'envy'. In fact, Rabindranath's happiness results in envy too;[108] he is en-
vious of not being able to seize the moment. The plastic moment that
Rabindranath encounters is the happiness of an experience in history
and of envy for staying alive as a possibility never to be fully actualized.
Tagore engages with history and Rabindranath with missed history, the
possible and deferred history in the irrealis, a cognition that sees history
in the present and leaves it open for the future too. Rabindranath relishes
unfulfilled history.

Both Rabindranath and Tagore see the possible in history and historical moment-formation: 'excess over anything that can become given;
excess over that which is; remainder that itself is not'.[109] Perhaps to see
Tagore's faith in a 'divine drive' in history as theological determinism
or as strict acts of destiny would not be appropriate. I would like to see
this drive or intention as recognition of possibility, a continuum of actualized, seized, happy moments in cohabitation with the unhappiness
of unseized and uncaptured moments, as a continued unfulfillment.
The fateful dimension of history integrates with the 'truth of emotion'
that Tagore so earnestly argued as removed from inflexible submission to evidential truths. History is not an unimpeachable serialization

---

[107] Ibid., 470.

[108] Tagore's sense of the *itihasa* would carry with it 'a secret index'; like Benjamin, he would
love to question: 'Does not a breath of the air that pervaded earlier days caress us as well? In the
voices we hear is not there an echo of now silent ones?' See Eli Friedlander, *Walter Benjamin: A
Philosophical Portrait* (Cambridge, MA: Harvard University Press, 2012), 196. Friedlander argues, 'because the image of happiness is so entrenched in the concreteness of one's life, future
generations lie outside the space of wishes, expectations and envy. It is because the future is
free from intricacies characteristic of present relations in the human world that a different bond
between it and its past can be forged. This other bond can be explored insofar as we reverse the
perspective and consider not the expectations of the present towards its future but the relation
of the present to its past in remembrance' (ibid. 197). 'Rabindranath' has freed himself from
the future and all connection with public history to develop a happiness that does not redeem
but merely contributes to his creative suffering, his *viraha* with the presentness of the past—the
index of *itihasa* in the *aaj-kal*.

[109] Werner Hamacher, '"Now": Walter Benjamin on Historical Time', in *Walter Benjamin and
History*, ed. Andrew Benjamin (London: Continuum, 2005), 41.

of the factual, the realized, and the 'taken place'; historical reading can depotentialize itself to include the fleeting, the non-archivable—an invitation to the 'hidden index'. Werner Hamacher's exegesis on Benjamin is relevant to understanding the Rabindranath-predicament: 'the present, if it is one, does not make claims on the future, but is present alone as that upon which the past makes demands: present is always present out of the past and present for the past. And second, the past not only has in this present its intentional object but its intention comes in it to a standstill: what-has-been shines in the present, if it is one, and unites with the Now of its cognition.'[110] Tagore believes in the now-ing of history, the interruptions that historical consciousness might produce on the ruins of the past, the hunger and drive of history breaking off at moments of fulfilment to digressively produce an emotion, reflection, and romance in historical meaning-generation. Theodor Adorno's commentary on thesis VII of Benjamin's 'Theses on the Philosophy of History' is relevant here:

> If Benjamin said that history had hitherto been written from the standpoint of the victor, and needed to be written from that of the vanquished, we might add that knowledge must indeed present the fatally rectilinear succession of victory and defeat, but should also address itself to those things which were not embraced by this dynamic, which fell by the wayside—what might be called the waste products and blind spots that have escaped the dialectic. It is in the nature of the defeated to appear, in their impotence, irrelevant, eccentric, derisory.[111]

Tagore and Rabindranath play up the limits of historicism, create a dialectical understanding of the vanquished and victorious past, feel the potency of *Jetztzeit* (now-time), and also blast the moment of a homogeneous course of history.[112] Reflecting on Benjamin's 'angel of history', Ronald Beiner helps us to note that 'history is a sky-high pile of debris and the assertion of progress is meant to deflect our gaze from this unredeemed debris (thesis IX). Historical materialism means that the vanquished are not forgotten, and this means that one is never deterred by

---

[110] Ibid., 52.
[111] Quoted in Ronald Beiner, 'Walter Benjamin's Philosophy of History', *Political Theory* 12, no. 3 (1984): 425–26.
[112] Ibid., 427.

the idea of progress from continuing to wage "the fight for the oppressed past" (thesis XVIII).'[113] *Itihasa*, for Tagore, is the oppressed file waiting to be retold and not always in line with the colonial historiographical modes of representation and narration. The 'blast' produces a consciousness of an object beyond the object (object-diffusion) that the world materially formulates. Rabindranath has encountered the limitations of experience and the confinements that a dialectical materialist understanding of life produces. This results in the unselfing of Tagore into Rabindranath as an experience (another version of *yatra*) and subject-position that exist outside the empiricist and conservative epistemology of a subject–object understanding of life and history. It is a different kind of history of reason where the world 'looked at' and the world's 'looking back' are not necessarily congruent modes of experience. Rabindranath, for me, is the flaneur that all historicist selves possess, and Tagore's philosophy of *itihasa* knows its investments in the 'contrived corridors', 'cunning passages', and 'whispering ambitions' that constitute it.[114]

What impact might Tagore's plastic moments in historical formations have had on global disciplinary formations? Thomas Trautmann is concerned about disciplinary history's seeming shrinkage to 'an evernarrower band of the recent past, and losing interest in the uses of the deeper past. While it has become more global, its chronological depth has grown shallower; and that deeper past is left to others. At the very moment when history should be joining forces with the new technologies of the past, it is losing the capacity of doing so, thinning historians' understanding of the present, and the future.'[115] Rabindranath Tagore's contribution is in providing the *rasa* and rationale of a world (not always a fundamentally non-Western world) to the worlds of global history: an analytic and constructionist world of the *kavi-aitihāsik* with its

---

[113] Ibid., 428.
[114] See T. S. Eliot, 'Gerontion', in *T. S. Eliot: Selected Poems*, ed. Manju Jain (Delhi: Oxford University Press, 1992), 24.
[115] Trautmann, 'Does India Have History?', 200.

own imaginary and the logic of the given. Tagore's historical consciousness does not miss out on the emergence and dissemination of the politics of institution, technologies, and strategic stratification; it is also
alert to the impact of knowledge, fact, truth, opinion, detachment, and
evidence. Addressing a deep past, *itihasa* becomes a way to free history
from the univocality of world history; it flourishes at its limits, in its own
'worlding', and, thus, never fails to plasticize our notions of global history.

5

The Plastic Kavi ...

The plastic kavi writes with a transformative impetus, not trying to create a system but rather an experience which has its own holes and through which the coin can sink. Michel Foucault observes, 'I am an experimenter and not a theorist. I call a theorist someone who constructs a general system, either deductive or analytical, and applies it to different fields in a uniform way. That isn't my case. I am an experimenter in the sense that *I write in order to change myself* and in order not to think the same thing as before.' And further, '[As an author] my problem is to construct myself and to invite others to share an experience of what we are, not only our past but also our present, an experience of our modernity in such a way that we might come out of it *transformed*. Which means that at the end of a book we would establish new relationships with the subject at issue.'[1] There is a strong force of beyonding in his plastic consciousness as the *kavi-darshanik* (poet-philosopher) frames a philosophy beyond philosophy which is an absorption into instants (moments of revelation and awakening), and in a time longer than we can think of (Infinite). This combines well with the transitional and happening time. The *kavi-darshanik* can see things we would not otherwise see through our layered encounters with the world of egos, habits in passive repetition, and memories. He is not up to solving problems for experimenters are not meant to work under the force of habit and molar indoctrinations. More than solving problems, the *kavi-darshanik* as 'experimenter' creates and discovers problems. All his plastic arts are experimental. The plastic kavi is problematic.

---

[1] Michel Foucault, 'Interview with Michel Foucault', in *Power: Essential Works of Foucault, 1954–1984*, ed. James D. Faubion, trans. Robert Hurley et al. (New York: New Press, 2001), 240, 242; my italics.

Plastic Tagore. Ranjan Ghosh, Oxford University Press. © Ranjan Ghosh 2024.
DOI: 10.1093/9780198922995.003.0005

Plastic Nature

To explore another instance of the plastic-problematic, we can commit to figure a few plastic moments in Tagore's negotiations with nature. Tagore's intimacy with nature is a long story narrated many times over. Writing to Dinabandhu Andrews, he points out that 'I feel I am going nearer to myself... it is becoming easier for me to feel that it is *I who bloom in flowers, spread in the grass, flow in water, and scintillate in (the) stars, lives in the life of all men of all ages.*'[2] Tagore poetizes, sublimizes, and musicalizes nature in a kind of nostalgia and ideology of essential interrelation. This nature is not the one that has been triggering alarm bells all across the planet today. How would this intimacy manifest today when the grasses are steeped in plastic and other waste, the water is precariously toxified, and plant and animal species are going extinct at a frightening speed? His emergence as the man living 'in the life of all men' sounds fallacious today and the connection with the non-human world and its ceaseless materialization and processes of inter-being struggles to experience the flow and transfusion of and in *ananda* (joy). Feeling this *ananda* is no protection against a nature whose grasses, flowers, water, and soil are announcing an eco-precarity on a scale unimaginable to human cognition. In the face of a climatocenic imminence, his ideas about nature may seem anachronistic when the meaning of nature and 'natural contracts' have come in for major refigurations in the last fifty years. There is a Gothic surplus in our understanding of nature today where going back to pristinity (there cannot, in fact, be any) and finding homeostasis in the face of relentless anthropogenic intervention can never be a reality; a return to nature is saving nature and such instinct and interest is inspired by the urge to save humans.

The will to save nature is the will to save humans as Tagore's supervising and universal man is under a serious threat of being decentred and left disjoint; he, however, does not lose holding a place in a different space and order within a fresh natural contract. The universal man today is an endangered *anthropos*; he is a split man. And the wonder of nature has changed and so has the nature of its behaviour where more accidents and

---

[2] C. F. Andrews (ed.) *Rabindra Nath Tagore Letters To A Friend* (London: George Allen & Unwin Ltd, 1926), 74.

unexpected turns have surfaced and the foundation of having an opportunity of natural retreat has become close to a delusion. But does Tagore's
idea of nature look 'stupid' now when stupidity is a serious provocation
to rethink the surplus emerging out of a changing nature, a nature 'yet to
come', and the universal man caught in anthropocenic constructs? This
surplus, unlike the one Tagore experiences in art and sāhitya, terrifies; it
is no longer the supersensible aesthetic. If the nature Tagore proposes and
promises to negotiate and ally with is gradually disappearing from this
planet, what happens to his thesis, his claims and understanding? Does the
kavi become irrelevant? The dynamic of the plastic kavi, however, does
not allow this irrelevance when transactional plasticities make attachment
get seen not as bondage, when being with Earth is not exchanging roles
of a big Other (first man and now nature) but an interface with stupidity
that declares how the art and science of living together can be reframed.
Tagore made nature present to itself as much as man presented to nature is
always presenting himself before him. We are never out of each other; we
never were. Being present to oneself is a being in process. By considering
him as *ananda-rupam* where the kavi's true form is not in flesh and blood
but in 'joy', a profound statement on the living togetherness with a nature
and the new forms of alienation is established. Tagore writes:

> I have often thought that the profound joy we have from nature is be-
> cause of our feeling of an enormous relationship with her—these
> ever-reviving green and sappy grass and creepers, trees and bushes,
> this flow of waters, this blowing of winds, this continuous revolving
> of the shadows, this cycle of seasons, this ever-moving stream of stars
> and planets filling up the boundless sky, the endless kingdom of life on
> earth—with all this is our blood-stream in the arteries linked—we are
> set to the same rhythm as the whole universe—where this rhythm is
> taking a pause, or where it is ringing out, there from inside our heart
> comes a consent—if all the particles and atoms of nature not our kin,
> not ever throbbing in our heart out of a sense of beauty and profound
> joy, then we would never have had such inner happiness to be in contact
> with the world outside us.[3]

---

[3] Tagore, *Chinnapatra*, 23 August 1895; quoted from Amiya Dev, 'Tagore's Truth', in *Tagore, Einstein and the Nature of Reality: Literary and Philosophical Reflections*, ed. Partha Ghose (London: Routledge, 2019), 65.

This joy within our contemporary green consciousness (the *ananda* is never irrelevant whether with a less harmed Earth or an Earth under fierce anthropogenic stab marks) makes a powerful case for rebuilding a 'living' companionship with nature, a *sambandha* that is deep and unifying. I agree with Michael Bess that nature is 'no longer a static, rigid taxonomy; it becomes protean, upwelling, a vital force erupting forth, proliferating, unpredictable, and metastasizing. We may actually be facing the most extraordinary frontier—the frontier of nature as an ultimately creative, responsive, and transformative power, which regards human beings simply as a trace that is overcome and left behind.'[4] Nature is more than what takes place without the voluntary and intentional agency of man; it is also functionally multivalent, historically complex, and an ideological and paradoxical concept. We must appeal to the 'pathologies of epistemology'—the disruption of the loops of communicative feedback between mind and matter, nature and culture. Nature has the opportunity to function within the argument that does not see 'ideas of nature' as simply the 'projected ideas of men', as Raymond Williams has argued. What Bernard Charbonneau sees as human 'freedom' (a version of natural dialecticism) is born out of seeing nature's otherness as a self: a deconstructed self emerging from thoughts about the death of nature, a death that is a promise of a fresh lease on life—a postendism that transcends imponderable thresholds. Tagore's proclamation of the event of afforestation and a reconstructive understanding of nature in the laboratory of his ashram and Sriniketan are trembling exposures to a postendist prospect, the struggle to stay 'present', as the plastic nature gradually slips beyond the representable to the undetermined.

Man does not live by bread alone. He is unhinged by a plastic desire to go beyond his immediate necessities. His fund of emotional energy is invested beyond the material immediacy of living. 'In our highly complex modern conditions,' Tagore writes, 'mechanical forces are organized with such efficiency that the materials produced grow far in advance of man's capacity to select and assimilate them to suit his nature and needs. Such an overgrowth, like the rank vegetation of the tropics, creates

---

[4] Michael Bess, 'Deconstructing Nature', *Letters* 8, no. 1 (Fall 1999): 2.

confinement for man.'[5] However, the kavi knows that the 'nest is simple. It has an easy relationship with the sky; the cage is complex and costly, it is too much itself, excommunicating whatever lies outside. And modern man is busy building his cage. He is always occupied in adapting himself to its dead angularities, limiting himself to its limitations, and so he becomes a part of it.'[6] It is the limitation in existence and the *ananda* in the limiting premises of man's (in)dwelling that struggle to find the right nodes to flow. Through what Heidegger calls the 'technological way of revealing', humans have lost almost all claims to a 'simple nest'. The 'dead angularities' to which humans adapt are a sort of surrender of lives at source to an authoritarian system, that, in the words of Lewis Mumford, 'gives back as much of it as can be mechanically graded, quantitatively multiplied, scientifically sorted, technically conditioned, manipulated, directed, and socially distributed under supervision of a centralized bureaucracy'.[7] The lure of 'automated superfluity' dehumanizes techno-loaded Mumfordian machine-addicts who are ready to relinquish 'their prerogatives as living beings: the right to be alive'.[8] This fearful reality rationalizes an existence in *ananda*—the necessity and surplus of *ananda* as ways of existing and possibilities of surviving.

Within the thought-space that the phenomenon of the plastic kavi provides, the *anthropos* as geological agency can be seen to have overstepped his limits—surplus can never be a productive reality without limits—and faces the 'shapeability' of his being under anthropocenic conditions.[9] He writes:

---

[5] Tagore, 'A Poet's School', in *Towards Universal Man* (London: Asia Publishing House, 1961), 289.

[6] Ibid.

[7] Lewis Mumford, *The Myth of the Machine: The Pentagon of Power* (New York: Harcourt Brace Jovanovich, 1970), 322; Being alive for Mumford is to act holistically as humans which is about trying to 'exercise all their organs without officious interference, to see through their own eyes, hear with their own ears, to work with their own hands, to move on their own legs, to think with their own minds, to experience erotic gratification and to beget children in direct sexual intercourse—in short, reacting as whole human beings to other whole human beings, in constant engagement with both the visible environment and the immense heritage of historic culture, whereof technology is only a part' (ibid.).

[8] Ibid.

[9] Magdalena Hoły-Łuczaj, 'Shapeability: Revisiting Heidegger's Concept of Being in the Anthropocene', *Cosmos and History: The Journal of Natural and Social Philosophy* 15, no. 1 (2019): 402–26.

As I sat by the open window of my house-boat and behold the rays of sunlight focused on the ochre-coloured soils of the dear old earth, at that moment all my body felt like, as, if, spread out freely over the layer of dust and grasses up to the end of the horizon. As an auspicious moment, when it rings in clear notes in my mind that *I do exist all along with the stars, planets and satellites, with the rocks, soils and waters*, then my body and mind became delighted at the great joy of wide existence.[10]

Existing with all and finding the *ananda* in a 'wide existence' speak of a dwelling. But the dynamic of dwelling clamours for revision as the fact and philosophy of being with the Earth and its living and non-living occupants is being with a becoming Earth, a degenerate Earth, a plastic Earth. What Tagore sees as the deep unity of man and nature, the planet and our being, is what the Anthropocene has made us realize in an ironical way. After the Industrial Revolution, two world wars, and relentless anthropogenic agency at work, the Earth is at a melting point, making us realize that the predator and the victim are not removed from each other; within a 'wide existence', both shape and impact each other struggling for survival. Although Sen Gupta observation that Tagore's anthropocentrism does not entail any kind of human-centred 'imperialism' or speciesist 'chauvinism'[11] cannot be denied, there is no denying either that Tagore sees a threat in the reckless footprints of man, disrupting the rhythm of a nature of being that he has always been devoted to hold on to.

How is *ananda* leading us to argue about 'using' nature? Is use only about instrumental and calculative thinking, only a ready-to-use way of inhabiting nature where the being of the 'nest' stands unmanifested? Tagore's deep intimacy is not aesthetic only; it is ethical and ecologically necessitated. Disconnection with the *ananda* is our anthropocenic fatality. This joy necessitates preservation, inspires us to undo what we are suicidogenically committed to and is a relievement in finitude amidst the throes of extinction. The plastic kavi demonstrates a separate 'use' of nature that can have life-enriching and being-sustaining disclosures on us. This 'use' is not 'utilization' (*Benützen, Ab- und Ausnützen*) and

[10] S. C. Sengupta, 'The Surplus in Man: The Poet's Philosophy of Man', in *Rabindranath Tagore and the Challenges of Today*, ed. Bhudeb Chaudhuri and K. G. Subramanyan (Shimla: Indian Insitute of Advanced Studies, 1988), 39–54; my italics. Tagore. *Chithi-patra*, Vol. 15, 72.

[11] Kalyan Sen Gupta, *The Philosophy of Rabindranath Tagore* (Aldershot: Ashgate, 2005), 72.

not 'exploitation' (*Fördern*), because it asks for more care and attention to the calls of living. In a sense, the *ananda* in nature is about 'letting be' where the being in nature is not an overwhelming utilization of its potential and availability but allowing a way of being for us to encounter. Despite claiming human exemplarity, plastic Tagore can be seen to argue for a 'proper use' (following on Heidegger) which is not imperialistically anthropocentric. The surplus in man is the energy that learns to 'adjust', to fit better into the dynamics of relationship. All relationship is a kind of 'use' but not without the potency of 'letting be'. Caged humanity with furious investment in material use and utilization has the harmony of adjustment. Heidegger writes that 'when we handle a thing for example, our hand must fit itself to the thing. Use implies fitting (*anmessende*) response.'[12] Conforming to the 'use' is not about being hegemonized by the other; conforming in joy is considering the measure of the activities, the limitation and availability of the other. Nature under the monstrosity of the material and acquisitive culture has become a negotiation without this kind of conformity. For Tagore, much more than Heidegger, this extends to the non-human other as Tagore's being before the Padma river or the ecstatic exposure one day to the morning sun on the edges of the trees, speak of a way of revealment beyond the river or the sun as objects of material and sensual use only. The Padma river for Tagore is not outside the 'proper use' in that the river for Tagore is not the river that irrigates or is ready at hand for other commercial uses. The Padma withdraws to become the 'non-granting being' whose presence is in the withdrawal itself. The joy that courses through the poet comes from the river but whose use is in the withdrawal, the refusal to be utilized in bald mechanical and instrumental ways. The *ananda* here sheds new circulation to the relationality of beings where the river, water, light, sound, sky, boat, banks, and others come into shaping the experiencing being. The search for joy, the dwelling in joy, the rupture in joy from denial through anthropogenic arrogance, come to question the radical changes in nature's ways that have led to a serious man–nature divide.

Living in nature is affecting nature and being affected by it. Magdalena Hoły-Łuczaj sees 'shapeability' (in German it would be *Gestaltbarkeit*) as

---

[12] Martin Heidegger, *What Is Called Thinking?*, trans. J. Glenn Gray (New York: Harper & Row Publishers, 1968), 12.

similar to 'plasticity' which 'in Catherine Malabou's view, is the equilibrium of receiving and giving form, but in contrast to this idea, shapeability indicates that the activity in question does not create identity nor entirely model it. It rather shows that it leaves some imprint—not necessarily a negative one. Shapeability is also related to the form (*Gestalt*) in which something appears to us.'[13] For me, the *ananda* shapes and is shaped by the flow and movement through other beings and habitations. *Ananda* can be the recuperative mood, a process that strictly does not lead to identity-formation within the anthropocenic tremble. Hoły-Łuczaj notes further that Malabou's concept of plasticity 'describes the inner possibility of a being to change, or more specifically to destroy itself due to accident, trauma, or without any cause. As a result an entity is transformed into a completely new being: there is a radical break, contradicting the existing identity. This would be compatible with Heidegger's use of the word "shape" (Gestalt). It is not a technical term for him; actually the only passage in which it plays a major role is in Mindfulness, where he links it with "being-set-unto-itself", which means arising into pure presencing.'[14] *Ananda* is presencing—a contingency and essentiality in the impress of anthropocenic trauma. Not being affected by nature and not affecting nature are two impossible acts; they are inconceivable. Shapeability is not within the force of personal agency only. We put our marks on nature as much as nature does not let us go without marks. The acts of being present for each other and the presencing 'mark' us out. Tagore encounters nature where meeting a river is about marking many other circumambient things or connecting to them. His being in nature is a being enfolded in other entities that *shape* him both consciously and unconsciously. This is an entanglement whose threads are not always in the hands of man that declares *ami* (I). Tagore has to admit this shapeability and his *ami* is no longer a willed activity with a transfigural subjective imagination to boost but an admittance of shapeability by and of things that *ami* cannot deny. *Ami* uses nature as much as nature uses *ami*: this is true of the relationship that Tagore has with other beings and things. The plastic kavi is the I in 'Ami' in *Syamali*, Tagore's book of poems (1936); but this *ami* is far more vexed and meshed than any ordinary understanding of a romantic

---

[13] Hoły-Łuczaj, 'Shapeability', 412.
[14] Ibid., 413.

poet would allow. He writes that 'when a feeling is aroused in our hearts which is far in excess of the amount that can be completely absorbed by the object which has produced it, it comes back to us and makes us conscious of ourselves by its return waves'.[15] The kavi returns much more than he receives—a surplus in transactional imbalance that leads to greater plasticities of meaning-generation. The *ami* explodes and in such plastic explosion the love and music of this world is determined: nature speaks but it is *ami* who articulates the excess that translates into love and intimacy. Where is this *ami* today? Is it just an actor-network force in the manifestation of nature as a totality? The *ami* is overbalanced into a self-depredating crisis of gradual extinction as nature now is the *ami* speaking back to man. If it was the kavi-*ami* whose declaration of a rose as beautiful made the rose beautiful, it is the nature-*ami* who determines the attribute of a rose today. The kavi-*ami*'s saying and being are threatened with revision and morphing as the dominant subjectivity of a multivalent and diffusive nature and a 'yet to come' nature-reality influence the quotient of the surplus. In short, *ananda* becomes a force in the shapeability and the gestaltic presence within such deep transactions. But what would the disruption of *ananda* do to such intense interconnection? Tagore knows that *ananda* exists as a discovery that comes with its own limits and measure. *Ananda* is the possibility of understanding nature differently and a way of letting the human know the necessity of overcoming his self-aggrandizing depravity. *Ananda* is about finding the axis in co-sharing and bio-egalitarianism and how the reality of it being threatened and disrupted becomes the anthropocenic tremor. Tagore's insistence on *ananda* is coeval with the consternation of seeing how the limits and possibilities of such interconnection are precariously exceeded and undermined.

Tagore and Heidegger are on the same page when one sees both disturbed by the modern 'enframing of the real' under the relentless pressure of science and technology where the Earth stands to subjection and oppression at the hands of an instrumentalist *anthropos*. Heidegger, much in the way Tagore complains, points out how, having lost the autopoesis, we are no longer 'capable of listening, tuning in, and singing back, to its

---

[15] Tagore, 'What is Art', in *On Art and Aesthetics: A Selection of Lectures, Essays and Letters* (Kolkata: Orient Longmans, 1961), 16.

song'.[16] And 'as Heidegger says elsewhere, by "positioning," "ordering," "requisitioning," and "conscripting" whatever there is, modern technology frames reality as a "standing reserve" (*Bestand*) in which all things are placed "at the ready" to be appropriated, investigated, classified, experimented with, manipulated, modified, exchanged, destroyed, and replaced by something else when needed'.[17] In one of his courses on Heraclitus, Heidegger writes:

> We do not listen because we have ears: rather, we have and can have ears because we listen. However, we humans are only able to listen—for example, to the thunder of the heavens, to the rustling of the woods, to the flowing of a spring, to the tones of the harp, to the clattering of motors, and to the noise of the city—insofar we belong, or do not belong, to all of this. We have ears because we can listen in a hearkening way, and through such hearkening are allowed to listen to the song of the earth [*das Lied der Erde*], its shudders and shakes, a song that nevertheless remains untouched by the colossal noise that the human is now causing upon earth's battered surface.[18]

Tagore advocates a retuning, tuning back, asking for ears to listen to the Earth. Tagore's *ananda* in nature, the depth and calm, has a parallel narrative with the gross materialization that he fears and discounts; this dual narrative bears the intimations of an anthropocenic unconscious. If *ananda* is a mode of revealment and appearance, so are the anxiety of technology and the harm that threaten the *ananda*. For plastic Tagore human exceptionalism cannot be an event outside the care and responsibility for nature; and, as with art so with Earth, where the totality of both cannot be subjects of rational scrutiny all the time. The aesthetic of both has its mode of manifestation where a painting can hold a space and meaning outside the rational and rigorous interpretation and the river Padma is a presence which, in its mystery and maya, evokes a separate being in the conjugation of the human and the non-human: 'evening, beside the Padma, stands close to him, like a human presence, "with such intensity

[16] Quoted in Sofya Gevorkyan and Carlos A. Segovia, 'Earth and World(s): From Heidegger's Fourfold to Contemporary Anthropology', *Open Philosophy* 4, no. 5 (2021), 59.
[17] Ibid., 71–72.
[18] Quoted ibid., 71.

that the whole vast scene, from the starry realm of the sky to the distant shaded shoreline of the Padma, encloses me like a secret, secluded, restful little room. The two beings within me, I and my soul dwelling in me, have this entire room to ourselves: everything comprised in the scene, all birds and beasts and other creatures, become part of our being." '[19] Having an 'entire room to ourselves' speaks of dwelling as an inclusive mode of appearance and an entangled encounter with the world. Within the dynamics of enframing, man, in his role as the manager of this planet, forgets how the enframing starts to speak to him. As the acts of listening to Earth change, man's exposure to the alternatives of revealment is nullified to a point where enframing becomes dangerously an ordering principle. There is the saving principle that associates with the enframing. Destruction pairs with a saving power and the frenziedness of biodegradation works in concert with a saving grace achieved through a separate level of encounter with the world and the world of nature. Tagore's investment in *brikkaropon* and rural 'green' reconstructionism is not in the spirit of conservation and geo-engineering only. It is also about a mode of revealing, a response to both the ontological and ontic level of being. The ashram, Sriniketan, and all other green commitments clear spaces for 'releasement' that includes technologies into our lives as much as it leaves them outside for a different kind of emergence. Putting nature to use is not about technolozing it but also a 'proper use' where a meaning exists despite technology in a kind of possibility for a different world of experience.

Tagore observes that the 'glorious march of cement-concrete' civilization in India did not begin in the city but grew out of the forest. Humans have not jostled and lumped themselves together to help create this growth. It happened because of the ways by which humans decided to conjoin with nature around them—not in fearful and perspiring congestion but through spaces that were both open and crowded. This openness, this decongestion, he argued, kindled the consciousness of India and prevented her soul from being a congealed immobile entity.[20] Tagore

---

[19] Aseem Shrivastava, 'An Ecology of the Spirit: Rabindranath's Experience of Nature', in *The Cambridge Companion to Rabindranath Tagore*, ed. Sukanta Chaudhuri (Cambridge: Cambridge University Press, 2020), 329–30.

[20] Tagore, 'Tapovan', in *Rabindra Rachanabali*, vol. 14 (Kolkata: Government of West Bengal, Saraswati Press Limited, 1992), 384.

finds an 'energy' in the forest—the cult of *tapovan*—which is dominantly independent and internal in its inception and dissemination. This is the energy that has not grown through extrinsic forces born out of necessity, contesting contingencies and overpowering centripetal material persuasions. This immense, immanent, immutable energy is a 'quiet power' that infuses the spirit of the world; it is a power in solitude that, on most occasions, emerges in meditation. Tagore writes:

> the sub-conscious remembrance of some primeval dwelling place, where in our ancestors' minds were figured and voiced the mysteries of the inarticulate rocks, the rushing water and the dark whispers of the forest, was constantly stirring my blood with its call. (Some living memory in me seemed to ache for the playground it had once shared with the primal life in the illimitable magic of land, water and air.) The thin shrill cry of the high-flying kite in the blazing sun of a dazed Indian midday sent to a solitary boy the signal of a dumb distant kinship. The few coconut palms growing by the boundary wall of our house, like some war captives from an older army of invaders of this earth, spoke to me of the eternal companionship which the great brotherhood of trees have ever offered to man.[21]

This vital 'kinship' with nature determines the temper of the ashram and its enviable communitarian space. In 'Ashramer Siksha' Tagore makes an interesting point:

> Once I was a guest in the house of a Japanese friend. My host was a gardening enthusiast. He used to say: I love trees and plants. The power of my love enters into their being and comes out in the form of fruits and flowers. It goes without saying that his words are particularly apt for the gardener who has to look after the tender young shoots of the human soul. When one mind meets another in perfect harmony, the outcome is spontaneous joy. This joy is instinct with creative energy. Education in an ashram is the gift of this bounteous joy.[22]

---

[21] Tagore, 'A Poet's School', 290–91.
[22] See Tagore, 'Ashramer Siksha', in *Rabindra Rachanabali*, 14:431; translation by the poet himself.

This interdependence, this unconstrained *sambandha*, speaks of the core of ashram education where man, nature, and the greater spirit are threaded together in 'joy' (Tagore writes, 'The gifts of nature, unconsciously, build the human race'[23]). Endowed by a 'curiosity' to establish 'contact with their immediate environment', students and teachers seek for worlds beyond the textbooks and desire to find 'joy' in direct experiences—the *ananda* that is creative. The ashram school grows an 'atmosphere' (a significant word in Tagore's philosophical vocabulary) which is responsive to 'colour, perfume, music and movement'.[24] Tagore complains that 'in his society man has about himself a diffuse atmosphere of culture. It keeps his mind sensitive to his racial inheritance, to the current of influences that come from tradition; it enables him to imbibe unconsciously the concentrated wisdom of ages. But in our educational organisations we behave like miners, digging only for things and not like the tillers of the earth whose work is a perfect collaboration with nature'.[25] The 'green space' of the ashram fosters a *sambandha* that keeps the dynamics of human condition and its collaterality with nature firmly in place. It thrives in a dialectic of communication and conformity. The teacher, the taught, and nature are caught in non-hierarchical gestaltic games of 'mutual domination' and 'interchangeable supremacy' involving imagination, empathy, and tolerance.

What does this *ananda* and *sambandha* mean in the face of an ever-changing nature? Does the relentless advocation and search for *ananda* speak of an anthropocenic anxiety, a phobic being unsure about the ontology and character of *ananda* within a growing consciousness of impermanence? Plastic Tagore betrays an anxiety of a changing nature, a negative surplus that made him commit to a biocentric pedagogy or rural reconstruction within a nature–culture *sambandha* or a life amidst the nourishing and recuperative shelter of forests, trees, and plants—an inclusive and intensive green consciousness. Within this anthropocenic imaginary I would like to see these commitments as part of an anxiety of

---

[23] Ibid., 463.

[24] Tagore writes, 'An atmosphere was created, and what was important, this atmosphere provided the students with a natural impulse to live in harmony with it'. See 'Conversations in Russia', in *English Writings of Rabindranath Tagore*, ed. S. K. Das, vol. 3 (Delhi: Sāhitya Akademi, 1996), 933.

[25] 'Ashramer Siksha', 300.

living, a fear of losing the touch of *ananda* in nature, and, hence, an exposure to eco-inimicality. This love of the forest is not a love wired into the utilitarian fruits of existence and the mere urge of conservation. The plastic kavi sees a rhythm of limit in nature's forms of revelation and continuance, in processes and becomings, for beauty is the delicate distribution of proportion. Nature through its own existence lives and sustains as much as it throws open an alternative nature that we consider as a reality for our consumption and experience. But all overenthusiastic engagement with the nature we know has put us before a nature again that we don't know—human-ushered, and yet indescribably alien—forthcoming in an undisclosed power that unhinges all forms of rhythmic living. This nature responds to human intervention at the limits of excess: if creativity is a product of a surplus, this prospective planetary reconstruction is another manifestation of a human-generated surplus. The experience is unfamiliar; the impact is noisy and chaotic. Neither objective nor removed, the kavi speaks of a love for nature as an experience that exists outside us but is intense enough to stimulate the 'sense of our own existence'.[26] This existence owes to the 'superfluous' that determines our relationship with the world: the affective and aesthetic experience of nature is built into an excess as much as the instrumentalist understanding of it. This means excess opens us into two forms of nature—one that expresses the rhythm of the heart and the earth-being and the other that leaves us dithering on the edge of existence struggling to make sense of what discloses on us (the arrhythmic). The plastic kavi commits to the former and is apprehensive of the latter. The plasticization of this green consciousness is never outside a tremble and suffering as this over-insistence on *ananda* is existential and elemental and also connects with a growing alienation that the human world has inescapably thrown him into.

Tagore does not subscribe to a strict dichotomization of nature and culture into mutually exclusive categories of reality. Within a philosophy of green integralism, he is in favour of promoting a version of being that sees both the social self and the eco-self in a dynamic interaction. He has always sought a balance but the search for it has never been easy. Tagore rues man's inability to see the living whole of nature—

---

[26] Tagore, 'The Religion of an Artist', in *On Art and Aesthetics*, 690.

This vast and wonderful process is happening every day outside us, but we scarcely respond to it fittingly from within, so far removed are we from the universe! The light of a star reaches this earth after travelling through the infinite darkness for hundreds of thousands of years, but it cannot enter our hearts, as though that were another hundred thousand leagues away! ... The people inhabiting this world to which I have been consigned are very strange creatures. Day and night, they are busy constructing rules and walls, assiduously putting up curtains so that their eyes might not catch sight of anything. ... It's remarkable that they have not screened off flowering plants, or set up a tent to shut out the moon[27]

—and laments man's failure to avoid seeing nature as only 'an object of control, alteration and exploitation' where nature becomes a force to be subdued and not a territory to be respected with certain boundaries.[28] Probably, the 'modern understanding of nature' predicated on objectivity and differently attitudinized towards the non-human nature—what Neil Evernden calls 'the epistemological policing of nature'[29]—does not leave much room for an integralist connect with nature. Tagore's naturalism seeks to reverse the attitudinal legacies under which nature has continually been bracketed for disinterested examination. He looks into the 'ecological self', a self that can transcend both individualism and holism. This non-Cartesian process of learning amidst nature—human consciousness as an extension of the environment—is an energy flow where individuals are like 'local perturbations' having an awareness of individualism and a sense of being a part of the whole. Endorsing friluftsliv, Tagore's ecosophy sees this learning amidst nature as partaking of the energy flow—the *lila*, the *ananda dhara*, whose nature is not one of domination, not self-gratification, but communion (*sahit*). This is a joy whose foundation lies in *tapasya*, the mediation of restraint (*bodher tapasya*, cultivation of feeling); it is the inscribing of an awareness of a greater movement that often eludes us in our atomistic consciousness of things and existence.

[27] Quoted in Shrivastava, 'An Ecology of the Spirit', 327–28.
[28] Quoted in Thomas B. Colwell, 'The Ecological Basis of Human Community', *Educational Theory* 21, no. 4 (1971): 427.
[29] Neil Evernden, *The Social Creation of Nature* (Baltimore, MD: Johns Hopkins University Press, 1992), 55.

John Seed has argued that ' "I am protecting the rain forest" develops into "I am part of the rain forest protecting myself ". I am that part of the rain forest recently emerged into thinking. The thousands of years of separation are over and we begin to recall our true nature.'[30] This is not *unio mystica*, rather a separate investment in transpersonality with nature— an 'earth wisdom.'[31] Tagore vindicates the growth of an 'ecological self ' necessary to the 'pedagogic' and complementary to the 'cultural'. I would term this the 'ecological capital', the intervention and poaching of which can end up in multiple personalities—green low, green high, green deep. Without being 'partist', Tagore accented the 'relational' aspect between holism and individualism—dividualism. Within the collective cooperative of the ashram, for instance, Tagore intends to fasten a green sky over all but not in a reductive way which would have disabled individual experiences from speaking out in different tones. The ashram creates 'personal moods, values, aesthetic and philosophical convictions which serve no necessarily utilitarian, nor rational ends'. Within an integral ecologics, it forms itself around goodness, truth and beauty of the natural world, and of a human being's biological and psychological need to be fully integrated into it.[32]

Although largely concerned with the deep interdependence between nature and culture, Tagore sees a certain 'human need' to affirm ecological interdependence. Within such a metaphysics his students in the ashram need a certain order of growth and maturity drawing upon a conviction of their embeddedness in a vast web of life, in the efficacy of a co-evolutionary perspective. It is, to an extent, an act of being let loose in nature with a purpose (a freedom that is both mindless and alert); this cultivates a 'conscience' that extends from people to land, from commodity to community, from clothes to nakedness, from knowledge to mysteries, changing intellectual emphasis, affections, and fealties. The 'sacred' that Tagore proposes for his ashramites and the ashram campus to touch is transformative, vital, rejuvenative, and resuscitatory, requiring what

[30] John Seed, 'Anthropocentrism', in *Deep Ecology: Living as if Nature Mattered*, ed. B. Devall and G. Sessions (Salt Lake City, UT: Peregrine Smith, 1985), 243.

[31] For more on this, see Doris LaChapelle, *Earth Wisdom* (San Diego, CA: Guild of Tudors Press, 1978).

[32] See Devall and Sessions, eds., *Deep Ecology*, 66.

Aldo Leopold terms as 'intelligent tinkering'.[33] This 'sacred' denies an-thropocentric mastery and discloses on the students a charm and a mys-tery that non-human nature can only unleash—an act that is not mere intuitive-instinctive in nature but requires the growth of a 'conscience' whose understanding of bio-egalitarianism is of a different order and de-gree. The ashram campus—the nature–culture workshop—has a world view grounded in ethical and spiritual appreciation of interrelatedness—ecopsychological, ecosophical, and ecotechnological—which is, also, a 'participant consciousness' (in the words of Morris Berman) and a 'trans-personal identification with life'.[34] This is not merely the world produced by material objects but an energy whose production is of a different char-acter and consequence. Tagore's vexed 'deep' ecological position, how-ever, has nothing to do with the mystical. The connection that Tagore wants to imbibe is both material and non-material, psychological and corporeal, mediated and non-mediated and yet not 'mystical'. His deep ecological base to plastic pedagogy is performative, reflective, trans-formative, and non-utopic.

The submission to nature in the ashram, however, is not a commitment to return to a pre-technological age. The difficulty of sundering science and nature into mutually conflicting discourses is not the norm of 'pro-gress'. For Tagore, nature speaks not amidst the muteness of science but in the background of consistent throes of the abuse of science; it does not signal any intractable divide between the science-blessed human and the science-hurt non-human but projects an embodied self-nourished state in the duality of the two forces. Is this the provocation to reinterpret the 'use value' of existence in nature? Does Tagore direct us to redefine self-preservation beyond the domains of the instrumental reason? Tagore's appropriation of nature in his understanding of green pedagogy has a kind of internal limit to it. Under a regulative idea of reason, he chooses to minimize the opposition between nature and man. For me, Tagore by his choice of the locale makes nature available to his students in a liber-ating way, reducing considerably the dichotomy between *res cogitans* and *res extensa*. Tagore envisages a human good within the discursive ethics

---

[33] Aldo Leopold, *A Sand County Almanac, with Essays on Conservation from Round River* (New York: Ballantine Books, 1966), 190.
[34] Morris Berman, *The Reenchantment of the World* (Ithaca, NY: Cornell University Press, 1981).

of the ashram but cannot deny the anthropomorphic ends to it ('soft anthropocentrism'). The ashram, as a discursive space, is not a green submission to autotelic nature but an extrapolation of a space which declares the continued knowledge accumulation that human and the non-human have always developed through negotiation and opposition. It is a human settlement in nature which clearly emphasizes that nature could not have been left in her inviolability. Hence, the ethics of 'use value' and 'mastery' begs consideration within Tagore's principles of aesthetic education. Liberation in nature is about allowing nature the space to articulate back its values—both intrinsic or extrinsic—and the ashram accommodated them in its infrastructural bareness, spartan life habits, and remarkably conscious ways of connecting with the earth (for instance, the ashram students walked barefoot on ruddy muddy roads, students sat on the bare earth underneath the tree for their classes, a part of the teaching between the teacher and student was conducted while walking between the rows of trees). Tagore's resurgent motives to help create a space in the ashram that respects the intrinsic values of nature are, however, a little different from the Naessian school of deep ecology. Kalyan Sen Gupta observes that 'If the "deep" ecologist's talk of intrinsic value in nature is intended to counter subjectivism and instrumentalism about values, it is perfectly in order. But if the intention is to ascribe to nature values that it possesses in isolation from how nature engages with a human sense of significance, then, for Tagore, this "deep" ecological rhetoric is unintelligible. Tagore's broadly aesthetic case for protecting the natural environment is certainly not an instrumentalist one.'[35] Disinvested of 'shallow environmentalism' and yet not completely espousing of a post-anthropocentric ecosophy, Tagore comes close to redefining his own 'biospherical egalitarianism'. Tagorean ecosophy saw *sanmilan* (communion) of nature and human forces, not in a piecemeal, shallow approach to problems of integration and opposition, but within the framework of a philosophico-religious world view. So, it is out of order to see any dissolution of reason into nature. Rather this reasons nature out in a meaningfully consonant dialogue with man achieved within a separate truth and value regime. This is no 'de-development' (in the words of Ted Trainer),[36] but prioritization

---

[35] Sen Gupta, *The Philosophy of Rabindranath Tagore*, 73.
[36] See F. E. Trainer, *Abandon Affluence* (London: Zed Books, 1985), 176–78.

of the non-instrumental reason which, without being extremist in its interpretation of nature as either a space for wholesome consumption or brute untainted vitality, treats nature as a text of meaningful 'suffering'. Herein exists a fresh poesis of *ananda*.

The philosophical imaginary of the earth-connect unveiled and problematized at ashram school refigures its politics at Siksha-Satra (the school at Sriniketan) through a remarkable biopolitics in self-expression, *atmasakti*, and sensualization of pedagogy. This projected a series of plastic moments. The complex principle of love manifesting through his concern for poverty and underdevelopment in the villages ('Gradually the sorrow and poverty of the villagers became clear to me, and I began to grow restless to do something about it. It seemed to me a very shameful thing that I should spend my days as a landlord, concerned only with money-making and engrossed with my own profit and loss'[37]), accompanied by the raging requirement to produce the fruits of self-independent education, makes him restive, always ill-adapted to situations at hand, and relentlessly in need for what Paulo Freire calls 'integration'.[38] Caught in deep and disturbing plastic rhythm, the kavi connects with moments of unease and the politics of 'counter' and, in a near existential authenticity and positive angst, brings about his own ways of nature–culture dwelling. Sriniketan reveals love in ways that makes nature a life web, inviting him to participate in an unfinished universe—an earthbound and biocentric pedagogy and liberalism that stay an unfinished project always caught in the passion of reconstruction and imagination. The tactility and sense-drive (the performative and aesthetic investments through 'garden plots'[39]) in education inserted the existential quotient at the heart of learning and educational maturity. Students are

---

[37] Tagore, 'The History and Ideals of Sriniketan', *The Modern Review* (November 1941), 433.

[38] He points out that 'the education, the desires and the pursuits of those whom we call gentle folks and the opportunities they enjoy belong to the dry cave on one side of the dead river: an impassable distance separates them from those who are on the other side in knowledge and beliefs, customs and habits and the mode of daily life. The villagers have neither education, nor medical care, nor do they possess wealth, food and clothing. On the other side those who read in the college, practise law or medicine or pile up money at the banks find themselves on an island surrounded by bottomless separation'. Tagore, 'Education for Rural India', *The Visva Bharati Quarterly* 13 (May–October 1947): 27–28. Paulo Freire, *Education for Critical Consciousness* (London: Continuum, 2005), 4.

[39] Leonard Elmhirst writes: 'The inclusion of garden within his home compound, properly supervised provides an ample basis for the widest and best form of education'. See Elmhirst, 'A Home School for Orphans', *The Visva Bharati Quarterly* (1924): 124–26.

made to undermine the schoolmaster and get exempted from 'banking education' within a politics of transmission that comes with a living connect with the earth—freedom and instruction, imagination and techne having an integrated manifestation in 'gardening, weaving, sewing their own clothes, constructing their own tables and boxes, cooking, painting, writing Bengali, reciting poems and solving mathematical problems in relation to life situations'.[40] The plastic kavi in such nature culture entanglement (in a non-hyphenated negotiation) could not have worked through a dispassionate bureaucratic logic but through a reasonableness stewed in imagination, the Eros of a possibility and empathy that brings temporary 'suspension' of loaded self-consciousness to 'glide with one's own feeling into the dynamic structure of an object' and an inclusivism which is 'the extension of one's own concreteness, the fulfilment of the actual situation of life, the complete presence of the reality in which one participates'.[41] It is love that settles deep into such reconstructive and experimental life-commitment. Plastic Tagore's self-conscious organized intelligence, positive abject and poetic Eros go out to meet the mind of the whole community and the rhythm of nature-ways.

Hwa Yol Yung observes that 'in sinography, "crisis" is spelled with two characters (sinograms): "danger" and "opportunity," which points to the transitional period of a paradigm change from old to new'.[42] These two paradigms speak of a plasticity where opportunity inspires the imagination and agency to stand up to danger and create spaces for thought and action. Such an opportunity can be in the form of the rural 'nature–man' construction in Sriniketan and can also be an investment in *brikksharopon*. Alongside a calm and silent listening to nature's articulation and affect, there is an ensouled and enfleshed ecopiety that is both interhuman (homopious) and interspecific (geopious) that constructs the possibility of both an aesthetic and ethical understanding of the Earth. For the plastic kavi difference is no deterrent for it prepares the grounds for relationality, and, hence, a rhythm of co-living.

---

[40] Kathleen M. O'Connell, *Rabindranath Tagore: The Poet as Educator* (Kolkata: Visva Bharati, 2002), 298.

[41] Martin Buber, *Between Man and Man*, trans. Roger Gregor Smith (New York: Macmillan, 1969), 97.

[42] Hwa Yol Jung, 'A Prolegomenon to Transversal Geophilosophy', in 'East Asian and Comparative Approaches to the Environment', special issue, *Environmental Philosophy* 10, no. 1 (Spring 2013): 83–112.

Negotiations built around the ethics of 'suffering'—the dynamics that provide the ethos of imaginative reconstruction and non-aggressive mutuality—leverage the post-technological or non-substantive reason. This reason—humanist and green in nature—acknowledges the self-preservative dimensions of existence and yet notionalizes a 'freeing-up', an unboundedness, that argues for a life beyond self-preservation. This makes allowance for an attitude of domesticating nature and letting nature 'be'. This is a difficult axis to inhabit as we realize that at every point in the unfolding state of nature today. The disquiet in our intimacies with nature has forced us to change our habits as much as the habits of the planet. Earth has been changing its habit mechanism as our ethics of 'being' and 'doing' is continually under revision and stress. A repremised biocentrism has changed the human exemplarity in its relationship with nature as an 'eccentric' Earth invariably keeps altering our definitions of *ananda*. All of plastic Tagore's conceptual facilitators in the form of rhythm, surplus, union, and love face a separate understanding as the heavy denomination of 'staying together' and 'living together' within a changing green politics demands refiguration.

Do these fiercely biocentric ways of being and becoming; the insistence on staying profoundly in touch with the earth-needs and earth-ways; a disturbing urgency to revive the value and valence of living with trees, fresh water, and air; the ever-degenerative and precarious equations of the life web affecting the *ananda*; and the increasing obliteration of a consciousness of the 'eternal' (so typical of Tagore) leave us with a nature that is 'unborn'—an intimacy with a speculative nature in slow and certain turns and unexpected emergences? Plastic Tagore, I am deeply convinced, knows that 'Virgin nature' is a deeply problematized phenomenon. Walter Truett Anderson observes that 'there is no place on Earth—certainly not on an Earth whose sunlight filters through an ozone layer that has been accidentally altered by human technology—that is truly, as the saying goes, untouched by human hands. Indeed, all the things we do to preserve "nature," everything from wilderness management to endangered species legislation, are in one way or another human interventions.'[43] However, this comfort of the inhuman has made nature

---

[43] Walter Truett Anderson, *To Govern Evolution* (New York: Harcourt Brace Jovanovich, 1987), 7.

manifest in ways that are different from conventional understanding. Nature unnatured is still nature. Interestingly, our understanding of nature has become even more anthropocentric than in the past. This anthropocentrist approach probably persists in a different way even where human intervention ironically fosters the perpetuation of nature (Tagore's *brikksharopon* programme is one such instance). This nature, however, has lost some of its primitive diversity and seemingly inviolate independence. It is a human regeneration of nature—pastoralization with clear anthropomorphic ends—implying human continuity and the domination of nature for a human cause. Likewise, the exploitation of nature is for human advantage, and is more often about survival than obvious economic ends. Sequestering nature from human intervention is clearly impossible, hence the need to create a 'new nature': a dynamic, functional nature, revised and devised—supported by human technology and made sustainable in the face of human growth and commercial exploitation. Rejuvenated commitment to plant trees and a 'return to forest' consciousness and nature–culture dialogism as a reconstructive project of staying together, are clear indicators of an unconscious that brings home the prospect of the 'unborn' (phobic) incarnation of nature and the nature that is being 'helped' in its birthing.

Tagore finds nature coursing through his being—as he sees himself in clouds, in grasses, in the skies—but nature interestingly does not include him in its becoming. The unity and life web that he commits to experience are a complicated expression of a non-instrumentalist nature, an indifferent and ever-evolving life process where he is just a part. This nature is outside the kavi, building and existing in greater forms of expression. Tagore knows a change in nature is inevitable and seeks means to preserve a rhythm that speaks of unity and less discordance. However, this connection with a nature whose personality infuses and evidentializes a unity is an unknown nature with a different articulation that the kavi never expects to have his being become a prisoner to. Tagore's human-centric Earth and world is no longer able to sustain its conqueror for whom the definition of 'staying together' is never without the overbalanced accent of human species. He has a guilt about man's expression of himself on this planet—the misplaced *ami*.

If civilization is in crisis, it is because the planet is in outstanding crisis. He feels that the human can express himself differently through a separate understanding of the 'wealth of human life'[44] whose potential and delivery can remove many anxieties of existence. In a deeply theocentric way, he plasticizes his green consciousness by believing in the 'vision of Paradise' to be seen 'in the sunlight and the green of the earth, in human face, in human life, and in objects that are seemingly insignificant and unprepossessing.'[45] This is a force, a spirit, that spreads across the face of this Earth, not always logicalized into a pattern of meaning, but something that enters our being without making us know of its presence. This is a state of living beyond the finite as finitude has had its overpowering domination through machinery, industrialization, capitalist exploitation, and an enormous cult of greed that appropriates all the non-human planetary representation within the human judgement and order. Perhaps, this 'Paradise is awake'[46] consciousness and the state of earthly being is eventful in bringing an awe back into our lives—an awe for a nature that is not what man thinks exists for his instrumentality and manipulations alone. This awe is a way of thinking in the face of a 'yet to come nature', a nature 'to come'. There is a spirit that manifests in nature, an expression in surplus, as all things we give to nature come back to us as 'nature returns'. Nature is expression; a profound expressive principle works through her. Mark Wallace contends that

> an earth-centered reenvisioning of the Spirit as the 'green face' of God in the world is the best grounds for hope and renewal at a point in human history when our rapacious appetites seemed destined to destroy the earth. From this perspective, hope for a renewed earth is best founded on belief in God as Earth Spirit, the benevolent, all-encompassing divine force within the biosphere who continually indwells and works to maintain the integrity of all forms of life [. . .] the enfleshment of God within every thing that burrows, creeps, runs, swims, and flies in and across the earth.[47]

---

[44] Tagore, 'The Religion of an Artist', 57.
[45] Ibid.
[46] Ibid.
[47] Mark I. Wallace, 'Earth God: Cultivating the Spirit in an Ecocidal Culture', in *The Blackwell Companion to Postmodern Theology*, ed. Graham Ward (Malden, MA: Blackwell Publishing, 2005), 211.

This is green pneumatology where the concept of spirit is less metaphysical given its obvious correspondence with consciousness or intellect and proximity to Earth Spirit. The plastic kavi's celebration of and commitment to a Vedantic Earth wisdom works towards a sustainability and 'care' of nature against the anthropocenic menace. The 'vision of Paradise' builds the counter-discourse against a disanthropic imaginary gradually breaking loose on us.

Being born into nature is being born into an Earth that is a living system—interactive, transactional, assimilative, and accommodative. Keeping aside human exemplarity and anthropogenic superiority, the kavi imagines himself as a tree, growing out of an ancient sea-drenched earth: 'I drank in the first sunlight that touched the earth with my entire body under the blue sky, stirred by a blind joy in living, like a newborn child. I clutched this mother of mine, this clay, with all my roots and sucked at her breast.... Ever since, I have been born on this earth's soil with every new era. I seem to recall that old *relationship*, little by little, when I sit face to face with her in solitude.'[48] This relationship is the rhythm of 'living together' brought forth through a memory of the Earth; importantly, this togetherness goes back to the prehuman past in moments of visualized submission and this memory articulates an 'old relationship' that needs its own moments of revaluation and reaccommodation. Ecotheologically, the kavi connects with the memory and sacredness of the changing Earth. But the sacredness with which we may look at the Earth is not confining and limiting. Sacred is a restive totality and memory is no indoctrination and instruction: it changes, transforms, and accommodates. This comes from embeddedness and co-evolutionary existence. We invited the Anthropocene by dismantling the sacred of co-sharing and co-formation and co-occurrence. We lost our memory of the earth for, as Tagore knows, that 'staying together' has become a difficult reality with a growing technological and anthropocentrical superiority. As part of his relational ontology, the staying togetherness demands a premising where harmony is caring, manifests as a less instrumental understanding of non-human other, and exists as a strong support for ethical imagination. This earth is quintessentially interspecies and nature is more plastic than ever before. The memory of a deep friendship with

---

[48] Tagore, 'Nature', Kindle edition; my italics.

its changing plasticities brings out a sense of a time which the plastic kavi knows is about enlivement.

Always Plastic

Whether with art or life or socio-educational projects or nature, the temptation and risk to hold the plastic kavi as schizophrenic is enormous. His states of detachment, self-torment, loneliness, mournfulness, distraction, restlessness, libidinal vitalism, have rendered deep fissures through which we experience, to an extent, a depth of understanding that only schizophrenia can generate. It is a creative critical condition—a deficit as surplus and surplus as want—where a sovereign poet if he is not mad would become schizophrenic.[49] I identify two plastic 'schizophrenic' moments—one in the making of a university (without him ever going to one) under fiercely limiting and exiguous circumstances and the second in his obsessive indulgence into painting (without the slightest of formal training). These moments speak of the forces of 'capture'; they are experiences that dissolve the formal stratified self and its expressive ways. What is identified as schizophrenic vitalism is the plunge into the zones of indetermination, molecularity, and individuation. The plastic kavi has its own birth clinic.

In his paintings, philosophy of art, the vision and the concretization of the university, and the nature–culture collaborative reconstructionism, the plastic kavi is caught in molar, molecular lines and lines of flight. His plastic art holds in its ambit self-portraits, paintings in general, doodle art, the construction of the ashram school, Visva Bharati, Sriniketan, understanding of politics and nationalism, and the art of poetry and music. The plastic kavi, 'hopelessly entangled in the spell that the lines have cast all around' him,[50] can join voices with Deleuze who claims that 'whether we are individuals or groups, we are made up of lines'.[51] In such entanglement in lines, in entropic manifestation between lines, and the

---

[49] See Gilles Deleuze and Félix Guattari, *Anti-Oedipus: Capitalism and Schizophrenia*, trans. Robert Hurley, Mark Seem, and Helen R. Lane (London: Continuum, 2004).

[50] Tagore, 'Letter', in *On Art and Aesthetics*, 101.

[51] Gilles Deleuze and Claire Parnet, *Dialogues II*, trans. Hugh Tomlinson, Barbara Habberjam, and Eliot Ross Albert (New York: Columbia University Press, 2007), 124.

surplus in lines of flight we encounter plasticity as both rest and motion, a state of acceptance and disruption, equilibrium and disrupture. Plastic art is a process, a momentary stay against transition and an irresistible desire in becoming. Whether in art-tradition or colonial system of education or composition of music, the plasti kavi is never outside the molar lines of inveterate segmentarities; hegemonic stratification in social, economic, cultural, and educational discriminations; and choked desires of administrative and bureaucratic regimes. However, the molecular lines, as saving grace, determine the constitutive desire in Tagore as his mind and action, thoughts and activities, build their points of dispersion and kinesis. Art is in motion as is education and culture and religion. Desire in mere forms and functions is transposed with flows and forces. It is molecularity that signals 'border ante' and in it we have Deleuze and Guattari's 'lines of flight'. If nepantla through its liminality constructs 'bridges', the lines of flight produce desire lines of escape. Windsor explains that 'if molar lines represent desire as refracted through the prism of power and interest, the line of flight is a molecular revolution coextensive with 'the proliferation of desire' itself and the 'production of radically different experiences of "becoming".'[52] The plastic kavi is inconsistently brilliant because every project that he conceives is not without the restless urge to escape. All have fluctuating schedules and wavering fixtures, as scripts keep changing and actions get freshly generated. This escape urge is not to run away from something but to emerge out of a subject within a transformative aesthetics and praxis. His paintings and experiments with education are solid announcements in this respect.

The plastic poet invents and supplements and does not entertain the dour intent of a schoolmaster. Tagore's plastic pedagogy in Sriniketan, for instance, is a project in unveiling love and desire lines of molecularizaion where he seeks a utopic politics that is not built on the inane harmony between the empowered and the disprivileged. It turns out to be the theatre of the oppressed—poetics of inequality—where disharmony or rupture is a way to reconstruct further knowledge and reaestheticize what Jacques Rancière describes as connecting with the unconnected. In fact, what Peter McLaren says of Paulo Freire is true of Tagore: the 'politics

---

[52] Joshua Windsor, 'Desire Lines: Deleuze and Guattari on Molar Lines, Molecular Lines, and Lines of Flight', *New Zealand Sociology* 30, no. 1 (2015): 164.

of liberation resists subsumption under a codified set of universal principles; rather, it animates a set of ethical imperatives that together serve as a precipitate of our answering the call of the other who is suffering and of a heavy heart. Such imperatives do not mark a naive utopian faith in the future; rather, they presage a form of active, irreverent, and uncompromising hope in the possibilities of the present'.[53] Plastic worldings are marked by irreverence and irrelevance and a creative humanization that declares aesthetic-political counter-education; they are affective hope. Writing to Elmhirst, Tagore makes his creative Eros evident which is no mere construction but the expression of his being: 'The ideal which I cherish in my heart for the work I have been struggling to build up through the best portion of mature life does not need qualifications that are divided into compartments. It was not the kingdom of the Expert in the midst of the inept and ignorant which we wanted to establish— although the experts' advices are valuable. The villages are waiting for the living touch of creative'.[54] This requires a new order of desire and wisdom which John Dewey qualifies as a 'conviction about moral values, a sense for the better kind of life to be led'. The morality of the Sriniketan project calls for choice 'about something to be done, a preference for living this sort of life rather than that. It refers not to accomplished reality but to a *desired future* which our desires, when translated into articulate conviction, may help bring into existence'.[55] All of Tagore's projects are plastic explosives resulting in longing, hope, desire, beyonding, and rupture. Hence, much in character with the relationship that disappointment has with the supersensible and the indeterminate, the plastic kavi's experience and experiments bleeds on the stubs of anxiety—an inconsummation which builds at the heart of all creativity. His experiments, as plastic worldings, cannot be niched as 'problem posing, problem shooting' acts because of their inherent sublimic nature which, again, disallows hardened

[53] Peter McLaren, 'Paulo Freire's Pedagogy of Possibility', in *Freirean Pedagogy, Praxis, and Possibilities: Projects for the New Millennium*, ed. H. Mark Krank, Peter Mclaren, and Robert E. Bahruth (New York: Falmer Press, 2000), 14.

[54] Letter from Tagore to L. K. Elmhirst, 3 September 1932. See Leonard Elmhirst, 'Rabindranath Tagore and Sriniketan', *The Visva Bharati Quarterly* 24, no. 2 (Autumn 1958): 132.

[55] Quoted in Jim Garrison, 'Dewey, Eros and Education', *Education and Culture* 11, no. 2 (Fall 1994): 2; my italics.

institutionalization. Ideal is agony, vision is struggle, thinking is power, anxiety is reality, and life love as rhythm is the plastic kavi.

Tagore's philosophical and conceptual explorations get him close to Gloria Anzaldúa's 'border artist' who 'constantly reinvents her/himself. Through art s/he is able to re-read, reinterpret, re-envision, and reconstruct her/his culture's present as well as its past';[56] this is the unfamiliar, unenvisioned, and unexpected liminality whether in music or paintings or education—the plastic kavi's 'nepantla'. More than radicality I prefer seeing Tagore in the in-between state with his own molecularity. This nepantlic state is the surplus. Anzaldúa observes that 'Bridges are thresholds to other realities, archetypal, primal symbols of shifting consciousness. They are passageways, conduits, and connectors that connote transitioning, crossing borders, and changing perspectives. Bridges span liminal (threshold) spaces between worlds, spaces I call nepantla, a Náhuatl word meaning tierra entre medio. Transformations occur in this in-between space, an unstable, unpredictable, precarious, always-in-transition space lacking clear boundaries. Nepantla es tierra desconocida, and living in this liminal zone means being in a constant state of displacement—an uncomfortable, even alarming feeling.'[57] It is in such bridges that complex overlapping of worlds lie, with varying traditions, lineages, resistance, and ideologies. Anzaldúa's 'nepantleras' commit to such plastic moments that 'create new topographies and geographies of hybrid selves who transcend binaries and de-polarize potential allies.'[58] The plastic kavi 'listens' to issues and problems differently. He has *conocimiento* which Anzaldúa sees as a way of knowing and acting, a form of creativity that suspends conventionality and conservatism. Tagore's *conocimiento* is border arte where 'we enter the silence, go inward, attend to feelings and to that inner cenote, the creative reservoir where earth, female, and water energies merge. We surrender to the rhythm and the grace of our artworks. Through our artworks we cross the border into other subjective levels of awareness, shift into different and new terrains

[56] Gloria E. Anzaldúa, 'Border Arte: Nepantla, el Lugar de la Frontera', in *The Gloria Anzaldúa Reader*, ed. Ana Louise Keating (Durham, NC: Duke University Press, 2009), 183.
[57] Gloria E. Anzaldúa, '(Un)natural Bridges, (Un)safe Spaces', in *The Gloria Anzaldúa Reader*, 243.
[58] Gloria E. Anzaldúa, *Light in the Dark/Luz en lo Oscuro* (Durham, NC: Duke University Press, 2015), 82.

of mestizaje.'[59] All the artistic and social projects of the plastic kavi are invested in the aesthetic of the border arte in that it challenges the dominant molar discourse of understanding and acceptance. Border arte builds a transformative imagination that enables 'seeing through reality's roles and descriptions'.[60] In such modes of perception and performance the plastic kavi keeps inventing himself.

Caught amidst figural plasticities, Tagore's plastic art is never without form and never without the bursting torrent of expression, an *ananda*, that following on Deleuze comes from 'breaks' and 'ruptures'. This is the intensity of trying to overcome the steepest slope. His engagements with society, culture, and politics have their own 'crack lines' that are outlets for the expression of energy, the excess, the *ananda*. Tagore has relentlessly built infra-individuality. A dialectical relationship with the Real, which is what I would like to argue as the Infinite, makes this infra-individuality a 'swarm of differences'.[61] In thinking about sāhitya, social reconstructionism, nuanced pedagogy, and the deep loneliness and detachment, the plastic kavi becomes the incident point of elastic forces of differential variations. These variations and perturbations produce the crack and rupture lines bringing out the vital excess, the *jiban devata*. The Infinite is not a product of straight lines but an overabundance, a totality that leaks always. Tagore's universality or the Infinite is non-molar in that it evokes the singularity of the subject, cultivates an invitation and a source of joy, is an evocation that outbounds us whether in art, life, or philosophy. The *ananda* rejoices in others by which it means that *ananda* fills you with fulfilment when its rejoicement happens with others. The *ananda dhara* is the desire line, the ego-breaking flow, where contemplation is the conversation with what makes and unmakes us. Luis de Miranda explains the Deleuzian line of arguments by pointing out that 'every single thing is a contemplation of that which it derives from, which is life becoming difference, flesh of endless disparity. What is it that the rock contemplates? Its own parts. The rock contemplates the silicon, the carbon, the micro-elements from which it derives. The wheat is contemplation of the elements from which it derives and which it takes from the

---

[59] Anzaldúa, 'Border Arte: Nepantla, el Lugar de la Frontera', 182.

[60] Anzaldúa, *Light in the Dark/Luz en lo Oscuro*, 44.

[61] Gilles Deleuze, *Difference and Repetition*, trans. Paul Patton (London: Continuum, 2004), 61.

earth.'[62] The *ami*, as springing out of and submitting into something, exists in a plastic outburst—the vital upswelling; it is not the undifferentiated romantic subjectivity and is much more potent and diffractive than what the *ami* in the 'Ami' poem manifests. Miranda points out further that 'we have to understand that the difference comes before the lines but it underlies them: the line of flight is leak, ungrounding towards the difference; the rupture line is forcing back, burial of the difference; and the crack line is manifestation of the difference through the relentless repetition or exhaustion of the breaking repetition. In their relation to the difference, these three lines can be considered as being just one.'[63] The lines of flight of the plastic kavi take two directions where the one is towards 'a loss of destructive energy' (this comes from edification, unchanging habits, molar discourses of inflexibility) and the other is 'in the direction of a springing up of the sensible.'[64] The 'sensible' is difficult to derive for nothing comes out without the right kind of desire.

The *ami* of the plastic kavi is deeply signaturized into whatever aesthetic, social, and political actions and executions he chooses to be a part of and commits to. This is the Ami in the We, where the poet is the caesura in the molar lines of existence and settlement. Thought has its enemy within a system. The plastic Tagore is his own enemy, torturing the self into exploring and generating more sense out of the sensible, subjecting oneself to the hostility and indifference that one becomes aware of under the flow of desire. He can think differently where the centrality of his ego is overcome to release a new sense of being. This is a continued infidelity to the centrality of ego that builds the desire for the indifferent life. There is the revealment of the Ami in the thoughts that withdraw from the molar, the established, the substantive memory of being (whether it is the immanence of *visva sāhitya* or the reterritorialization of the colonial educational machinery or the radicality as fracture in paintings removed from the Bengal Art tradition). The 'irresponsible' plastic art of the plastic kavi is another name for his 'irresponsible' life where nothing is outside form and formations, for irresponsibility, importantly, needs a context to make its difference known and felt much like the lighting in the sky that

---

[62] Luis de Miranda, 'Is a New Life Possible? Deleuze and the Lines', trans. Marie-Céline Courilleault, *Deleuze Studies* 7, no. 1 (February 2013): 130.

[63] Ibid., 109.

[64] Ibid., 120.

needs a dark sky-canvas to express itself. A lighting during the day does not reveal in the same way as it does in the night. Irresponsibility has its own necessities, certain lines of desire, certain fractures to seep through without vanishing out of trace. The *ami* is the 'possibles' of the representation, and an 'individual who does not try to let the difference be made by himself or through himself does not reach singularity'. Deleuze puts his accent on the line that, as Miranda argues,

is a rising or falling flux with a zigzag course sometimes bursting egotist plugs, colliding here with a break, there with a relapse. It is not only through work of the thought that difference is made singularly, because thought is not able to tell the difference between the possible and the real. In order to be singular, singularity has to let the real be expressed and told through the body, the senses. But the real that shows up is difference coupled with the possibles of thought and egotist breaks.[65]

The *ami* is then a flux for itself. It is a movement that repeats itself with a difference. It is his own resistance. The plasticity of the *ami* comes through three coordinates that are remarkably relevant to the 'production' of the plastic kavi: one is to 'hypo-stasiate our will-to-bring-into-existence-that-which-does not-yet-exist in a conscious and felt repetition'; the second is 'to keep being untimely by refusing the normative temporality of the breaks'; and the third is about never giving 'in to the fatalism of believing that the real is fixed.'[66] *Ami* creates but, in such creations, it creates multiple *ami(s)*.

For the plastic kavi 'forms' determine the being: forms that are not always subservient to necessity and knowledge, not fixated on utility. Tagore asks, 'Where is the source of the great stream of formative energy man has released in words, in lines, in melodies?'[67] It is the formative energy that lends the power and shape to the lines that one draws to construct life with all its tasks, trials, and tribulations. He writes that 'man was forced to struggle and fight unceasingly, but in the midst of the insecurity and turmoil of his life he decorated his water jar and found time to

---

[65] Ibid., 127.
[66] Ibid., 151.
[67] Tagore, 'My Pictures (III)', in *On Art and Aesthetics*, 104.

paint designs around the door of his cave. He did not regard the world as taken up entirely with necessity. Something had touched him which was beyond his immediate material needs'.[68] It is in this sense of beyonding, in aesthetic-cultural manifestations that are not always products of information, 'ethical deliberation or logical argument', and in the 'extra exertion of man's consciousness',[69] that plastic art finds its true measure. It is a kind of form-impulse, a hunger for 'self-unfoldment', a form-ability and form-fulfilment. The plastic kavi, unlike many others, has the ability to intensify this form-expression to the 'point of illumination'.[70] He observes that 'the real lies scattered about in many diverse objects'; he 'cannot see it in its pure unfragmented state immediately'.[71] However, in artistic creation 'the real stands before us in all its immediacy'; this immediacy owes to a plastic figural imagination that, inspired by the sense of the beyonding and the flights from burdens of material necessity, helps the kavi to behold form. Standing before form is passing through forms as the immediacy of the experience is suffused by a shaping principle that overcomes the identical necessity of a kerosene tin and an earthen water jar to carry and draw water. Necessity has a power to transcend utility; this transcendence makes the plastic kavi say: 'I can behold its form'.[72] The plastic kavi is the man who 'shapes'.[73]

How is Art the 'guest that comes and remains'?[74] Aren't guests meant to depart? If they don't, how do they stay back and yet refuse to be the host? Plastic art allows such transformative 'staying back', the irresponsibility that comes from not being similar with every engagement, the inconsistency that makes art 'inexplicable' and 'inevitable'. Art as host is art as settlement; plastic art is settlement as host guest whose configurations are transient and transformative. It is the love not for the forms that endure for ages, but for the 'forming', the yet to be, the prepositional 'to come'. Being in dialogue with Tagore is being in the midst of creative supplement. Plastic Tagore has the philosopher's crisis in that he is unable to resolve the tension between theory and practice (this is, as I have argued,

---

[68]   Tagore, 'Maker of Forms', in *On Art and Aesthetics*, 83.
[69]   Ibid.
[70]   Ibid., 84.
[71]   Ibid., 86.
[72]   Ibid.
[73]   Ibid.
[74]   'My Pictures (III)', 104.

theoreticism with a difference), his ideals and prospective enactments. But the poet's 'dream of the other' gives exceptionality to this space and, distinct from the unified community that the German Idealists propose, it anticipates de-referentialization of culture and, in a certain sense, a post-historical position which has a separate logic of cultural syncretism and performativity. This ensures the endless supply of the surplus. Plastic Tagore's trial with the surplus makes him dwell on the notions of confinement, border and the margin of discourse, ideology and power. He looks into the logic of the margin and the centre in a new reckoning which sees the ferment on the borders as a way of negotiating traffic at the centre, of sponsoring new formations that appreciate locations, instances, and structures. It re-premises academic topology, investing distinct values into 'academic reason' where finitude is not about drawing up the 'yes' and the 'no', but is a dialecticism in disclosures and enclosures, bordering the inside and the outside of the reflexive unbound cosmopolitan venture. 'Doing' Tagore, then, is not just knowing Tagore; it is about rehearsing our un-legislated everydayness, our deepest thoughts and emotions, our un-thoughts, our secrets, our unclaimed and acclaimed life experiences. Tagore speaks to us from the line and beyond the line, speaks through us and speaks about us. As a provocation and surplus, plastic Tagore is not what Tagore possibly was; he is the image of a self that most often he was not aware of. Plastic Tagore is his own unhingement, a state of 'to come' that is alive in living the impurity of present, disrupting teleology, and upsetting self-identity: a stranger emerging out of a familiarity with a different planetarity whose discovery can only be controversial and deeply ambiguous. Tagore, plastic Tagore, what next? Play again ...

Bibliography

Acharya, Chandrika. 'Rabindranath Tagore's Sky of Colours'. *Artery India*, 8 May 2021. https://arteryindia.com/blog/post/sky-of-colours-rabindranath-tagore?artist=rabindranath-tagore.

Aichele, K. Porter. *Paul Klee, Poet/Painter*. Rochester, NY: Camden House, 2006.

Alam, Fakrul, ed. *The Essential Tagore*. Cambridge, MA: Harvard University Press, 2014.

Alvarez, Walter. 'Laws or Comets'. *Aeon*, 3 November 2016. https://aeon.co/essays/how-chance-and-probability-affect-the-path-of-big-history.

Anderson, Walter Truett. *To Govern Evolution*. New York: Harcourt Brace Jovanovich, 1987.

Andrews, C. F. 'An Open-Air School', *Visva Bharati News*, Silver Jubilee Number (1957).

Andrieu, Bernard. *Le Corps disperse: Histoire du corps au XXe siècle*. Paris: L'Harmattan, 1993.

Ankersmit, Frank. *Sublime Historical Experience*. Stanford, CA: Stanford University Press, 2005.

Anzaldúa, Gloria E. 'Border Arte: Nepantla, el Lugar de la Frontera'. In *The Gloria Anzaldúa Reader*, edited by Ana Louise Keating, 176–86. Durham, NC: Duke University Press, 2009.

Anzaldúa, Gloria E. '(Un)natural Bridges, (Un)safe Spaces'. In *The Gloria Anzaldúa Reader*, edited by Ana Louise Keating, 243–48. Durham, NC: Duke University Press, 2009.

Anzaldúa, Gloria E., and Analouise Keating, eds. *this bridge we call home: radical visions for transformation*. New York: Routledge, 2002.

Anzieu, Didier. *The Skin Ego*. New Haven, CT: Yale University Press, 1989.

Apter, Emily. 'Philosophizing World Literature'. *Contemporary French and Francophone Studies* 16, no. 2 (March 2012): 171–86.

Archer, W. G. 'The Paintings of Tagore'. *East and West* 12, nos. 2–3 (June–September 1961): 147–51.

Armstrong, Philip, Jason Smith, and Jean-Luc Nancy. 'Politics and Beyond: An Interview with Jean-Luc Nancy'. *Diacritics* 43, no. 4 (2015): 90–108.

Asia Society. 'Rabindranath Tagore: The Last Harvest'. https://asiasociety.org/new-york/rabindranath-tagore-last-harvest

Attridge, Derek. *The Singularity of Literature*. London: Routledge, 2017.

Auerbach, Erich. 'Philology and *Weltliteratur*'. Translated by Maire Said and Edward Said. *Centennial Review* 13, no. 1 (Winter 1969): 1–17.

Axtell, James. 'History as Imagination'. *Historian* 49, no. 4 (1987): 451–62.

Bagchi, Amiya Kumar. 'Rabindranath Tagore and the Human Condition'. *Economic and Political Weekly* 49, no. 12 (2014): 38–46.

Bahun, Sanja. 'Politics of World Literature'. In *The Routledge Companion to World Literature*, edited by Theo D'haen, David Damrosch, and Djelal Kadir, 373–82. Abingdon: Routledge, 2012.

Bartky, Sandra Lee. 'Heidegger and the Modes of World-Disclosure'. *Philosophy and Phenomenological Research* 40, no. 2 (1979): 212–36.

Bassel, Leah. *The Politics of Listening: Possibilities and Challenges for Democratic Life*. London: Palgrave Macmillan, 2017.

Battles, Matthew. 'In Praise of Doodling'. *The American Scholar* 73, no. 4 (Autumn 2004): 105–8.

Becquer, Marcos, and José Gatti. 'Elements of Vogue'. *Third Text* 5, no. 16/17 (1991): 65–81.

Beiner, Ronald. 'Walter Benjamin's Philosophy of History'. *Political Theory* 12, no. 3 (1984): 424–34.

Benjamin, Walter. *The Arcades Project*. Translated by Howard Eiland and Kevin McLaughlin. Cambridge, MA: Harvard University Press, 1999.

Benjamin, Walter. *Selected Writings of Walter Benjamin*. Vol. 4, *1938–1940*, edited by Howard Eiland and Michael W. Jennings. Cambridge, MA: Harvard University Press, 2003.

Berman, Morris. *The Reenchantment of the World*. Ithaca, NY: Cornell University Press, 1981.

Bess, Michael. 'Deconstructing Nature'. *Letters* 8, no. 1 (Fall 1999): 2.

Bessière, Jean. 'What Is Left of Comparative Literature and World Literature? Notes on International Literature, Its Concrete Universality and Enigmacity'. *Canadian Review of Comparative Literature / Revue Canadienne de Littérature Comparée* 44, no. 3 (September 2017): 407–19.

Bhagath, Sujatha [sujnaturelover]. 'The Last Harvest'. https://sujnaturelover.wordpress.com/2013/07/17/the-last-harvest/.

Bhandar, Brenda, and Jonathan Goldberg-Hiller, eds. *Politics, Legality, and Metamorphosis in the Work of Catherine Malabou*. Durham, NC: Duke University Press, 2015.

Bhargava, P. L. 'A Fresh Appraisal of the Historicity of Indian Epics'. *Annals of the Bhandarkar Oriental Research Institute* 63, no. 1/4 (1982): 15–28.

Blanchot, Maurice. 'Everyday Speech'. *Yale French Studies*, no. 73 (1987): 12–20.

Boisvert, Raymond D. *John Dewey: Rethinking Our Time*. Albany, NY: State University of New York Press, 1998.

Boucher, David. 'The Creation of the Past: British Idealism and Michael Oakeshott's Philosophy of History'. *History and Theory* 23, no. 2 (1984): 193–214.

Bourneuf, Annie. *Paul Klee: The Visible and the Legible*. Chicago: University of Chicago University Press, 2015.

Braidotti, Rosi, and Rick Dolphijn, eds. *This Deleuzian Century: Art, Activism, Life*. Leiden: Brill, 2015.

Brewer, John. 'Microhistory and the Histories of Everyday Life'. *Cultural and Social History* 7, no. 1 (2010): 87–109.

Buber, Martin. *Between Man and Man*. Translated by Roger Gregor Smith. New York: Macmillan, 1969.

Bunyard, P., and F. Morgan-Grenville, eds. *The Green Alternative*. London: Methuen, 1987.

Bushnell, Albert Hart. 'Imagination in History'. *American Historical Review* 15, no. 2 (1910): 227–51.

Caduff, Carlo. 'Canguilhem's Vital Social Medicine'. *History of Anthropology Review* 4 (February 2019). https://histanthro.org/notes/vital-social-medicine/.

Caranfa, Angelo. 'Into the Unseen, the Unsaying, the Unknowing: Whitehead's Mystical Aesthetics in Paul Klee'. *American Journal of Theology & Philosophy* 39, no. 3 (September 2018): 5–28.

Chakraborty, Bikash. *Byahato Shawkhyo: Rabindranath o Jadunath Sarkar.* Kolkata: Visva Bharati, 2011.

Chan, A. K. L., ed. *Mencius: Contexts and Interpretations.* Honolulu: University of Hawai'i Press, 2002.

Chattopadhyay, Jayanti. 'Tagore's Aesthetics'. In *The Cambridge Companion to Rabindranath Tagore,* edited by Sukanta Chaudhuri, 366–78. Cambridge: Cambridge University Press, 2020.

Chaudhuri, Amit. 'Foreword: Poetry as Polemic'. In *The Essential Tagore.* Edited by Fakrul Alam, xv–xxxiv. Cambridge, MA: Harvard University Press, 2014.

Chaudhuri, Rosinka. 'The Flute, Gerontion, and Subaltern Misreadings of Tagore'. *Social Text* 22, no. 1 (78) (Spring 2004): 103–22.

Cheah, Pheng. 'What Is a World? On World Literature as World-Making Activity'. *Daedalus* 137, no. 3 (Summer 2008): 26–38.

Cheah, Pheng. 'Worlding Literature: Living with Tiger Spirits'. *Diacritics* 45, no. 2 (2017): 86–114.

Claviez, Thomas, ed. *The Conditions of Hospitality.* New York: Fordham University Press, 2013.

Colwell, Thomas B. 'The Ecological Basis of Human Community'. *Educational Theory* 21, no. 4 (1971): 418–33.

Conley, Verena Andermatt. 'Nancy's Worlds'. *Diacritics* 42, no. 2 (2014): 84–98.

Cusinato, Guido. 'Hunger for Being Born Completely: Plasticity and Desire'. *Philarchive.org,* 2017. https://philarchive.org/archive/CUSHFB.

Das Gupta, Uma. *Rabindranath Tagore: A Biography.* New Delhi: Oxford University Press, 2004.

Das Gupta, Uma. *Rabindranath Tagore: An Illustrated Life.* New Delhi: Oxford University Press, 2013.

Davis, Brent. 'Complexity and Education: Vital Simultaneities'. *Educational Philosophy and Theory* 40, no. 1 (2008): 50–65.

Davis, Natalie Zemon. *The Return of Martin Guerre.* Cambridge, MA: Harvard University Press, 1984.

Davis, Natalie Zemon. *Women on the Margins.* Cambridge, MA: Harvard University Press, 1997.

Deleuze, Gilles. *Difference and Repetition.* Translated by Paul Patton. New York: Columbia University Press, 1994.

Deleuze, Gilles. *Difference and Repetition.* Translated by Paul Patton. London: Continuum, 2004.

Deleuze, Gilles. *Empiricism and Subjectivity: An Essay on Hume's Theory of Human Nature.* Translated by Constantin V. Boundas. New York: Columbia University Press, 1991.

Deleuze, Gilles. *Negotiations: 1972-1990.* Translated by M. Joughin. New York: Columbia University Press, 1995.

Deleuze, Gilles. *Nietzsche and Philosophy.* Translated by H. Tomlinson. London: Continuum, 2002.

Deleuze, Gilles. *Proust and Signs.* Translated by R. Howard. Minneapolis: University of Minnesota Press, 2000.

Deleuze, Gilles, and Claire Parnet. *Dialogues II.* Translated by Hugh Tomlinson, Barbara Habberjam, and Eliot Ross Albert. New York: Columbia University Press, 2007.

Derrida, Jacques. 'The Future of the Profession or the University Without Condition'. In *Jacques Derrida and the Humanities: A Critical Reader,* edited by T. Cohen, 24–57. Cambridge: Cambridge University Press, 2001.

Derrida, Jacques. 'I Have a Taste for the Secret'. In Jacques Derrida and Maurizio Ferraris, *A Taste for the Secret,* edited by Giacomo Donis and David Webb, translated by Giacomo Donis, 1–92. London: Polity Press, 2001.

Derrida, Jacques. 'Mochlos ou le conflit des facultés'. In *Du droit à la philosophie,* 397–438. Paris: Galilée, 1990.

Derrida, Jacques. *Negotiations: Interventions and Interviews 1971-2001.* Edited and translated with an introduction by Elizabeth Rottenberg. Stanford, CA: Stanford University Press, 2002.

Derrida, Jacques. *Of Grammatology.* Translated by Gayatri Chakravorty Spivak. Baltimore, MD: Johns Hopkins University Press, 1998.

Derrida, Jacques. 'The Principle of Reason: The University in the Eyes of Its Pupils'. *Diacritics* 13 (Fall 1983): 3–20.

Dev, Amiya. 'Tagore's Truth'. In *Tagore, Einstein and the Nature of Reality: Literary and Philosophical Reflections,* edited by Partha Ghose, 59–72. London: Routledge, 2019.

Devall, B., and G. Sessions, eds. *Deep Ecology: Living as if Nature Mattered.* Salt Lake City, UT: Peregrine Smith, 1985.

Devi, Maitraye. *Mungpute Rabindranath.* Kolkata: Prajna Prakashani, 1943.

Devi, Maitraye. *Tagore by Fireside.* Kolkata: Rupa, 2002.

Dillet, Beniot. 'What Is Called Thinking?: When Deleuze Walks along Heideggerian Paths'. *Deleuze Studies* 7, no. 2 (2013): 250–74.

Dimock, Wai Chee. 'Literature for the Planet'. *PMLA* 116, no. 1 (2001): 173–88.

Dimock, Wai Chee. 'Nonbiological Clock: Literary History against Newtonian Mechanics'. *South Atlantic Quarterly* 102, no. 1 (2003): 153–77.

Dimock, Wai Chee. 'A Theory of Resonance'. *PMLA* 112, no. 5 (1997): 1060–71.

Dobson, Andrew. *Listening for Democracy: Recognition, Representation, Reconciliation.* New York: Oxford University Press, 2014.

Durkheim, Émile. *The Evolution of Educational Thought: Lectures on the Formation and Development of Secondary Education in France.* London: Routledge, 1977.

Durkheim, Émile. *Moral Education: A Study in the Theory and Application of the Sociology of Education.* New York: Free Press, 1961.

Dworkin, A. *Intercourse.* London: Arrow Books, 1988.

Eckersley, A., and T. Bird. 'Speculation as Surplus-Value'. *MaHKUscript: Journal of Fine Art Research* 3, no. 1 (2019): 1–6.

Eggers, J. Philip. 'Memory in Mankind: Keats's Historical Imagination'. *PMLA* 86, no. 5 (1971): 990–98.

Eliot, T. S. 'Gerontion'. In *T. S. Eliot: Selected Poems*, edited by Manju Jain, 23. Delhi: Oxford University Press, 1992.

Elmhirst, Leonard. 'A Home School for Orphans'. *The Visva Bharati Quarterly* (1924): 124–26.

Elmhirst, Leonard. 'Rabindranath Tagore and Sriniketan'. *The Visva Bharati Quarterly* 24, no. 2 (Autumn 1958): 122–44.

Evernden, Neil. *The Social Creation of Nature*. Baltimore, MD: Johns Hopkins University Press, 1992.

Figlio, Karl. 'Historical Imagination/Psychoanalytic Imagination'. *History Workshop Journal* 45 (1998): 199–221.

Fitzgerald, James L. 'History and Primordium in Ancient Indian Historical Writing: *Itihasa* and Purana in the Mahabharata and Beyond'. In *Thinking, Recording, and Writing History in the Ancient World*, edited by Kurt A. Raaflaub, 41–60. Malden, MA: John Wiley and Sons, 2013.

Follett, Mary Parker. *The New State: Group Organization and the Solution of Popular Government*. New York: Longmans, Green and Co., 1918.

Foucault, Michel. 'Interview with Michel Foucault'. In *Power: Essential Works of Foucault, 1954–1984*, edited by James D. Faubion, translated by Robert Hurley et al., 239–97. New York: New Press, 2001.

Friedlander, Eli. *Walter Benjamin: A Philosophical Portrait*. Cambridge, MA: Harvard University Press, 2012.

Frost, Robert. 'Remarks on the Occasion of the Tagore Centenary'. *Poetry* 99, no. 2 (November 1961): 106–19.

Fusco, Coco. *English is Broken Here: Notes on Cultural Fusion in the Americas*. New York: New Press, 1995.

Gadamer, Hans-Georg. *Truth and Method*. New York: Bloomsbury, 2013.

Gamboa, Shaun. *Canguilhem Notes: Normal and Pathological*. Self-published, Academia, 2013.

Garrido, Juan Manuel, and Vanessa Doriott Anderson. 'The Poetry of the World'. *Diacritics* 43, no. 4 (2015): 52–64.

Garrison, Jim. 'Dewey, Eros and Education'. *Education and Culture* 11, no. 2 (Fall 1994): 1–5.

Gevorkyan, Sofya, and Carlos A. Segovia. 'Earth and World(s): From Heidegger's Fourfold to Contemporary Anthropology'. *Open Philosophy* 4, no. 5 (2021): 58–82.

Ghose, Sisir Kumar. 'Rabindranath and Modernism'. *Indian Literature* 11, no. 3 (July–September 1968): 12–20.

Ghosh, Ranjan. 'India, *itihasa* and Inter-historiographical Discourse'. *History and Theory* 46, no. 2 (2007): 210–17.

Ghosh, Ranjan. 'Intra-active Transculturality'. *Modern Language Notes* 130 (December 2015): 1198–220.

Ghosh, Ranjan. 'Introducing a Surplus'. *South Asia: Journal of South Asian Studies* 35, no. 1 (2012): 7–12.

Ghosh, Ranjan. 'Jugalbandi'. *Comparative Literature Studies* 55, no. 4 (2018): 953–62.

Ghosh, Ranjan. *Trans(in)fusion: Reflections for Critical Thinking*. New York: Routledge, 2020.

Ginzburg, Carlo. *The Cheese and the Worms: The Cosmos of a Sixteenth-Century Miller*. Translated by John and Anne C. Tedeshi. Baltimore, MD: Johns Hopkins University Press, 2013.

Gladstone, W. E. 'Indian Art in London'. *The Times of India*, 4 January 1938, 18.

Glissant, Edouard. 'History-Histories-Stories'. In *Caribbean Discourse: Selected Essays*, translated by J. Michael Dash, 61–96. Charlottesville: University Press of Virginia, 1989.

Godin, Christian. 'The Notion of Totality in Indian Thought'. *Diogenes* 48, no. 189 (2000): 58–67.

Goethe, Johann Wolfgang von. *Goethe Edition*. Vol. 12, *Scientific Studies*, edited by D. Miller. New York: Suhrkamp, 1988.

Goethe, Johann Wolfgang von. *Schriften zur Morphologie*. Createspace Independent Publishing Platform. 2014. First published 1824.

Goethe, Johann Wolfgang von. *The Sorrows of Young Werther and Selected Writings*. Translated by Catherine Hutter. New York: New American Library, Inc., 1962.

Goldberg, Ellen. 'The Romanticism of Rabindranath Tagore: Poetry as Sadhana'. *Indian Literature* 45, no. 4 (July–August 2001): 173–96.

Goldman, Robert P. 'Historicising the Ramakatha: Valmiki's Ramayana and Its Medieval Commentators'. *India International Centre Quarterly* 31, no. 4 (2005): 83–97.

Gomez-Pena, Guillermo. *The New World Border*. San Francisco, CA: City Lights Books, 1996.

Gregory, Brad S. 'Is Small Beautiful? Microhistory and the History of Everyday Life'. *History and Theory* 38, no. 1 (1999): 100–110.

Guha, Ranajit. *History at the Limit of World-History*. New Delhi: Oxford University Press, 2003.

Gumbrecht, Hans Ulrich. *Our Broad Present: Time and Contemporary Culture*. New York: Columbia University Press, 2014.

Gumbrecht, Hans Ulrich. *Production of Presence: What Meaning Cannot Convey*. Stanford, CA: Stanford University Press, 2004.

Gupta, Amita. *Early Childhood Education, Postcolonial Theory, and Teaching Practices in India*. New York: Palgrave Macmillan, 2006.

Hamacher, Werner. ' "Now": Walter Benjamin on Historical Time'. In *Walter Benjamin and History*, edited by Andrew Benjamin, 38–68. London: Continuum, 2005.

Heidegger, Martin. *What Is Called Thinking?* Translated by J. Glenn Gray. New York: Harper & Row Publishers, 1968.

Heine, Steven. 'History, Transhistory, and Narrative History: A Postmodern View of Nishitani's Philosophy of Zen'. *Philosophy East and West* 44, no. 2 (1994): 251–78.

Helm, Bert P. 'Emerson Agonistes: Education as Struggle and Process'. *Educational Theory* 42, no. 2 (1992): 165–80.

Hogstad, Kjetil Hornand, and Catherine Malabou. 'Plasticity and Education—An Interview with Catherine Malabou'. *Educational Philosophy and Theory* 53, no. 10 (2021): 1049–53.

Hoły-Łuczaj, Magdalena. 'Shapeability: Revisiting Heidegger's Concept of Being in the Anthropocene'. *Cosmos and History: The Journal of Natural and Social Philosophy* 15, no. 1 (2019): 402–26.

Hope, Alexander. 'The Future is Plastic: Refiguring Malabou's Plasticity'. *Journal for Cultural Research* 18, no. 4 (2014): 329–49.

Hurwitz, Harold M. 'Yeats and Tagore'. *Comparative Literature* 16, no. 1 (1964): 55–64.

Inada, Kenneth K. 'Time and Temporality: A Buddhist Approach'. *Philosophy East and West* 24, no. 2 (1974): 171–79.

Ingold, Tim. *Lines: A Brief History*. Abingdon: Routledge, 2007.

James, Ian. '(Neuro)plasticity, Epigenesis and the Void'. *parrhesia* 25 (2016): 1–19.

Johnson, Galen A. 'On the Origin(s) of Truth in Art: Merleau-Ponty, Klee, and Cézanne'. *Research in Phenomenology* 43, no. 3 (2013): 475–515.

Jung, Hwa Yol. 'A Prolegomenon to Transversal Geophilosophy'. In 'East Asian and Comparative Approaches to the Environment', special issue, *Environmental Philosophy* 10, no. 1 (Spring 2013): 83–112.

Klee, Paul. *The Diaries of Paul Klee 1898–1918*. Edited by Ralph Klee. Berkeley and Los Angeles: University of California Press, 1964.

Klee, Paul. *Notebooks*. Vol. 1, *The Thinking Eye*. Edited by Jurg Spiller. Translated by Ralph Manheim. London: Lund Humphries, 1961.

Klee, Paul. *Paul Klee*. New York: Parkstone International, 2013.

Klee, Paul. *Pedagogical Sketchbook*. Edited and translated by Sibyl Moholy-Nagy. New York: Frederick A. Praeger, 1960.

Kuge, Shu. 'Politics of Doodling: Tamura Toshiko's "A Woman Writer"'. *positions: east asia cultures critique* 15, no. 3 (Winter 2007): 487–509.

Kumar, R. Siva. *Rabindra Chitravali: Paintings of Rabindranath Tagore*. Vols. 1–4. Kolkata: Pratikshan, in association with Visva-Bharati (Santiniketan) and Ministry of Culture, Government of India, New Delhi, 2011.

LaChapelle, Doris. *Earth Wisdom*. San Diego, CA: Guild of Tudors Press, 1978.

Latour, Bruno. *The Pasteurization of France*. Translated by Alan Sheridan. Cambridge, MA: Harvard University Press, 1993.

Le Bris, Michel, and Jean Rouaud, eds. *Pour une littérature-monde*. Paris: Gallimard, 2007.

Leopold, Aldo. *A Sand County Almanac, with Essays on Conservation from Round River*. New York: Ballantine Books, 1966.

Leservot, Typhaine. 'From *Weltliteratur* to World Literature to *Littérature-monde*: The History of a Controversial Concept'. In *Postcolonialism and Litterature-monde*, edited by Alec G. Hargreaves, Charles Forsdick, and David Murphy, 36–48. Liverpool: Liverpool University Press, 2010.

Leyden, W. von. 'History and the Concept of Relative Time'. *History and Theory* 2, no. 3 (1963): 263–85.

Liakos, Antonis. 'The Transformation of Historical Writing from Syntagmatic to Paradigmatic Syntax'. *Historein* 2 (2000): 47–54.

Lyotard, Jean-François. 'Foreword: Spaceship', translated by Rosemary Arnoux. In *Education and the Postmodern Condition*, edited by Michael Peters, xix. Westport, CT: Bergin & Garvey, 1995.

Machwe, Prabhakar. 'Tagore: The Oriental and Modern'. *Indian Literature* 19, no. 5 (September–October 1976): 80–94.

Maggiore, Valeria. 'Is Aesthetic Mind a Plastic Mind? Reflections on Goethe and Catherine Malabou'. *Aisthesis: Pratiche, linguaggi e saperi dell'estetico* 12, no. 1 (2019): 55–60.

Malabou, Catherine. 'An Eye at the Edge of Discourse'. *Communication Theory* 17, no.1 (2007): 16–25.

Malabou, Catherine. *The Future of Hegel: Plasticity, Temporality and Dialectic.* Translated by Lisabeth During. London: Routledge, 1996.

Malabou, Catherine. *The Future of Hegel: Plasticity, Temporality and Dialectic.* Translated by Lisabeth During. New York: Routledge, 2005.

Malabou, Catherine. *The Heidegger Change: On the Fantastic in Philosophy.* Translated by Peter Skafish. Albany, NY: Suny Press, 2011.

Malabou, Catherine. 'Superhumanity'. e-flux, February 2018. https://www.e-flux. com/architecture/superhumanity/179166/repetition-revenge-plasticity/.

Malabou, Catherine. *Plasticity at the Dusk of Writing: Dialectic, Destruction, Deconstruction.* New York: Columbia University Press, 2010.

Malabou, Catherine. *What Should We Do with Our Brain?* Translated by S. Rand. New York: Fordham University Press, 2008.

Malabou, Catherine. 'Who Is Afraid of Hegelian Wolves?' In *Deleuze: A Critical Reader*, edited by Paul Patton, 114–38. London: Wiley-Blackwell, 1997.

Margaronis, Maria. 'The Anxiety of Authenticity: Writing Historical Fiction at the End of the Twentieth Century'. *History Workshop Journal* 65 (2008): 138–60.

Masschelein, Jan. 'Experimentum Scholae: The World Once More . . . But Not (Yet) Finished'. In *Making Sense of Education*, edited by Gert J. J. Biesta, 101–7. Dordrecht: Springer, 2012.

Massumi, Brian. *99 Theses on the Revaluation of Value: A Post-Capitalist Manifesto.* Minneapolis: University of Minnesota Press, 2019.

Massumi, Brian. 'Virtual Ecology and Questions of Value'. In *General Ecology: The New Ecological Paradigm*, edited by Erich Hörl with James Burton, 345–73. London: Bloomsbury, 2017.

McLaren, Peter. *Multiculturalism: Pedagogies of Dissent for the New Millennium.* Boulder, CO: Westview Press, 1997.

McLaren, Peter. 'Paulo Freire's Pedagogy of Possibility'. In *Freirean Pedagogy, Praxis, and Possibilities: Projects for the New Millennium*, edited by H. Mark Krank, Peter Mclaren, and Robert E. Bahruth, 14. New York: Falmer Press, 2000.

Merleau-Ponty, Maurice. *Phenomenology of Perception.* London: Routledge & Kegan Paul, 2003.

Merleau-Ponty, Maurice. *The Primacy of Perception.* Edited by James M. Edie. Translated by William Cobb. Evanston, IL: Northwestern University Press, 1964.

Merleau-Ponty, Maurice. *The Visible and the Invisible.* Evanston, IL: Northwestern University Press, 1968.

Miranda, Luis de. 'Is a New Life Possible? Deleuze and the Lines'. Translated by Marie-Céline Courilleault. *Deleuze Studies* 7, no. 1 (February 2013): 106–52.

Moder, Gregor. 'Catherine Malabou's Hegel: One or Several Plasticities?' *Filozofija I Drustvo* 4 (2015): 813–29.

Mohanty, Jitendra Nath. *Reason and Tradition in Indian Thought.* New Delhi: Oxford University Press, 1992.

Moraru, Christian. 'Fringes, Margins, Diaphragms: The University and Textual Reason after Derrida'. *Crossings* 3 (1999): 79–100.

Mukherjee, Himangshu Bhushan. *Education for Fullness.* London: Asia Publishing House, 1962.

Mumford, Lewis. *The Myth of the Machine: The Pentagon of Power*. New York: Harcourt Brace Jovanovich, 1970.

Murray, Timothy. 'Prepositional Oscillations: Politics, Ontology, Poetics'. *Diacritics* 43, no. 4 (2015): 3–6.

Nancy, Jean-Luc. *Being Singular Plural*. Translated by Robert D. Richardson and Anne E. O'Byrne. Stanford, CA: Stanford University Press, 2000.

Nancy, Jean-Luc. *The Creation of the World or Globalization*. Translated by François Raffoul and David Petigrew. Albany, NY: State University of New York, 2007.

Nancy, Jean-Luc. *Expectations*. Translated by Jean Michel Rabate. New York: Fordham University Press, 2017.

Nancy, Jean-Luc. ' "Our World": An Interview'. *Angelaki* 8, no. 2 (2003): 43–54.

Nancy, Jean-Luc, and Aurelien Barrau. *What's These Worlds Coming To?* New York: Fordham University Press, 2015.

Naravane, V. S. 'The Place of Aesthetics in Tagore's Thought'. *Indian Literature* 4, no. 1/2 (October 1960–September 1961): 146–54.

O'Connell, Kathleen M. *Rabindranath Tagore: The Poet as Educator*. Kolkata: Visva Bharati, 2002.

Paine, M., and J. Schad, eds. *Life After Theory*. New York: Continuum, 2003.

Panikkar, Raimundo. 'Toward a Typology of Time and Temporality in the Ancient Indian Tradition'. *Philosophy East and West* 24, no. 2 (1974): 161–64.

Patil, Sharad. 'Myth and Reality of Ramayana and Mahabharata'. *Social Scientist* 4, no. 8 (1976): 68–72.

Pennycook, Alistair. 'English, Universities and Struggles over Culture and Knowledge'. In *East–West Dialogue in Knowledge and Higher Education,* edited by Ruth Hayhoe and Julia Pan, 64–82. New York: M. E. Sharpe, 1996.

Phillips, Charles. 'Bend, Engage, Wait, and Watch: Rethinking Political Agency in a World of Flows'. PhD diss., Johns Hopkins University, 2014.

Phillips, Mark Salber. *On Historical Distance*. New Haven, CT: Yale University Press, 2013.

Plato. *The Collected Dialogues of Plato*. Edited by Edith Hamilton and Huntington Cairns. Princeton, NJ: Princeton University Press, 1963.

Poovey, Mary. *A History of the Modern Fact*. Chicago, IL: University of Chicago Press, 1998.

Proudfoot, I. 'Interpreting Mahabharata Episodes as Sources for the History of Ideas'. *Annals of the Bhandarkar Oriental Research Institute* 60, no. 1/4 (1979): 41–63.

Quint, David. ' "Alexander the Pig": Shakespeare on History and Poetry'. *boundary 2* 10, no. 3 (1982): 49–67.

Radhakrishnan, R. *History, the Human, and the World Between*. Durham, NC: Duke University Press, 2008.

Radhakrishnan, S. *The Philosophy of Rabindranath Tagore*. Baroda: Good Companions Publishers, 1961.

Raghavan, V. 'Sahitya'. In *An Introduction to Indian Poetics*, edited by V. Raghavan and Nagendra, 82 (Bombay: Macmillan, 1970).

Robbins, Bruce. 'Uses of World Literature'. In *The Routledge Companion to World Literature*, edited by Theo D'haen, David Damrosch, and Djelal Kadir, 383–92. Abingdon: Routledge, 2012.

Robinson, Andrew. *The Art of Rabindranath Tagore*. Vols. 1–4. Foreword by Satyajit Ray. London: Andre Deutsch, 1989.

Rockas, Leo. 'The Rhetoric of Doodle'. *College English* 40, no. 2 (October 1978): 139–44.

Rorty, Richard. *Contingency, Irony, Solidarity*. Cambridge: Cambridge University Press, 1989.

Rosenstone, Robert A. 'Rethinking History: Theory, Practice, and New Ways of Telling the Past'. *Perspectives on History*, 1 April 1998. https://www.historians.org/research-and-publications/perspectives-on-history/april-1998/rethinking-hist ory-theory-practice-and-new-ways-of-telling-the-past.

Rotenstreich, Nathan. 'Historical Inevitability and Human Responsibility'. *Philosophy and Phenomenological Research* 23, no. 3 (1963): 380–96.

Sankalia, H. D. 'Ayodhya of the Ramayana in a Historical Perspective'. *Annals of the Bhandarkar Oriental Research Institute* 58/59 (1977): 893–919.

Sauvagnargues, Anne. *Deleuze and Art*. Translated by Samantha Bankston. London: Bloomsbury, 2005.

Schama, Simon. *Citizens: A Chronicle of the French Revolution*. London: Viking, 1989.

Seed, John. 'Anthropocentrism'. In *Deep Ecology: Living as if Nature Mattered*, edited by B. Devall and G. Sessions, 236–42. Salt Lake City, UT: Peregrine Smith, 1985.

Sen, Amartya. 'Indian Traditions & the Western Imagination'. *Daedalus* 134, no. 4 (2005): 168–85.

Sen, Paritosh. 'Pandora's Box: The Original Art of Rabindranath Tagore'. *India International Centre Quarterly* 17, no. 3/4 (Winter 1990–91): 270–80.

Sen Gupta, Kalyan. *The Philosophy of Rabindranath Tagore*. Aldershot: Ashgate, 2005.

Sengupta, S. C. 'The Surplus in Man: The Poet's Philosophy of Man'. In *Rabindranath Tagore and the Challenges of Today*, edited by Bhudeb Chaudhuri and K. G Subramanyan, 39–54. Shimla: Indian Institute of Advanced Studies, 1988.

Serres, Michel. *The Birth of Physics*. Translated by Jack Hawkes. Manchester: Clinamen Press, 2001.

Serres, Michel. *Hermes: Literature, Science, Philosophy*. Baltimore, MD: John Hopkins University Press, 1982.

Serres, Michel. *The Troubadour of Knowledge*. Translated by S. F. Glaser with W. Paulson. Ann Arbor: The University of Michigan Press, 1997.

Shrivastava, Aseem. 'An Ecology of the Spirit: Rabindranath's Experience of Nature'. In *The Cambridge Companion to Rabindranath Tagore*, edited by Sukanta Chaudhuri, 323–36. Cambridge: Cambridge University Press, 2020.

Shusterman, Richard. *Performing Live: Aesthetic Alternatives for the Ends of Art*. Ithaca, NY: Cornell University Press, 2000.

Siegel, D. J. *The Mindful Brain: Reflection and Attunement in the Cultivation of Well-Being*. New York: W. W. Norton, 2007.

Simmons, James C. 'The Novelist as Historian: An Unexplored Tract of Victorian Historiography'. *Victorian Studies* 14, no. 3 (1971): 293–305.

Sisk, John P. 'The Literary Imagination and the Sense of the Past'. *Salmagundi* 68/69 (Fall 1985–Winter 1986): 76–86.

Smith, Page. *The Historian and History*. New York: Vintage, 1964.

Stevenson Stewart, Jessica. 'Toward a Hermeneutics of Doodling in The Era of Folly'. *Word & Image* 29, no. 4 (2013): 409–27.

Stunkel, Kenneth R. 'Rabindranath Tagore and the Aesthetics of Postmodernism'. *International Journal of Politics, Culture and Society* 17, no. 2 (Winter 2003): 237–53.

Tagore, Rabindranath. *Angel of Surplus*. Edited by Sisirkumar Ghose. Kolkata: Visva Bharati, 1978.

Tagore, Rabindranath. *The Complete Works of Rabindranath Tagore*. New Delhi: New Delhi General Press, 2017.

Tagore, Rabindranath. *Creative Unity*. London: Macmillan and Co., 1922.

Tagore, Rabindranath. 'Education for Rural India'. *The Visva-Bharati Quarterly* 13 (May–October 1947): 27–28.

Tagore, Rabindranath. *English Writings of Rabindranath Tagore*. Edited by S. K. Das. Vol. 3. Delhi: Sahitya Akademi, 1996.

Tagore, Rabindranath. 'The History and Ideals of Sriniketan'. *The Modern Review* (November 1941): 421–33.

Tagore, Rabindranath. *On Art and Aesthetics: A Selection of Lectures, Essays and Letters*. Kolkata: Orient Longmans, 1961.

Tagore, Rabindranath. *On the Edges of Time*. Visva Bharati, 1958.

Tagore, Rabindranath. *Personality*. London: Macmillan & Co., 1945.

Tagore, Rabindranath. *Personality*. London: Macmillan & Co., 1970.

Tagore, Rabindranath. *Personality*. Kolkata: Rupa, 2002.

Tagore, Rabindranath. *Rabindra Rachanabali*, vol. 2. Kolkata: Government of West Bengal, Saraswati Press Limited, 1992.

Tagore, Rabindranth. *Rabindra Rachanabali*, vol. 10. Kolkata: Government of West Bengal, Saraswati Press Limited, 1989.

Tagore, Rabindranath. *Rabindra Rachanabali*, vol. 13. Kolkata: Government of West Bengal, Saraswati Press Limited, 1990.

Tagore, Rabindranath. *Rabindra Rachanabali*, vol. 14. Kolkata: Government of West Bengal, Saraswati Press Limited, 1992.

Tagore, Rabindranath. *Rabindra Rachanabali*, vol. 15. Kolkata: Government of West Bengal, Saraswati Press Limited, 1994.

Tagore, Rabindranath. *The Religion of Man*. London: George Allen & Unwin Limited, 1958.

Tagore, Rabindranath. *Sadhana*. New York: The Macmillan Co., 1914.

Tagore, Rabindranath. *Selected Letters of Rabindranath Tagore*. Edited by Krishna Dutta and Andrew Robinson. Cambridge: Cambridge University Press, 1997.

Tagore, Rabindranath. 'Schooling'. *The Visva Bharati Quarterly* 29, no. 4 (1963–64): 273–79.

Tagore, Rabindranath. *A Tagore Reader*. Edited by Amiya Chakravarty. New York: Macmillan, 1961.

Tagore, Rabindranath. 'Thoughts on Education'. *The Visva Bharati Quarterly* 13 (May–October 1947): 1–7.

Tagore, Rabindranath. *Towards Universal Man*. London: Asia Publishing House, 1961.

Tagore, Rabindranath. *A Vision of India's History*. Kolkata: Visva Bharati Bookshop, 1951.

Tagore, Rabindranath. 'Visva Sāhitya'. Translated by Rijula Das and Makarand R. Paranjape. *Journal of Contemporary Thought* 34 (2011): 277–88.

Tagore, Saranindranath. 'Tagore's Conception of Cosmopolitanism: A Reconstruction'. *University of Toronto Quarterly* 77, no. 4 (2008): 1070–81.

Talbot, Ann. 'Chance and Necessity in History: E. H. Carr and Leon Trotsky Compared'. *Historical Social Research / Historische Sozialforschung* 34, no. 2 (2009): 88–96.

Taylor, Charles. *Sources of the Self*. Cambridge, MA: Harvard University Press, 1989.

Thapar, Romila. *The Past Before Us*. New Delhi: Permanent Black, 2013.

Trainer, F. E. *Abandon Affluence*. London: Zed Books, 1985.

Trautmann, Thomas R. 'Does India Have History? Does History Have India?' *Comparative Studies in Society and History* 54, no. 1 (2012): 174–95.

Vajpayi, Ananya. *Righteous Republic*. Cambridge, MA: Harvard University Press, 2012.

Waldron, Jeremy. 'Minority Cultures and the Cosmopolitan Alternative'. In *The Rights of Minority Cultures*, edited by Will Kymlicka, 93–122. Oxford: Oxford University Press, 1995.

Wallace, Mark I. 'Earth God: Cultivating the Spirit in an Ecocidal Culture'. In *The Blackwell Companion to Postmodern Theology*, edited by Graham Ward, 208–28. Malden, MA: Blackwell Publishing, 2005.

Watkin, Christopher. 'A Different Alterity: Jean-Luc Nancy's "Singular Plural"'. *Paragraph* 30, no. 2 (July 2007): 50–64.

Weber, Max. *Political Writings*. Edited by Peter Lassman and Ronald Speirs. Cambridge: Cambridge University Press, 1994.

Wegenstein, Bernadette. *Getting Under the Skin: Body and Media Theory*. Cambridge, MA: MIT Press, 2006.

Whitaker, Thomas R. 'The Dialectic of Yeats's Vision of History'. *Modern Philology* 57, no. 2 (1959): 100–12.

White, Hayden. 'Interpretation in History'. *New Literary History* 4, no. 2 (1973): 281–314.

Whitehead, Alfred North. *Adventures of Ideas*. New York: Macmillan, 1961.

Whitehead, Alfred North. *The Aims of Education and Other Essays*. New York: Mentor Books, 1929.

Whitehead, Alfred North. *Science and the Modern World*. New York: Macmillan, 1954.

Williams, Dave, and Chris Taylor. 'Peripheral Expressions: Samuel Beckett's Marginal Drawings in Endgame'. *Journal of Beckett Studies* 19, no. 1 (April 2010): 29–55.

Williams, Louise Blakeney. *Modernism and the Ideology of History*. Cambridge: Cambridge University Press, 2002.

Williams, Louise Blakeney. 'Overcoming the "Contagion of Mimicry": The Cosmopolitan Nationalism and Modernist History of Rabindranath Tagore and W. B. Yeats'. *American Historical Review* 112, no. 1 (2007): 69–100.

Williams, Tyler. 'Plasticity, In Retrospect: Changing the Future of The Humanities'. *Diacritics* 41, no. 1 (2013): 6–25.

Wills, John E. 'Taking Historical Novels Seriously'. *The Public Historian* 6, no. 1 (1984): 39–46.

Windsor, Joshua. 'Desire Lines: Deleuze and Guattari on Molar Lines, Molecular Lines, and Lines of Flight'. *New Zealand Sociology* 30, no. 1 (2015): 156–71.

Wong, Aida Yuen. 'Rabindranath Tagore's Mysterious Faces and India's Encounter with Modernism'. In *Behind the Masks of Modernism: Global and Transnational Perspectives*, edited by Andrew Reynolds and Bonnie Roos, 24–54. Gainesville, FL: University Press of Florida, 2016.

Wormald, Thomas. 'Habitués'. In *Thinking Catherine Malabou: Passionate Detachments*, edited by Thomas Wormald and Isabell Dahms, 123–38. New York: Rowman and Littlefield, 2018.

Wormald, Thomas. 'On Plasticity's Own Conceptual Epigenesis: Malabou on the Origin and History of Plasticity'. *Cosmos and History: The Journal of Natural and Social Philosophy* 16, no. 1 (2020): 102–24.

Wright, Thomas. 'Wilde the Doodle Dandy: A Scholarly Doodle'. *The Wildean: Journal of the Oscar Wilde Society* 47 (July 2015): 65–89.

Yuasa, Yasuo. *The Body: Toward an Eastern Mind–Body Theory*. Edited by Thomas P. Kasulis. Translated by Nagatomo Shigenori. Albany, NY: State University of New York Press, 1987.

Index